Christian and Islamic Theology of Religions

Theologians have had to increasingly engage with beliefs and practises outside of their own traditions. The resultant "theology of religions" is, however, often formulated in isolation from the religions they are describing. This book provides a comparison of the development of theology of religions in Western Christianity and its application in an Islamic context. It also shows the parallels between some specific forms of theology of religions, i.e. exclusivism, inclusivism or pluralism, in both Islamic and Christian traditions.

The arguments of Christian and Muslim theologians, including the specific contributions of Rowan Williams and Jerusha Lamptey, are examined in order to reveal the interconnections and contradictions of their pluralist, exclusivist and inclusivist approaches. This provides a rounded picture of Christian-Muslim understanding of religious others and prepares the ground for a stronger and more sophisticated Islamic theology of religions.

This is vital reading for those studying theology of religions, comparative theology and interfaith relations.

Esra Akay Dag is a research assistant in religious studies at Sakarya University, Turkey.

Routledge studies in religion

For a full list of titles in this series, please visit www.routledge.com

47 **Translating Religion**
What Is Lost and Gained?
Edited by Michael P. Dejonge and Christiane Tietz

48 **Refractions of the Scriptural**
Critical Orientation as Transgression
Edited by Vincent L. Wimbush

49 **Innovative Catholicism and the Human Condition**
Jane Anderson

50 **Religion and Ecological Crisis**
The "Lynn White Thesis" at Fifty
Edited by Todd LeVasseur and Anna Peterson

51 **Secular Cosmopolitanism, Hospitality, and Religious Pluralism**
Andrew Fiala

52 **Religion, Migration, and Mobility**
The Brazilian Experience
Edited by Cristina Maria de Castro and Andrew Dawson

53 **Hans Mol and the Sociology of Religion**
Adam J. Powell with Original Essays by Hans Mol

54 **Buddhist Modernities**
Re-inventing Tradition in the Globalizing Modern World
*Edited by Hanna Havnevik, Ute Hüsken, Mark Teeuwen,
Vladimir Tikhonov and Koen Wellens*

55 **New Perspectives on the Nation of Islam**
Edited by Dawn-Marie Gibson and Herbert Berg

56 **Christian and Islamic Theology of Religions**
A Critical Appraisal
Esra Akay Dag

Christian and Islamic Theology of Religions
A Critical Appraisal

Esra Akay Dag

LONDON AND NEW YORK

First published 2017
by Routledge
2 Park Square, Milton Park, Abingdon, Oxon OX14 4RN

and by Routledge
711 Third Avenue, New York, NY 10017

Routledge is an imprint of the Taylor & Francis Group, an informa business

© 2017 Esra Akay Dag

The right of Esra Akay Dag to be identified as author of this work has been asserted by her in accordance with sections 77 and 78 of the Copyright, Designs and Patents Act 1988.

All rights reserved. No part of this book may be reprinted or reproduced or utilised in any form or by any electronic, mechanical, or other means, now known or hereafter invented, including photocopying and recording, or in any information storage or retrieval system, without permission in writing from the publishers.

Trademark notice: Product or corporate names may be trademarks or registered trademarks, and are used only for identification and explanation without intent to infringe.

British Library Cataloguing-in-Publication Data
A catalogue record for this book is available from the British Library

Library of Congress Cataloging-in-Publication Data
A catalog record for this book has been requested

ISBN: 978-1-138-70449-7 (hbk)
ISBN: 978-1-315-20267-9 (ebk)

Typeset in Sabon
by Apex CoVantage, LLC

To my little boy, Omar.

Contents

	Preface	ix
	Abbreviations	xi
	Introduction	1
1	Christian theology of religions	8
2	Rowan Williams's theology of religions	54
3	Islamic theology of religions	82
4	Jerusha Lamptey's theology of religions	126
5	Theology of religions reassessed	150
	Conclusion	182
	Index	185

Preface

This book is from a long PhD journey. In this book, I will basically provide a critical analysis of Christian and Islamic theology of religions. The first section of the research, utilising Alan Race's threefold typology together with alternative typologies, presents diverse Christian theologians' responses to religious pluralism. It argues that although Race's typology provides a good overview of current discussion on Christian theology of religions, it fails to do justice to more complex theologies. After paying specific attention to Rowan Williams's theology, I will show that Rowan Williams's Trinitarian theology of religions, with its complexities, challenges both the threefold and other typologies and the pluralist assumption that only pluralism provides sufficient openness towards other religions.

In the second section, I will question the applicability of Race's threefold typology to Islamic theology of religions. I will argue that Race's typology does not fully help present Islamic theology of religions as the application of inclusivist theology to Islamic theology seems to be problematic. Subsequently, providing diverse Islamic responses to religious diversity under the types of exclusivism and pluralism, I will argue that both approaches do not satisfactorily respond to religious similarities and difference. In this respect, after careful consideration of Jerusha Lamptey's Muslima theology of religions, I will argue that she offers a sophisticated theology which pays attention to the problem of doing justice to both religious similarities and differences.

After presenting diverse Christian and Islamic responses to religious pluralism, I will conclude that there is a need to pay attention to the specific details of other religious traditions and show how this complicates theology of religions questions.

I am deeply grateful to the many people, more than I can mention, who supported and encouraged me during my entire PhD journey and the publication of this book process. To begin, I must acknowledge my whole gratitude to my PhD supervisor Prof. Gavin D'Costa for his intellectual support and encouragement. From the first moment, he has always been supportive. I would not have been able to complete this project without Prof. D'Costa's generous support. Throughout my PhD, sometimes I lost my confidence, but he has always convinced me that what I have been working on is important

x *Preface*

and that I have the ability to do it. After the PhD, he has also been very supportive to publish my research as a book. I am sincerely grateful to my husband, Rahman, for his sacrifice, forbearance and encouragement. Although he was also studying his research, he has always prioritised mine by providing extra psychological and intellectual support. I must extend my deep gratitude to my parents and my sisters and brothers for their prayers, love and encouragement. I am very grateful to my fellow Luke Perera, with whom I shared the same faculty and house during our PhD life. Luke has proofread all my research and also provided some assistance where I had difficulties. I must extend my gratitude to the editors at Routledge, Joshua Wells and Jack Boothroyd, who have kindly responded to every question I asked and also to two anonymous reviewers for their insights.

Abbreviations

ACT	A Common Word
Lumen Gentium	Dogmatic Constitution on the Church
NIFCON	Anglican Communion Network for Interfaith Concerns
Nostra Aetate	Declaration on the Relationship of the Church to Non-Christian Religions

Introduction

In the twentieth century with increasing interaction with the believers of non-Christian religions in the Western world, Christian theologians have developed different approaches towards non-Christians. Different responses to religious pluralism have shaped a specific intellectual subtopic within Christian theology, namely theology of religions. In 1983, with the publication of *Christians and Religious Pluralism*, Alan Race categorised diverse responses to religious pluralism into three different approaches, exclusivism, inclusivism and pluralism. Since then, some theologians have used his classification; some have offered alternatives, whereas some comparative theologians[1] have added another dimension to the discussion by offering to move beyond theology of religions. Diverse Christian responses to religious pluralism and discussion on theology of religions occupy the first half of this research.

The discussions by Christian theologians on religious pluralism also in some way have influenced Muslims who live or are educated in Western countries. In the contemporary era, Muslims have not studied the area of theology of religions systematically. However, contemporary Christians' proposals, especially those made by liberal pluralist theologians, have had an effect on the development of Islamic pluralist approaches by liberal Muslim theologians, who in the last five or four decades have produced a number of important and systematic works on the subject. While Islamic pluralism is influenced (directly or indirectly) by Christian liberal theologies, there have been some other responses to religious pluralism in the contemporary period. Some theologians have revised a classical form of theology which regards Islam as the only religion accepted by God and as superseding other religions. From this perspective, two opposing positions (exclusivism and pluralism) occupy the main place in the Islamic response to religious pluralism. The second half of this thesis addresses Islamic responses to religious pluralism.

Christian and Muslim theologians who promote world peace, social harmony and openness towards others have generally focused on commonalities between religions to put aside their history of conflict. The Second Vatican documents, *Lumen Gentium* and *Nostra Aetate*, emphasised the commonalities between Christianity and non-Christian religions. Moreover,

2 Introduction

the Catholic theologian Hans Küng in 1991 came up with an important slogan: 'no world peace without peace among religions; no peace among religions without dialogue between religions.'[2] In the following years, religious leaders and scholars from diverse religions gathered in Chicago and issued the 'Declaration of the World Parliament of Religions', which summarises the core elements of a global ethic: 'respect for the humanity of persons, non-violence, just economics, tolerance, truthfulness and gender and racial equality.'[3] The document *A Common Word Between Us and You* also underlined the commonalities between Islam and Christianity from an Islamic point of view. While these kinds of noteworthy attempts promote religious peace and coexistence, they also create the unfortunate impression that talking about the real differences between religions will lead to conflict and harm coexistence and social harmony. Of course, there are good reasons to support such initiatives for the common good. For instance, Samuel Huntington in 1993 published an essay, 'The Clash of Civilizations', which basically claimed that the different cultures in the world would be the main source for conflict post-Cold War, for example, Muslim-Middle East versus Christian-Western. He presented Islam and Christianity as two rival religions: both are missionary and universal in nature, and thus both claim to be only true religion.[4] This kind of simplified division sometimes leaves us to choose either to insist upon commonalities to cut down boundaries between religious communities or to insist upon differences that may lead to divisions of 'us' and 'them', 'good' and 'bad', 'true' and 'false'.

The commonalities/similarities and differences of religions play important roles for theologians' shaping of their position towards other religions. From the Christian and Islamic traditions, specifically in academic circles, while responding to religious diversity, the general tendency has been to confirm commonalities. With commonalities confirmed, some theologians go further and offer pluralistic approaches which regarded diverse religions as equally true. This approach has left less space for religious orthodoxy. Moreover, the advocates of pluralism have sometimes been insistent on the point that only pluralism can bring openness towards other religions, and this idea has created a lasting impression in some circles, although the idea is far from universally accepted. Recently some Christian theologians from the more orthodox wing have shown us that openness towards other religions does not depend on the adoption of a pluralistic position.

My aim is thus to present pluralism as one possible approach, not as the only approach which shows openness towards other religions. While pluralism successfully opened up a new period for interfaith engagement, its dependence on similarities and downplaying of differences has left little space for the believers of different faiths who hold to more orthodox versions of their own religions. It is worth mentioning a small autobiographical anecdote to contextualise this point.

My PhD journey has led my personal transformation in terms of my approach towards other religions. When I started my PhD project, I held a pluralistic position, more specifically an ethical-theological form of pluralism mainly inspired by Paul Knitter and Farid Esack. The main reason why I held this position was that since I started my undergraduate education, I had been heavily influenced by modernist reformist Muslims who have offered different approaches to the traditional ones long established in Islamic studies. Thus, differing from traditional Islamic perspectives, the pluralist position developed by modern Muslim theologians convinced me that Islam and the Qur'an accept pluralistic views. I was also convinced by the idea that the pluralist position shows more openness towards others. Furthermore, Christian theologians' challenges to orthodox Christian doctrines were another reason for me to adopt a pluralist position. What some Christian pluralists proposed, that is, the removal or reinterpretation of doctrines of incarnation and Trinity, was something which I can easily support because of my Islamic background. Thus, the pluralist position was for me the safest position that I could advocate. However, engaging more deeply with the subject of theology of religions and comparative theology and experiencing the real diversity of Christians in my faculty environment led me to revise my own position. I realised that the position I was holding did not show enough openness towards the believers of other religions, specifically Christians, who take their orthodox beliefs seriously. Thus I started to consider the difference of Christianity more carefully, and at the end of my PhD journey, I found that I was no longer holding to a pluralist position so seriously.

This research deepens the discussion on Christian and Islamic theology of religions. Specifically, it provides a comparison of the development of theology of religions in the Western Christian context and its application in the Islamic context. It also shows the parallels between some specific forms of theology of religions, that is, exclusivism, inclusivism or pluralism, in both traditions. To this end, the arguments of certain Christian and Muslim theologians are taken under consideration to figure out the interconnections and contradictions of their pluralist, exclusivist and inclusivist approaches. Based on this research, it can be claimed, as the fundamental contribution of this study, that it draws a rounded picture of Christian-Muslim understandings of religious others. In this way, it also includes Christian approaches to Islam and vice versa. Therefore, this study also serves an important goal, together with other works on this subject, in exploring the massive theological discussion in this area and preparing the ground for a stronger and more sophisticated Islamic theology of religions.

There have been diverse studies on theology of religions in Christian circles, but Islamic studies of theology of religions have been limited. Despite its limitations, different responses to religious pluralism by Muslims have formed an Islamic-based theology of religions. However, Muslim theologians have offered their own form of theology of religions without delving deeply into discussions on Christian theology of religions.[5] Furthermore, studies on Islamic theology of religions also generally have focused on a particular form of theology of religions, which in most cases is pluralist theology in general or a comparative perspective of two theologians from

4 Introduction

Islamic and Christian traditions.[6] However, in this study I aim to offer a rounded study of Christian and Islamic theology of religions. In this respect, I aim to present diverse Christian and Islamic responses to religious pluralism in conversation with each other through interceptions and contradictions among their ideas.

Apart from contribution to the area of theology of religions, this research also aims to contribute a possible Islamic comparative theology which can be seen as an important way for theorising non-Islamic religions from the Islamic perspective. It offers comparative theology, not something as alternative to theology of religions but rather as something which can contribute Islamic theology of religions itself. To this end, this research shows how comparative theology can challenge the questions raised within theology of religions and how Islamic theology of religions can work in conjunction with comparative theology and so on.

Methodologically, I will only focus on contemporary discussions of how Christian and Muslim theologians respond to religious diversity in the light of the threefold typology provided by Alan Race: exclusivism, inclusivism and pluralism. Alternative typologies to Race's will also be assessed, and I will also question the applicability of the threefold typology to Islamic theology of religions discussion.

This study basically consists of an analytical survey of selected bodies of literature from Christian and Islamic perspectives. This book consists of three main sections. The first section examines Christian perceptions of others in the light of epistemological and soteriological concerns about whether or not Christianity is the only true religion and/or the only one which leads to salvation. In the second section the same methodological approach has been applied in the Islamic context; thus, the diverse answers to the question of whether Islam is the only valid religion which leads its believers to heaven will be examined. Through these two discussions I will show that one important problem faced by both Christian and Muslim thinkers is the challenge of negotiating religious similarity and difference. In my final section I will return to this problem. I will show that some criticisms made against Christian inclusivists and pluralists are also relevant for Muslim theology of religions. I will also argue that there is a need to pay attention to the specific details of other religious traditions and show how this complicates theology of religions questions by looking at two issues between Christianity and Islam: whether or not Christians and Muslims worship the same God and whether or not they have the same understanding of revelation. This section will contain some comparative analysis and will also indicate the potential implications for future Islamic theology of religions thinking.

The book has five main chapters:

The first chapter outlines Christian theology of religions, including Race's threefold typology, exclusivism, inclusivism and pluralism, and particularism, which has been offered as a fourth alternative position. Prominent advocates of each position's theology of religions will be presented, and then criticisms and objections to their ideas will be evaluated. Moreover, it will also outline comparative theology and will offer the comparative theological approach as a framework to contextualise any theological position. The main object of this chapter is to outline the deficiencies and insights of each position and to show that the discussions, especially among pluralist and post-liberal theologians, have been a fruitful contribution to the development of Christian theology of religions.

The second chapter outlines Rowan Williams's theology of religions in light of the discussion of typologies given in the first chapter. I have chosen to look at Williams's work because he offers a sophisticated theology which attempts to do justice to both the similarity and difference of other religions, and he also has some statements explicitly addressing Islam. This chapter will firstly give some biographical information about Williams and then attempt to locate his theology of religions within the typologies given in the first chapter. Finally, his theology of religions will be evaluated. The main argument of this chapter is that although Williams's theology of religions seems to be particularist, which is considered by pluralists to be insufficiently open to religious others, the form of theology which Williams offers (Trinitarian theology of religions) is open to other religions and able to interact with other religions' doctrines. It will be also argued that Williams's theology of religions challenges typologies of theology of religions by not easily fitting any category.

The third chapter focuses on Muslims' diverse responses to religious pluralism. As in the first chapter, it will present a number of well-known theologians as representatives of diverse positions and will aim to show the inadequacies, insights and consequences of each position. One of the main objects of this chapter is to present that in Islamic theology of religions the problem of salvation is not as central as in Christianity. Another object of this chapter is to show that in contemporary Islamic discourse, despite its variety, there are two distinct groups: exclusivists and pluralists. On the one hand, there are exclusivists who hold the idea that Islam is the only true religion; on the other hand are pluralists who claim the opposite. In other words, in current discussion on Islamic theology of religions, theologians either take supersessionist theory as a starting point or develop theology which rejects the supersessionist theory. As a result of these two different positions, which in nature oppose to each other, I argue that Race's threefold paradigm, whilst heuristically useful as a starting point for considering Islamic theology of religions, is not fully applicable to it as finding Muslim thinkers who fit easily into the inclusivist category is problematic.

The fourth chapter examines Jerusha Lamptey's Islamic theology of religions as an alternative to the two forms described in the previous chapter. Like Williams, Lamptey offers a sophisticated theology which pays attention to the problem of doing justice to both religious similarities and differences and which does not fit easily into a single category on a typology. I will argue that in the contemporary discussion of religious diversity, theologians either present non-Islamic religions as invalid or corrupted or simply reject the real differences of other religions by placing emphasis on similarities.

6 *Introduction*

Lamptey's theology of religions, however, considers religious difference while at the same time aiming to affirm similarities or sameness. Despite her achievements, the deficiency of her position also will be provided.

The fifth chapter reassesses theology of religions in light of the discussion provided in previous chapters. I will argue that every attempt to formulate a theology of religions is valuable, but any alternative theology of religions might appear to solve the problems of others and simultaneously create new problems. Thus, rather than judging theologies of religions as a whole, I will consider Keith Ward's definition of 'open' and 'closed' theology and aim to apply it to a number of possible theological options. The object of this chapter is to propose that if theology of religions works in conjunction with comparative theology, then it will be much more capable of recognising the difference of other religions. To this end, it will compare two central notions, God and revelation, in Islam and Christianity. On the basis of this comparative discussion, I will argue that we should not be left with an either/or dilemma when considering the pluralist claim that Islam and Christianity (and other religions) come from and lead to the same source.

Overall, then, I will show that Christian and Muslim theology of religions share similar problems and can be subject to similar criticisms. In particular, there is the problem of doing justice to religious difference even in the context of emphasising common ground. Even sophisticated thinkers sympathetic to other religions like Rowan Williams and Jerusha Lamptey do not offer a completely satisfactory resolution to this problem, although they make some helpful suggestions. Attention to comparative analysis shows that theology of religions questions need not always end in an either/or answer and convinces us of the importance of paying attention to religious differences. Thus, this study will be a preliminary study to developing a more satisfactory Muslim position (by using the tools of comparative theology) that I would hope to proceed postdoctorally.

Notes

1 Contemporary comparative theology in Christian theology is a new area. Unlike theology of religions, the comparative theology aims to postpone theorising non-Christian religions after the engagement. In the first chapter, more detailed information will be provided.

2 Hans Küng, *Global Responsibility: In Search of a New World Ethic* (London: SCM Press, 1991).

3 Hans Küng and Karl-Josef Kuschel (eds.), *A Global Ethic: The Declaration of the Parliament of World's Religions* (Munich: SCM Press, 1993).

4 Samuel Huntington, "The Clash of Civilizations," *Foreign Affairs* (Summer 1993).

5 I will show these interconnections mainly in Chapter 3.

6 For instance Rifat Atay in *Religious Pluralism and Islam: A Critical Examination of John Hick's Pluralistic Hypothesis* (doctoral thesis, University of St Andrews, 1999) analyses John Hick's theology of religions from an Islamic perspective. Similarly, Adnan Aslan in *Religious Pluralism in Christian and Islamic Philosophy: The Thought of John Hick and Seyyed Hossein Nasr* (Abingdon, Oxon: Routledge, 1994) and Lewis Winkler in *Contemporary Muslim and Christian*

Responses to Religious Pluralism: Wolfhart Pannenberg in Dialogue with Abdulaziz Sachedina (Eugene: Pickwick Publications, 2011) present two different theologians' responses to religious pluralism in conversation with each other. Muhammad Hassan Khalil in *Islam and the Fate of Others: The Salvation Question* (New York: Oxford University Press, 2012) also explores Muslim theologians' response to religious pluralism on the theme of the question of salvation. Jerusha Lamptey in *Never Wholly Other: A Muslima Theology of Religions* (New York: Oxford University Press, 2014) also presents diverse Muslim responses to religious pluralism.

Bibliography

Aslan, Adnan. *Religious Pluralism in Christian and Islamic Philosophy: The Thought of John Hick and Seyyed Hossein Nasr.* Abingdon, Oxon: Routledge, 1994.

Atay, Rifat. "Religious Pluralism and Islam: A Critical Examination of John Hick's Pluralistic Hypothesis." PhD diss., University of St Andrews, 1999.

Huntington, Samuel. "The Clash of Civilizations." *Foreign Affairs* (Summer 1993): 22–49.

Khalil, Muhammad Hassan. *Islam and the Fate of Others: The Salvation Question.* New York: Oxford University Press, 2012.

Küng, Hans. *Global Responsibility: In Search of a New World Ethic.* London: SCM Press, 1991.

Küng, Hans and Karl-Josef Kuschel, eds. *A Global Ethic: The Declaration of the Parliament of World's Religions.* Munich: SCM Press, 1993.

Lamptey, Jerusha. *Never Wholly Other: A Muslima Theology of Religions.* New York: Oxford University Press, 2014.

Winkler, Lewis. *Contemporary Muslim and Christian Responses to Religious Pluralism: Wolfhart Pannenberg in Dialogue with Abdulaziz Sachedina.* Eugene: Pickwick Publications, 2011.

1 Christian theology of religions

Introduction

Religious pluralism has been a crucial case in the modern world. As a result of their experiences of religious pluralism, Western Christians have begun to ask fundamental questions to believers of non-Christian religions that they did not ask so frequently and with such urgency as in the past. Locating Christianity among world religions and determining whether members of non-Christian religions would be saved or not through these religions and concerns such as these have urged Christians to respond to other religions. The responses to religious pluralism have been varied in the Christian world. From the late nineteenth century, Christian scholars have questioned the status of non-Christian religions within both academic and institutional circles. On the one hand, Christians continued missionary work; on the other hand, scholars of history of religions and comparative religion and theology have engaged in deep discussion of the Christian tradition.[1] Significantly, the discussion in the Christian tradition has given rise to a smaller, more specific subtopic, namely theology of religions within Christian theology.

In 1983, with the publication of *Christians and Religious Pluralism*, Alan Race offered a threefold typology, exclusivism, inclusivism and pluralism, concerning the Christian approach to non-Christian religions. Since then Race's typology has produced widespread discussion and debate. In this chapter I take Race's typology as a starting point and will present different theologies of religions in each section. Race's classification does not address post-liberal theology of religions;[2] however, I will present post-liberal theology after discussing Race's typology since I think post-liberal theology of religions occupies an important place in the current discussion in the area of Christian theology of religions. After presenting each section of the typology and considering post-liberal theology, I will evaluate Race's classification. While evaluating Race's typology I will present comparative theology's challenge to theology of religions with special attention to Francis Clooney and argue that if theology of religions works in conjunction with comparative theology, it could provide a better understanding of other religions. The chapter then offers a conclusion.

In current discussion on Christian theology of religions, there has been a movement from an exclusivist position toward a particularist position. In fact, pluralist and particularist positions occupy the central place in current discussion. For example Paul Hedges in *Controversies in Interreligious Dialogue and the Theology of Religions* takes pluralist and particularist positions as the primary stances to be addressed.[3] Although the exclusivist position introduced mainly by Karl Barth and early twentieth-century theologians is still stronger in some Christian churches, such as Evangelical and Fundamentalist ones,[4] post-liberal theology of religions has carried early exclusivist theology of religions into another dimension. Despite its popularity in some Churches, the early-formed exclusivist position does not fully take up a significant intellectual place in Christian responses to religious pluralism. For this reason, in this chapter I will give less attention to the exclusivist position than other positions. I will present major influential theologians for each type of theology of religions, that is, Karl Barth for exclusivism, Karl Rahner for inclusivism, John Hick for pluralism and George Lindbeck for post-liberal theology of religions. However, I will also give special attention to Paul Knitter's pluralist theology of religions as his theology of religions takes it roots from 'liberation theology', which in some ways challenges a standard pluralistic position. The next section explores exclusivist theology of religions.

1 Exclusivism

The exclusivist position has been the main theological option for the Christian world for many centuries. In *Christians and Religious Pluralism*, Race opens the section on exclusivism with two biblical texts, which are the sources of the exclusivist paradigm.[5] These texts are Act 4.12: 'And there is salvation in no one else, for there is no other name under heaven given among men by which we must be saved' and John 14.6: ' I am the way, and the truth, and the life; no one comes to the Father, but by me.' As can be understood from these two texts, the main argument of exclusivism is that salvation is only possible in Jesus Christ. To emphasise the point, exclusivist theology is shaped by two doctrines for Protestantism and three doctrines for Catholicism. The first doctrine is that salvation comes from Christ alone (*solus Christus*). According to this argument, Christ came into the world to bring salvation. The second doctrine is that salvation is only available through explicit faith in Christ that comes from the hearing the Gospel preached (*fides ex auditu*), from repentance, baptism and embracing of new life in Christ. The third doctrine, which is used primarily by Catholic theologians, is that the Church must be the means of salvation since Christ is the only cause to salvation (*extra ecclesiam nulla salus*).[6]

Indeed, exclusivist theologians develop their own theology according to these doctrines, though their emphasis may differ. Race summarises exclusivism as 'it counts the revelation in Jesus as the sole criterion by which all

10 *Christian theology of religions*

religions, including Christianity, can be understood and evaluated.'[7] It is necessary to offer an explanation of some exclusivist theologians' theories to see how they develop these doctrines. In this respect, I will focus on Barth's theology in detail and will also touch on some other theologians' theories.

1.1 *Barth's theology of religions*

Karl Barth has been considered one of the prominent exclusivist theologians of the twentieth century. As a Protestant (Swiss Reformed) theologian, Barth develops his own theology of religions in the light of the first two doctrines previously mentioned; salvation is only possible by explicit faith (second doctrine) in Christ (first doctrine).

Barth develops exclusivist theology by taking revelation as the starting point. For him revelation of God in Jesus Christ, as contained in the Holy Scripture, is where theology starts and finishes. Barth's theology of religions consists of two steps; firstly religion(s) is unbelief, and secondly Christianity is the only true religion. He comes to this conclusion through his understanding of revelation. For Barth, we can only know God by revelation, and any attempt to know God other than via God's revelation is an activity of unbelief. He says that 'religion is unbelief, it is a concern, indeed, we must say that it is the one great concern, of godless man.'[8] From this viewpoint, religion is an attempt by humans to know about God. In other words, religion is an attempt to replace God's revelation with a human manufacture, thus religion is a human creation, not God's divine creation.[9]

When Barth developed the idea of religion as unbelief, he set out two elements in which the necessity of revelation unmistakably became clear. The first element according to Barth is that only God can make God known; in essence, human beings can only know God if God tells them.

> Revelation is God's self-offering and self-manifestation. Revelation encounters man on the presupposition and in conformation of the fact that man's attempt to know God from his own standpoint are wholly and entirely futile; not because of any necessity in principle, but because of a practical necessity of fact. In revelation God tells man that he is God, and that such he is his Lord. In telling him this, revelation tells him something utterly new, something which apart from revelation he does not know and cannot tell either himself or others.[10]

The second element is related to the first element: that God gives revelation by His grace. Barth states that 'as self-manifestation and self-offering of God, revelation is the act by which in grace He reconciles man to Himself by grace.'[11] Thus according to Barth's theology of religions, there are two foundations of salvation. The first is that salvation is only through revelation of God in Jesus Christ. The second foundation is that salvation is only possible by the grace of God.

Turning to Barth's formulation that religion is unbelief, he is not only speaking about Christianity but about all religions of the world. Then the question should be asked, what makes Christianity special to other world religions? For Barth, Christianity is not special because of its own inward worthiness; however, the distinct feature of Christianity comes from the revelation of God and salvation offered only in Christ. Thanks to Jesus Christ, on the one hand, Christianity knows that it is a false and idolatry religion; on the other hand, it knows that it is saved through Jesus Christ. Thus, Barth separates revelation from religion. Despite this separation between revelation and religion, he still argues for the superiority of Christianity over non-Christian religions. He states that

> [a]t the end of road we have to tread there is, of course, the promise to those who accept God's judgment, who let themselves be led beyond their belief. There is faith in this promise, and, in this faith, the presence and the reality of grace of God, which, of course, differentiates our religion, the Christian, from all others as true religion.[12]

As a result Barth's perception of revelation leads him to confirm the superiority of Protestant Reformed Christianity over non-Christian religions. The reason Christianity is superior to other religions is because it has the only authentic revelation through which people would be saved. The question of whether non-Christian religions contain true elements is irrelevant since the only criteria for Barth is revelation. For example, when he compares Eastern religions' teaching, such as Yodoism of Japan (Yodo Shin-shu Buddhism) and the Bhakti form of Hinduism, with Christianity he contends that

> [i]ndeed, why should we not say it of a whole range of other religions, for which grace in different names and contexts is not a wholly foreign entity. Only one thing is really decisive for the distinction of truth and error. And we call the existence of Yodoism a providential disposition because with what is relatively the greatest possible force it makes it so clear that only one thing is decisive. That one thing is the name of Jesus Christ. . . . The truth of the Christian religion is in fact enclosed in the one name of Jesus Christ and nothing else.[13]

To summarise, Barth's position towards non-Christian religions is an example of exclusivism. Christianity is superior to other religions on the grounds that it necessitates the revelation of God in Christ. Other forms of religions are false because they do not have a true revelation.

1.2 Other forms of exclusivism and objections

Barth's theology of religions demonstrates his reaction to Enlightenment philosophy. From the Enlightenment to the early twentieth century, Enlightenment philosophy had replaced Christian theology as a dominant intellectual

12 *Christian theology of religions*

discourse. As Gunton states, Barth argues that after Kant, theology was fundamentally changed. Theologians followed the Kantian framework, extended the Kantian framework or offered an alternative.[14] Barth followed none of these options since to him all these philosophies (theologies) were less concerned with Christian virtues and more concerned with Enlightenment virtues; that is to say, all these frameworks create their own image of God or Jesus rather than extending the Christian image of God.[15] From this perspective Barth's theology of religions seems authentic. He has reconstructed the neo-orthodox view of Christianity and in such a way has influenced many theologians after him. As will become clear later in this chapter, the post-liberal theologies of religions have taken much from Barth's theology. On the other hand, certain aspects of his theology of religions seem problematic.

There are two methodological problems with Barth's theology of religions. Firstly, Barth's insistence on the notion that only Christianity has an authentic revelation seems problematic. He does not explore or offer any deep knowledge of non-Christian religions, yet still retains that idea. As Race contends, Barth's radical separation does not come from an exercise of comparative religion but arises from Barth's own understanding of Christian revelation.[16] For instance, when Barth is questioned as to how he knew Hinduism to be unbelief, while he had never met with any Hindus, his answer was interestingly 'a priori'.[17] Secondly, radical dependence on revelation also seems difficult. He paints a picture of the New Testament as if it is the only authoritative source about the knowledge of God; anything other than the Bible is irrelevant.[18] Knitter rightly criticises any position that takes the Bible as the only and final source of religious truth since this position would blind or blur the Christian vision to the beliefs of other religions, which in turn prevents an effective dialogue.[19]

Theologically, Barth's theology of religions seems to fail in certain aspects. The Bible itself claims other forms of revelation;[20] however, Barth dismisses these passages. Even though in the Christian tradition theologians have made a distinction between general revelation and a specific revelation of God in Jesus Christ, Barth does not engage with any kind of general or natural revelation. On the grounds that his theology's starting point is revelation, he disregards natural revelation. Even other exclusivist theologians, such as Kraemer, criticise Barth's theology on this point. Kraemer states that

> [i]f Barth says – and he does – that the Bible knows no other mode of revelation than Christ, he has the Bible against him. If he says that all modes of revelation find their source, their meaning and contention in Jesus Christ, and that the revelation of God's righteousness in Christ is the Truth, the *only* Truth, without whom no man comes to the Father – then he is quite right.[21]

From this point of view, it might be helpful to touch upon other exclusivist theologians' theology of religions to see the strengths and weaknesses of exclusivist theory.

Christian theology of religions   13

Both Emil Brunner and Hendrik Kraemer accept general revelation; however, they also pursue the exclusivist idea of the superiority of Christian religion over non-Christian religions. Kraemer is not as exclusivist as Barth; however, he still holds exclusivist ideas. Kraemer's theology of religions can be summarised using two main stages. Firstly, he goes a step further than Barth about revelation. Unlike Barth, he does not reject terms like 'general revelation' and 'natural theology'; rather, he redefines these terms. He contends that

> [g]eneral revelation can henceforth only mean that God shines revealingly through the works of His creation (nature), through the thirst and quest for truth and beauty, through the conscience and the thirst and quest for goodness, which throbs in man even in his condition of forlorn sinfulness, because God is continuously occupying Himself and wrestling with man, all ages and with all peoples.[22]

For Kraemer however, general revelation can only be understood through the lens of Jesus Christ. Secondly, he rejects any kind of 'point of contact' between Christianity and non-Christian religions to maintain the superiority of the special revelation of Jesus Christ. Although he appreciates the missionaries who are concerned with finding a connection so as to make sense of Christianity to the followers of non-Christian religions, he rejects comparing and finding similarities among the doctrines or practices of religions. He argues that 'when the world approach is taken in the sense of Christianity as total religious system approaching the non-Christian religions as total religious systems, there is only differences and antithesis, and this must be so because they are radically different.'[23] The second stage of Kraemer's theology of religions is a rejection of pluralistic theories that seek for common ground among religions, which as we will see in the forthcoming sections, is a common theological strategy among pluralist theologians. However, his emphasis on the radical differences of religions has also been developed more deeply by post-liberal theologians, which will also be discussed in the coming sections.

Brunner, like Kraemer, also accepts general revelation and natural theology. Yet, he argues there are three ways to know about God: natural theology, general revelation and revelation of Christ. He distinguishes among each of these kinds of revelation. For him, natural theology allows God's knowledge through human reason, yet there is no connection between natural theology and biblical knowledge of God since they are 'bitterly and fundamentally opposed'.[24] The second type is general revelation, which could be found within non-Christian traditions. However, general revelation can be understood only through revelation of Christ; 'as those whose eyes opened by Jesus Christ, on the basis of Biblical testimony we are able to speak of general revelation in the Creation is given to all.'[25] Yet, prioritising the revelation of Christ among other revelations, Brunner comes to the exclusivist argument of the superiority of Christian faith. Like Barth and Kraemer, Brunner's exclusivism also comes from his understanding of

14   *Christian theology of religions*

revelation. He locates Christology in the centre and tries to understand non-Christian traditions from this perspective. Thus, for him 'Jesus Christ is both the Fulfillment of all religion and the Judgment on all religion.'[26]

Even though Kraemer and Brunner offer a more tenable exclusivism than Barth, their theology of religions still faces the same criticism. They extend the boundary of revelation; however, this does not mean other kinds of revelations, other than Christ, are valid or meaningful. Thus, the exclusivist form of theology of religions has not satisfied some Christian theologians. Specifically, exclusivism's vision of salvation and its view of non-Christian religions have been criticised by other Christian theologians. Consequently, they have developed different forms of theology of religions. Gradually, inclusivist and pluralist theologies of religions have become alternatives to exclusivism in the modern period. In the next section, I will investigate how inclusivism has addressed the critiques of exclusivism.

2 Inclusivism

Inclusivist theology occupies a position between exclusivism and pluralism. On the one hand inclusivism retains the exclusivist belief that salvation is only possible through Jesus; on the other hand it accepts the spiritual power and essentially the salvific efficacy of non-Christian religions. Race describes inclusivism as 'both an acceptance and a rejection of other faiths, a dialectical "yes" and "no".'[27] Although inclusivism became a popular position in the Catholic tradition after the Second Vatican Council, some early Christian theologians have also been considered inclusivist.[28] Before moving on to a discussion of inclusivist theologians, it is necessary to note that there are two forms of inclusivism. The first form of inclusivism accepts the salvific means of non-Christian religions, whereas the second form does not view non-Christian religions as possible ways to salvation but only accepts some true elements of non-Christian religions. D'Costa labels these two forms of inclusivism as 'structural inclusivism' and 'restrictivist inclusivism', respectively.[29] In this section, I will use Rahner's inclusivism as an example of structural inclusivism, and then I will discuss some other inclusivist theologians and theories.

2.1 Rahner's theology of religions: theory of the 'anonymous Christianity'

Karl Rahner is regarded as the major figure responsible for shaping the Catholic Church's positive attitudes toward non-Christian religions.[30] He is also considered as the pioneer of an inclusivist theology of religions. He is also one of the most influential Catholic inclusivist theologians of the latter half of twentieth century.[31]

According to Rahner, God's grace operates in non-Christians. Making this argument, Rahner then develops his famous theory of the 'anonymous Christian', which suggests that all people implicitly have an awareness of God, even if they do not explicitly profess it. As a result, for Rahner, explicit belief in Christ is not necessary for all Christians; non-Christians can be saved by their implicit faith.

Rahner's perspective[32] is based on both Christology and the universal salvific will of God. From this basis he proposed four theses to outline a Christian theology of religions. Thus, his first thesis argues that 'Christianity understands itself as the absolute religion, intended for all men, which cannot recognize any other religion beside itself as of equal right.'[33] By presenting this as his first thesis, Rahner affirms the Christological statement that revelation from Christ is the absolute and there is nothing equal to it in other religions. Although this sounds like an exclusivist statement, the important point is that Rahner does not limit the salvation offered by Christ only to Christians; instead he emphasises the universal salvific will of God. His second thesis makes his position much clearer:

> Until the moment when the Gospel really enters into historical situation of an individual, a non-Christian religion (even outside the Mosaic religion) does not merely contain elements of a natural knowledge of God, elements, moreover, mixed with human depravity which is the result of original sin and later aberrations. It contains also supernatural elements arising out of the grace which is given to men as gratuitous gift on account of Christ. For this reason a non-Christian religion can be recognized as a *lawful* religion (although only in different degrees) without thereby denying the error and depravity contained in it.[34]

The second thesis deals with two statements. Firstly, it confirms that non-Christian religions contain supernatural and grace-filled elements. Rahner's interpretation of the relation between nature and grace makes the first statement clear. According to Rahner, there is always a preapprehension of infinite being, and therefore of God, in the human act of knowing and willing. God cannot be known directly and therefore cannot be the object of an act of knowledge unlike physical objects such as chairs and tables. In the case where the mind knows particular objects or wills some finite values, however, it never only chooses or knows the particular, rather it always strives to reach beyond, towards the whole being and thus towards God. For Rahner, nature and grace are not separate and distinct phases in the historical life of both the individual and the community. Rather he argues that human beings are oriented towards God by nature. He describes this nature as a 'supernatural existential'. That is, as a result of God's historical acts in the person of Jesus Christ, all men are called to develop an intimate connection with God. Rahner contends that every human is part of the plan of salvation, and his 'supernatural existential' theory supports this claim. Rahner commented that

> because the universal and supernatural will of God is working for human salvation, the unlimited transcendence of man, itself directed of necessity towards God, is raised up consciously by grace, although

16 *Christian theology of religions*

possibly without explicit thematic reflection, in such a way that the possibility of faith in revelation is thereby made available.[35]

Thus, he argues that grace is operative in a person's life in his very awareness of himself. He also claims however that

[i]n the acceptance of himself man is accepting Christ as the absolute perfection and guarantee of his own anonymous movement towards God by grace, and the acceptance of this belief is again not an act of man alone but the work of God's grace which is the grace of Christ.[36]

Therefore on the one hand, Rahner accepts the salvific will of God, including all human beings, while on the other hand, he claims that 'salvation willed by God is salvation won by Christ.'[37]

The second part of Rahner's second thesis confirms that non-Christian religions should be seen as lawful religions[38] and not regarded as if they have no positive significance. By a 'lawful religion' Rahner is referring to an institutional religion that can be regarded as having some form of 'right relationship' with God, and this inevitably entails also possessing positive significance as a means for achieving salvation. Thus, by recognising non-Christian religions as lawful religions, Rahner contends that God's grace operates to enable non-Christian religions to also serve as a way of salvation. Recognising non-Christian religions as lawful religions, however, does not entail believing that they are free from errors or depravations, and Rahner makes this point explicitly. In fact, Rahner claims that non-Christian religions contain serious religious, ethical and metaphysical aberrations both in theory and practice.[39] Despite these negative points, however, Rahner still considers non-Christian religions to be within God's salvific plan and thus to present a legitimate means to achieve salvation. In taking this position, Rahner presents his third thesis: 'Christianity does not simply confront the member of an extra-Christian religion as a mere non-Christian but as someone who can and must already be regarded in this or that respect as an anonymous Christian.'[40]

Rahner's third thesis leads him to the conclusion that everyone, regardless of whether they describe themselves as atheist, agnostic or any other label, retains an awareness of God. This awareness remains the case even when individuals explicitly deny the existence of God. Thus, according to Rahner, explicit faith in Christ is not necessary for salvation. Those who do not profess Christianity or do not grow up in a Christian tradition are still offered the grace of Christ through the depth of their personal experiences, even though they may not recognise it. These are the 'anonymous Christians'. It is for this reason that many scholars and theologians criticise that Rahner's theory imposes his Christian religious thought on non-Christians, thus robbing non-Christians of their agency. In doing so, he also prevents any recognition of the significant differences inherent in non-Christian religions.

This point is one of the major criticisms of Rahner's theory and is discussed in greater detail in the next section.

Rahner's fourth thesis is related to the missionary task and offers a re-evaluation of the Church itself. He states that

> the Church will not so much regard itself as the exclusivist community of those who have a claim to salvation but rather as the historically tangible vanguard and the historically and socially constituted explicit expression of what the Christian hopes is present as a hidden reality even outside the visible Church.[41]

In saying this, Rahner eliminates the common and long-held Christian claim that 'there is no salvation outside the Church.' Instead, he presents an extension to the boundaries of the Church. The belief that salvation exists outside the Church is the reason why exclusivist theologians disagree with Rahner and accuse him of denigrating the importance of Christianity and the Church.

2.2 Other forms of inclusivism

Rahner's 'anonymous Christian' theory has received both appreciation and support and harsh criticism from various Christian theologians. Until the Second Vatican Council, the primary Catholic teaching concerning non-Christian religions was simply that there was no possibility of salvation outside the Church. After the council however, the Catholic Church abandoned this exclusivist claim and appeared to broaden its stance on salvation to include non-Christians. Yet it should be noted that it is not entirely clear from the council's documents whether or not the Catholic Church officially accepts the salvific efficacy of non-Christian religions.[42] This is an important point, although it is beyond the scope of this study to address this controversy. What is clear, however, is that following the council, relations between Catholics and non-Christians were fundamentally changed, and Rahner's theology had a major influence on these changes.

At the same time, the mainstream Catholic teaching as constituted by the documents of the Second Vatican Council is not as radical as Rahner's theology of religions. The council has, however, opened a new path in the Catholic Church's history with Nostra Aetate (Declaration on the Relationship of the Church to Non-Christian Religions) and Lumen Gentium (Dogmatic Constitution on the Church) Paragraph 16. Before the council, for many centuries the majority of Christians had retained the exclusivist belief that '*extra ecclesiam nulla salus*' (there is no salvation outside the Church). The Church revised the older teaching,[43] which sees other religions as errors, and acknowledged the broadening of salvation to include non-Christian people. It was the first time in Church history that Catholics had spoken about the believers of non-Christian religions, namely, Jews,[44] Muslims,[45] Hindus and

18 *Christian theology of religions*

Buddhists,[46] positively. One the one hand the council declared that there are true elements in non-Christian religions, and thus salvation is open to them, while on the other hand the Church was still regarded as the necessary means for salvation.[47] The specific way in which non-Christians are connected to salvation is not given in the documents; however, it is stated that the Spirit of God is active in non-Christian religions to direct them towards Christ and the Church.[48] Despite the truth, holiness and secret presence of God, the salvific means of non-Christian religions are never confirmed. Thus, the fullness of salvation can only be found in the Catholic Church. Practically, the Church has placed its thoughts and doctrines at the centre and, by the Spirit of God's operation in non-Christian religions, has connected Catholicism to other religions. From this perspective, it is reasonable to argue that the Catholic Church's form of theology of religions is an example of restrictivist inclusivism, which accepts the salvation of non-Christians but rejects the salvific means of non-Christian religions.

Within the Catholic tradition, as an inclusivist theologian, Hans Küng developed a more liberal theology which accepts the salvific efficacy of non-Christian religions but does not require that individuals be regarded as hidden Christians. Küng criticises Rahner's anonymous Christian theory for not going far enough as, according to his account, the Church and knowledge of Christ are still ultimately necessary for salvation in Rahner's theory. For Küng however, sweeping all of humanity through the 'back door of the Catholic Church' represents a paper-thin bridge of 'theological fabrication'.[49] Thus for Küng, despite superficial appearances Rahner is fundamentally repeating the old formula that 'there is no salvation outside the Church.' On the one hand Küng accepts the salvific efficacy of non-Christian religions, while on the other hand, he considers Christ as normative. He sees Jesus as being 'ultimately decisive, definitive, archetypal, for man's relations with God'.[50] To him then, Jesus Christ is not only an archetypal man; he is also normative for all people.[51] Consequently, although Küng is critical of Rahner and attempts to find an alternative way to accommodate the salvation offered by non-Christian religions, his theology also seems to present Christ's superiority among other religious figures.

Inclusivist theory opens the gate of salvation to non-Christian religions while also maintaining the superiority of Christian doctrines or figures, thus it occupies a middle position between exclusivism and pluralism, and for this reason inclusivist theories and theologians have been criticised by both groups.

2.3 Objections to Rahner's theory and inclusivism

Rahner's understanding of non-Christians as 'anonymous Christians' has been criticised as he fails to recognise the very real differences between Christianity and the non-Christian religions. His approach has thus been regarded as patronising towards non-Christian religions as it suggests that Rahner knows the beliefs of non-Christians better than the individuals themselves. Hick points out that by labelling non-Christians as anonymous

Christians, '(t)he devout Muslim, or Hindu, or Sikh, or Jew can be regarded as an anonymous Christian, this being an honorary status granted unilaterally to people who have not expressed any desire for it.'[52] However, D'Costa argues that these criticisms misunderstand the intended context of Rahner's position. He points out that Rahner's anonymous Christianity theory is intended as an internal discourse within Christianity and as such addresses the relations between Christian and non-Christian religions. Consequently, his intention is not to gain approval of his theory from other religions but to present and alter the Church's own self-understanding.[53] A similar defence is presented by Boutin, who argues that the content and the notion are different: 'The person *to* whom the notion is communicated is not the person *about* whom the notion is formulated.'[54] Thus both D'Costa and Boutin emphasise that Rahner's use of the term 'anonymous Christian' was intended to characterise a Christian attitude towards other religions rather than to label them as Christian anonymously. These scholars quote from Rahner's conversation with the head of the Kyoto Zen Buddhist School, Keji Nishitani. When Nishitani asked Rahner how he would react if Nishitani treated him as an anonymous Zen Buddhist. Rahner replies:

> Certainly you may and should do so from your point of view; I feel myself honoured by such an interpretation, even if I am obliged to regard you as being in error or if I assume that, correctly understood, to be a genuine Zen Buddhist is identical with being a genuine Christian, in the sense directly and properly intended by such statements. Of course in terms of objective social awareness it is intended clear that the Buddhist is not a Christian and the Christian is not a Buddhist.[55]

It is quite clear that Rahner does not use the term 'anonymous Christianity' to label non-Christians but to open the way to salvation for them. By referring to non-Christian religions as being a form of anonymous Christianity Rahner is fundamentally attempting to extend salvation to non-Christian religions.

Nevertheless, both Rahner's theory and other forms of inclusivism actually do fail to recognise any real difference in non-Christians by implicitly equalising non-Christians with the explicit faith of Christians. As Race points out, such an inclusivist theory prejudges the issue of the truth in non-Christian religions. Moreover, he argues that labelling non-Christians as anonymous Christians suggests that Christians would have nothing to learn through interfaith dialogue, thus making such efforts meaningless.[56] Knitter raises a similar criticism against both Rahner's anonymous Christian theory and inclusivist theology of religions in general and argues that regarding Christianity or Christ as normative entails that inclusivist theologians are offensive to their partners in dialogue. Knitter argues that these kinds of inclusivist claims are a 'more subtle co-opting of dialogue',[57] and his quotation of Maurier illustrates how Christian inclusivist theology fails to pursue religious dialogue:

20 *Christian theology of religions*

> If Christianity (because of Christ) is the definitive truth, the absolute-
> ness of God's revelation to mankind, it only remains for the other reli-
> gions to convert to Christianity. . . . What we have, in fact, is a dialogue
> between the elephant and the mouse.[58]

Though these critics of inclusivism, and more specifically Rahner's anonymous Christianity, come from the pluralist circle, exclusivist theologians
also express similar criticisms related to the differences of religions. Exclusivist theologians conversely accuse inclusivists of reducing the importance
of Christianity and Christ. For example, in Balthasar's critique of Rahner's
methodology, he accuses Rahner of taking German idealism as his starting
point. Balthasar criticises the influence of the Enlightenment philosophical
system, which for him, reduces the central core of the Christian faith. He
argues that Rahner is trying to develop a Christian theology within an alien-
ating philosophical system. Moreover, he claims that the concept of anonymous Christianity leads to both a loss of the distinctiveness of Christianity
and a loss of commitment:

> Karl Rahner frees us from a nightmare with his theory of the anon-
> ymous Christian who is dispensed, at any rate, from the criterion of
> martyrdom and nevertheless thereby has a full claim to the name of
> Christian if he, consciously or unconsciously, gives God the honor.[59]

Aside from the methodological difficulty,[60] Balthasar's critique of anonymous Christianity as representing a reductive understanding of Christianity
is an important one. By classifying non-Christians as anonymous Christians, Rahner dismisses the real difference of Christianity as well. Specifically, the world religions have distinct sacraments and practices, and thus
by interpreting non-Christians as anonymous Christians, Rahner not only
fails to recognise the real distinctiveness of non-Christians but also dimin-
ishes what it means to be a Christian. It should also be noted, however, that
Rahner does not regard non-Christians as equal to Christians; while he talks
about the possibility of salvation for non-Christians, he still considers non-
Christian religions to be a mixture of errors and truths. Thus, Christianity
maintains its superiority among the world religions according to Rahner's
theory. Moreover, as Kilby points out, for Rahner, the offer of grace and
its acceptance only reach their full potential when non-Christians come to
express explicit recognition of Christianity.[61] Consequently, even though
Rahner considers non-Christians to be implicitly Christian, their version of
Christianity does not reach the full potential found within explicit Christianity, which is also the case in most inclusivist theories.

In fact, the criticism described here raised against inclusivism has also
been levelled against pluralism. Both pluralism and inclusivism share an
idea of 'the common ground'. Both typologies emphasise the importance of
God's universal salvific will and try to seek parallels between Christianity
and non-Christian religions. In contrast, pluralism differs from inclusivism

in terms of its locating Christianity among world religions and its emphasis on other salvific figures within other religions. The next section will explore the typology of pluralism.

3 Pluralism

The pluralist approach to the theology of religions is a recent phenomenon in Christian theology and the supporters of pluralism primarily come from the 'liberal' wing of Christianity.[62] Until the nineteenth century the dominant Christian approach to non-Christian religions was mainly exclusivist. With the development of empirical studies of non-Christian religions, however, especially in the field of the history of religions and comparative theology during the nineteenth century, pluralist Christian theologians have developed different approaches concerning Christian perspectives on and interactions with other religions in recent decades. Some theologians have emphasised a common religious object, 'the Real' (Hick),[63] whereas others, such as Smith, have underlined the importance of a common essence to religious faith.[64]

As has been mentioned in the previous sections, exclusivist and inclusivist theologians support the idea that salvation is only possible through either explicit (for exclusivists) or implicit (for inclusivists) faith in Jesus Christ. Thus, they consider non-Christian religions as invalid paths to the salvation promised in Christianity. In contrast, pluralist theology promotes the idea that both Christianity and non-Christian religions lead to salvation. Recently, in the Christian tradition, different pluralist theologies have been developed by different theologians. The most common theologies are what Knitter calls the 'philosophical-historical bridge', 'the religious-mystical bridge' and the 'ethical-practical bridge'.[65] John Hick and Paul Knitter's theology of religions as representing the philosophical-historical and ethical-practical forms, respectively, will be the subject of this section. Before moving on to their theology, I will briefly discuss the religious-mystical form of pluralism.

The religious-mystical form of the pluralist approach begins with Divine being. According to this approach, the object and content of religious life is infinite; that is to say, it is Mystery beyond all forms. Thus, the infinity of Mystery or God on the one hand requires religious pluralism, while on the other hand it leads to a rejection of the idea that only one specific religion has the final say on that Mystery.

Raimon Panikkar[66] is one of the most influential theologians to have developed the religious-mystical form of pluralism. His pluralism primarily emphasises the differences among religions rather than their similarities. In other words, his theology does not seek common ground among religions. He states:

> How can we pretend to deal with the ultimate problems of Man if we insist on reducing human being to only the American, or to only the

22 Christian theology of religions

> Christian or to black, or the male, or the exclusively heterosexual, or the healthy and 'normal', or the so called civilized? . . . pluralism is rooted in the deepest nature of things.[67]

His theology of religions does not reject the orthodox Christian doctrines, but rather he reinterprets these doctrines and offers his own pluralist theology of religions. In his theology, Jesus Christ is still the Logos: he maintains with seriousness the doctrine of the Trinity. He does, however, reject that Jesus totally circumscribes the Logos. Thus, he accepts other salvific figures in non-Christian religions. In terms of relating Christianity to non-Christian religions, he uses the metaphor of three rivers; the Jordan, the Tiber, and the Ganges. The Jordan represents early Christianity, which is exclusivist in nature. In that period Christian belief and practice needed to survive, and exclusivist beliefs were necessary for that survival. The Tiber represents the process of institutionalisation of Christianity, which shifts from exclusivism to inclusivism. Finally, the Ganges symbolises the diversity and pluralism of the present.[68]

3.1 Hick and philosophical-historical form of pluralism

John Hick is one of the most influential and also most criticised philosophers of the twentieth century. As mentioned, his theology of religions is an example of the philosophical-historical form of pluralism. He was an Evangelical Christian who held exclusivist views of Jesus Christ; however, after interacting more with his non-Christian neighbours of Birmingham, he refashioned his understanding of Jesus Christ and Christianity.

His theology of religions is opposed to both exclusivism and inclusivism. He has founded a 'Copernican revolution'[69] in Christology, a revolution that moves from a traditional Christological perspective on salvation to a new theocentric model. Hick proposes the idea that instead of recognising the figure of Christ or Christianity as the centre, God should be placed in the centre. As a result, Hick calls for a Copernican revolution in Christian theology of religions. The old Ptolemaic astronomy recognised the earth as the centre of the world; however, once it was observed that this fact does not fit with reality, there was a paradigm shift in belief. Taking this shift as a reference point, Hick claims that Christians should not regard themselves and their religion as the centre and should thus abandon the doctrine of 'no salvation outside the Church'.[70] Hick has come to the conclusion that all major world religions worship the *same* God, although He has been given various names. His proposal is thus for a major paradigm shift where Christianity is replaced by *God* as the focal point of salvation: 'we have to realize that [the] universe of faiths centres upon God, not upon Christianity or upon any other religion. He is the sun, the originative source of light and life, whom all religions reflect in their own different ways.'[71]

By removing Christ from the centre, Hick emphasises the universality of God and deemphasises traditional Christology. Hick's Copernican revolution excluded non-theistic religions based on the fact that not all world religions have the concept of God, which in turn has led him to redevelop his theology. Subsequently, he suggested 'Reality' in the centre rather than God to include non-theistic religions. In doing so Hick uses Kant's epistemological distinction between noumenal and phenomenal: the first 'exists independently of our perception', and the second is 'that same world as it appears to human consciousness'.[72] He comes to the conclusion that '[the] noumenal Real is experienced and thought by different human mentalities, forming and formed by different religious traditions.'[73] In making this argument, he distinguishes between the *personae* and *impersonae* of the Real. For him, the personae of the Real represent the God of theistic traditions such as Vishnu and Shiva, the heavenly Father, Allah, Yahweh[74] and more, whereas the impersonae of the Real represent the objects of non-theistic religions such as Brahman, Nirvana[75] and others. Moreover, Hick argues that even though the believers of each tradition experience the Real, they can only know it within their own social, historical and psychological forms. They can know the Real as phenomena, but they can never grasp it in its noumenal form. Thus, different religious traditions 'constitute different ways of experiencing, conceiving and living in relation to ultimate divine Reality which transcends all our visions of it'.[76]

As has been presented, Hick's theology of religions shows a clear separation from Christian orthodoxy. Hick still uses Christological language although completely differently from mainstream Christian tradition. He does not suggest that Christians abandon their traditional way of speaking about Jesus; instead he calls to Christians to revise their language. In essence, he suggests a metaphorical reading of Christology rather than a literal reading. According to Hick, Jesus neither taught nor claimed what Orthodox Christians have taught about his divinity.[77] In the New Testament and throughout Christian tradition, however, such language has been used to refer to Jesus as the Son of God, and Messiah. For Hick, thanks to New Testament or historical Jesus studies, Christians can understand the content of that language, knowledge they did not have a hundred years ago. The early Christians used these descriptions for Jesus to express their experience with Jesus. These descriptions are not what Jesus used to refer to himself, but rather his followers used these titles to express their feeling towards Jesus.

Hick claims that the language, which was created for Jesus in the New Testament, was already present in the Jewish culture.[78] Subsequently however that language was taken literally, thus Christian doctrines of incarnation became the Church's teaching specifically after the Nicene and Chalcedonian Councils. The title 'Son of God' was transformed into 'God the Son,' from a poetic image for Jesus to the second person of the Trinity.[79] As a result, there remained two descriptions of Jesus, a truly human and a truly divine. Hick argues that we should not take the divine nature of Jesus literally. The divine nature of Jesus should not necessarily lead us to think that metaphysically Jesus was God. Hick proposes that Jesus did not have

24 *Christian theology of religions*

two different natures; rather, he had two different minds. His divine mind prevented him from performing sinful actions. He further argues:

> We are left with the human Jesus, to whose mind God the Son has full cognitive access; and if, or whenever, the human mind began to make a wrong decision, God the Son prevented him from proceeding with it. That is to say, Jesus is God incarnate in the sense that God singled the human Jesus out for a special role – namely by not allowing him to go wrong.[80]

Two conclusions can be drawn from Hick's metaphoric reading of the incarnation of Jesus. Firstly, by the title Son of God, Christians learn more about themselves rather than about the nature of Christ; that is to say, modern Christians understand how the early Christians perceived Jesus. The early Christians called Jesus the Son of God since they thought God was communicating with them through Jesus. Secondly, Jesus had a divine mind, which protected him from sinful action. Thus we can say that there is a parallel between Hick's Copernican revolution and his understanding of the doctrine of incarnation. By removing Jesus Christ from the centre of salvation, Hick opens up the possibility of including other salvific figures. For Hick, different religions have different names for God acting as a saviour for humankind. For Christians these names are the eternal Logos, the cosmic Christ, the Son of God, the Second Person of Trinity and the Spirit. Hick, however, limits these names only to the Logos. He argues that '[if] we call God-acting-towards-mankind the Logos, then we must say that all salvation, within all religions, is the work of Logos and that under their various images and symbols men in different cultures and faiths may encounter the Logos and find the salvation.'[81] As a result, for Hick, the Logos is at work in different religious traditions such as in the Hebrew prophets, in the Buddha and in the Qur'an.

3.2 Knitter and ethical-practical form of pluralism

In his early writings,[82] Paul Knitter, a Catholic theologian, offers a 'theocentric Christology', which is critical of Evangelical, mainstream Protestant, and Catholic models. According to him, 'all these traditional Christian claims are insufficiently sensitive to the way they contradict contemporary awareness of historical relativity and to the way they impede authentic dialogue with believers of other faiths.'[83] Knitter still contends, however, that the theocentric model he was advocating represented an authentic Christian model since it did not contradict with the New Testament proclamations of Jesus.[84] Moreover, he argues that the pervasive message of the New Testament was undeniably Christocentric,[85] while the original message of Jesus is theocentric. Thus he states, 'the focus and core content of Jesus' original message was the 'kingdom of God.'[86] Like Hick, he contradicts one of the main Christological doctrines, namely the divinity of Jesus, arguing that

'Jesus never takes the place of God', echoing Hick's position that 'Jesus gave us no Christology'.[87]

While Knitter recognises that within the New Testament there are exclusivist statements such as 'There is 'no other name' by which persons can be saved (Acts 4:2), he offers an interpretation based on an understanding of the historical-cultural context. Thus, Knitter contends that the worldview proposed by early Christians includes a definitive view of Jesus. For Knitter the key to understanding this portrayal is to consider the specific contexts in which early Christians applied absolutist and exclusivist adjectives. For Knitter, it is necessary for early Christians to employ such language to ensure the survival of their communities rather than with the intention of offering a definitive description of the characteristics of Jesus. Thus he states that 'in discussing Jesus as "the only", Christians were not trying to elaborate a metaphysical principle but a personal relationship and a commitment that defined what it meant to belong to this community.'[88] As a result, Knitter maintains that modern Christians could retain the basic worldview of early Christians but were not required to adopt its absolutist and exclusivist language.[89]

In his later writings, Knitter moves from his own theocentric model to a soteriocentric model, inspired by liberation theology, in which a 'preferential option for the poor and the nonperson constitutes both the necessity and the primary purpose of interreligious dialogue.'[90] As a result, he explains that he finds his early model, proposed in his book *No Other Name*, to be incomplete as there is a need to move away from a theocentric approach to one that is more kingdom centric or includes a more universal soteriocentric orientation. Also, in his later work, Knitter considers post-liberalism's suggestion of the 'incommensurability of religions' and argues that we should stop our search for a 'universal theory' or a 'common source' of religion or 'one God', which represents the typical pluralist agenda. However, while he considers issues relating to incommensurability, ultimately he rejects them as he contends that ethics can function as a common ground uniting all religions. In this respect, he argues that liberation theology offers a solution in that it provides a 'common approach' or 'common context' from which dialogue can be initiated and a common ground created.[91] The common ground that liberation theology offers is the 'preferential option for the poor and the nonperson', and thus Knitter argues:

> If the religions of the world, in other words, can recognize poverty and oppression as a common problem, if they share a common commitment (expressed in different forms) to remove such evils, they will have the basis for reaching across their incommensurabilities and differences in order to hear and understand each other and possibly be transformed in the process.[92]

Furthermore, Knitter argues that searching for a shared locus of religious experience is of much more fundamental importance than attempts to seek

26 Christian theology of religions

agreement by identifying 'one God', 'one Ultimate' or a 'common essence'. Adopting such a perspective allows the adherents of different traditions to share their experiences of the struggle for liberation and justice, and thus, despite theological differences, they could be motivated to resolve their differences and share their inspiration and hopes for achieving their common concern of finding a way to overcome injustice and promote unity. Thus, for Knitter, the common ground for inter-religious dialogue cannot be the sharing of one Divine, one Theos or one Ultimate, but rather it is Soteria on the grounds that a soteriocentric approach is less inclined to ideological abuse as it is more difficult to impose insular perspectives in discussions, which is frequently the case when a theocentric approach is adopted.[93]

In Knitter's soteriocentric approach to other religions, the place of Jesus is not so different from that found in his previous theocentric model. He still considers the New Testament's exclusivist language about Jesus within the historical-cultural context of early Christianity, and thus the early Christians' rejection of religious pluralism is, for Knitter, a matter of orthopraxis rather than orthodoxy.[94] Instead he suggests a relational uniqueness in defining the salvific role of Jesus: Jesus is 'truly' a way for salvation but not the 'only' one. 'Truly' does not necessarily require 'solely'. Jesus Christ is unique in his own way but not the only representation of God; there may be others such as Buddha, Muhammad and Krishna.[95]

3.3 Objections to Hick's and Knitter's pluralism

There are many good reasons both to support and oppose the pluralist theology of religions. Even though pluralism seems pragmatically attractive, methodologically and theologically there are some issues with the approach. Starting with pragmatic reasons, the Christian past with world religions is not without conflict. As a result of religious wars, such as the crusades on one hand, and the imperialism of the Western world on the other, some theologians believed that the exclusivist claims of Christianity legitimised the crusades and colonialism and as such could be used as an excuse to suppress any claim that is different from Christianity. For example, the feminist theologian Ruether argues that the uniqueness of Christian beliefs led to the crusades, religious violence and the chauvinist history of Christianity.[96] Consequently, pluralist theologians urge Christians to abandon their exclusivist claims. It may be argued that it seems beneficial to get rid of the exclusivist claims of Christianity; however, it cannot change history, especially the violent history of a particular religion. This historically intolerant position should not necessarily lead Christians or followers of other religions to abandon their orthodox beliefs. Secondly, to show their openness, tolerance and kindness to non-Christian religions, many people may sympathise with the pluralist position since pluralism does not advocate the superiority of a single religion. These two reasons are pragmatic reasons why pluralism seems more attractive than the other two types of theology of religions.

Methodologically and theologically, however, pluralist positions have been criticised by many theologians. D'Costa is one of the most critical theologians of pluralism generally and Hick's and Knitter's forms of pluralism in particular. D'Costa criticises Hick and Knitter in two ways: firstly, he argues that their theology depends on modernity rather than the Trinitarian God, and thus their theologies represent the gods of modernity, namely' 'agnosticism' (in the case of Hick) and 'neo-pagan unitarianism' for Knitter.[97] It is true that both Hick and Knitter use the tools of modernity to present their theological arguments; however, this appears to be entirely unrelated to their theology being a product of non-Christian modernity. Rather their theological approaches represent different interpretations of Christianity, which in certain respects are not representative of mainstream Christian understanding. In Hick's case, his theology of religions is more closely related to philosophy, while Knitter's is based more obviously in theological reflection and reflection on the praxis of dialogue and social action. Hedges, in contrast to D'Costa's arguments, believes that pluralism does not necessarily entail a weaker commitment to Christian faith. As is the case for both Knitter and Hick, the main pluralist theologians originally come from exclusivist positions. Thus, for Hedges, pluralism is a response to tradition and must be considered as a serious and committed type of Christian theology.[98] D'Costa, as a Christian, may find pluralist theologies inconsistent with Christianity, but I interpret their theology of religions as different approaches within the Christian tradition. It is also true that their theologies are transferable to different religious traditions, and modernists or liberals within other religious traditions can defend similar positions within their traditions. It does not mean, however, that they do not have a basis in those specific religions. On this point, I find Panikkar's thoughts quite useful. He states:

> Different theologies can be recognised as Christian by their own self-affirmation. Their unity transcends the logos because one theology may consider the other incompatible with a Christian stance, and yet all declare themselves Christian. . . . All Christian theologies, for instance, may confer upon "Christ" a central role, but the meaning – and even referent – of this word may be radically different.[99]

Secondly, while D'Costa criticises pluralism, he also argues that pluralism is logically another form of exclusivism, and in fact, pluralism does not exist because it requires a denial of differences.[100] He believes that Hick mythologizes the differences away so that the different religious traditions can be fitted into his system. Similarly, in Knitter's model, religions are judged on the criteria of ecosystems. To D'Costa, both Knitter and Hick know the full truth and what is ethically required of the religions. Consequently they both remove ethics, which should be based on Jesus Christ, who is *sui generis*, and replace them with the ethics of modernity.[101]

28 *Christian theology of religions*

Based on these two criticisms, D'Costa contends that their pluralism is one of the strong forms of Kantian[102] exclusivist modernism.[103]Heim, like D'Costa, also criticises Hick's and Knitter's models of pluralism for falling into exclusivism; however, Heim's attack originates from the post-liberal foundation of the incommensurability of religions. He argues that the commitment of pluralist theologians like Hick, Smith and Knitter to inter-religious dialogue is based on the Western theory of tolerance and rationality, which is another form of exclusivism on the grounds that non-Western traditions do not have the same presuppositions. Therefore, dialogue can only take place on the condition that other traditions come to think in a more Western way.[104]

I will discuss the issue of whether pluralism is a form of exclusivism in a subsequent section of this chapter, when I evaluate Race's threefold typology. D'Costa's and Heim's critiques of the pluralist theologians which propose that they dismiss the real differences among religious traditions are compelling. Even though pluralist ideas expand the boundaries of salvation and knowledge of transcendence, they tend to achieve this by equating all religious traditions with the same goals. In Hick's case, he decentralises orthodox readings of any single religion. From his reading of religions, his pluralism seems coherent, but his reading of a single religion only represents one kind of interpretation of that religion, which we cannot say is the only interpretation of that religion. Hick himself is aware of this fact: he never states that his interpretation replaces all other interpretations, but rather he offers his pluralist view as an alternative. His pluralism fails to accept the real differences of diverse religions, however, since he sees all religions as the manifestation of the same Reality.

In Knitter's case, he recognises the deficiency of a theocentric or Real-centred form of pluralism, and believes that ethics may be useful tool to provide a common ground among religions. Though his attempt is fundamentally pragmatic, applicable to and useful in the current world, he minimises each religion's distinct ethical teaching. It is pragmatic because it offers solutions to problems that humanity faces. Its applicability has been demonstrated in recent years. For example, Küng's global ethics project can be seen as an example of Knitter's ethical-liberation form of pluralism in practice. Küng does, however, clarify that his global ethic presents a minimal ethical background for the world religions.[105] To summarise, Knitter's own form of pluralism is not specifically related to each religious tradition's ethics; it does not and cannot give the whole picture. Thus, both Hick's and Knitter's theology of religions achieves something but simultaneously leaves such major problems unsolved. Their theology aims to be open by equating world religions' truth claims; however, by doing so they in fact disregard the real difference of both Christianity and other world religions. Recently post-liberal theologians have tried to sort this problem by emphasising the real differences of each religion. The next section will evaluate post-liberal theology of religions.

Christian theology of religions 29

4 Post-liberal theology of religions

Post-liberal theology is another recent development within Christian theology. In the early 1980s, various forms of liberal theologies were found within mainstream theology in the United States, whereas Evangelical theology remained marginal in universities and intellectual environments. With the publication of Lindbeck's book *The Nature of Doctrine* in 1984 however, a new theological approach, namely post-liberalism, appeared in academia.[106]

William Placher describes four features of post-liberal theology. Firstly, this theology is non-foundationalist. It assumes that the experience of people is always shaped by their own language and previous experiences. Secondly, post-liberal theology does not engage in systematic apologetics. Thirdly, unlike liberals, post-liberal theologians place an emphasis on the differences among religions and downplay the commonalities that religions share. Finally, this approach underlines the narrative stories of the Bible through which God and Christian communities are identified. Unlike their liberal peers, post-liberals do not reduce the importance of the stories since they believe these narratives create and maintain the communal identity of Christians.[107]

4.1 Lindbeck's cultural-linguist form of theology of religions

Using the tools of post-liberal theology, George Lindbeck, a Lutheran theologian, has developed a cultural-linguistic model that provides new understanding in terms of how Christianity can be related to other religions. Lindbeck considers different religions as different cultural-linguistic systems. His cultural-linguistic system is a combination of Wittgenstein's analysis of language as a series of language games and Geertz's cultural theory. Thus he argues:

> it is just as hard to think of religions as it is to think of cultures or languages as having a single generic or universal experiential essence of which particular religions – or cultures or languages – are varied manifestations or modifications. One can in this outlook no more be religious in general than one can speak language in general.[108]

In the context of this statement Lindbeck offers three different types of understanding of religion or truth. The first type is the propositional-cognitive model of religion. This approach is inclined to take the cognitive aspect of religion as a primary consideration. This model was the most accepted within the Christian tradition for many centuries and can also be described as exclusivist. In this view, religious statements are connected with a correspondence theory of truth. In other words, religion is seen as the matter of knowing about the Divine through comprehensible propositions. Accordingly, each proposition or act of judgement either corresponds to or conflicts with true

30 *Christian theology of religions*

statements; that is to say, they are either eternally true or false. Thus, a superior religion would be one that claims the most veridical statements and the fewest false ones.

The second understanding of religion is through the 'experiential-expressivist' approach, which views the truth as a function of symbolic efficacy. This approach prioritises experience over language. In this sense of truth, different religious claims or contrary cognitive claims could all be regarded as truth if they are used in their own context. As Lindbeck notes, 'all religions are by definition capable of functioning truly in this nondiscursive, symbolic sense, but they can vary in their potential or actual degree.'[109] Lindbeck remains suspicious about the usefulness of this approach as he argues that using this approach makes it difficult to find a specific meaning for the notion of unsurpassable truths.[110] Nevertheless, following this model is a crucial part of what leads theologians to adopt either an inclusivist or pluralist approach.

Lindbeck rejects both of these described approaches and develops his own alternative approach. This third model for understanding religion is gained through adopting what Lindbeck terms the 'cultural-linguistic' approach. According to this interpretation, religions are considered 'different idioms for constructing reality, expressing experience, and ordering life'.[111] While the propositional-cognitive understanding of religion concerns the question of correspondence, Lindbeck's cultural-linguistic approach addresses the coherence of religion. This approach regards the differences among religions as incommensurable. In other words, one religion or language can contain some crucial terms which have no meaning in another context or tradition. Briefly, as Lindbeck describes, the cultural-linguistic approach of religion is

> open to the possibility that different religions and/or philosophies may have incommensurable notions of truth, of experience, and of categorical adequacy, and therefore also of what it would mean for something to be most important (i.e. 'God'). Unlike other perspectives, this approach proposes no common framework to compare religions such as those supplied by the propositionalist's concept of truth or experssivist's concept of experience. Thus when affirmation or ideas from categorically different religious or philosophical frameworks are introduced into a given religious outlook, these are regarded as being meaningless or like mathematical formulas employed in a poetic text-they have vastly different functions and meanings than they contained in their original settings.[112]

In some ways, Lindbeck accepts the efficacy of the experimental-expressive approach of religion in terms of its ability to foster inter-religious dialogue and offer salvation to other faiths. Lindbeck developed an alternative approach for inter-religious dialogue, however, with a contrary ideology to the experimental-expressive model based on his cultural-linguistic model. In Lindbeck's model, common experience remains important, although it is not central. Thus, Lindbeck describes how 'the cultural-linguistic approach can allow a strong case for interreligious dialogue, but not for any single type of such dialogue. The currently favorite motive of cooperatively exploring common experience is not entirely excluded, but it is not likely dominate.'[113]

Lindbeck contends that the cultural-linguistic approach may help believers of other faiths to be 'better' Muslims, Jews, Buddhists and others as the cultural-linguistic approach allows members of other faiths to develop their own reasons or to have different warrants for interfaith conversation and cooperation. Thus, Lindbeck's approach recognises that different religious groups will have different aims and objectives in any inter-religious dialogue. Although this lack of common ground could potentially weaken a shared dialogue, it could also become a strength through which more effective communication and dialogue are achieved. In this approach, in dialogue, partners cannot start with the conviction that essentially they agree or should come to a consensus, thus partners are not forced into the dilemma of considering themselves either as representatives of superior or inferior religions. They simply consider themselves as different and can therefore discuss their own agreements and disagreements without engaging in undesirable comparisons. In short, Lindbeck argues:

> while a cultural-linguistic approach does not issue a blanket endorsement of the enthusiasm and warm fellow-feelings that can be easily promoted in an experimental-expressive context, it does not exclude the development of powerful theological rationales for sober and practically efficacious commitment to interreligious discussion and cooperation.[114]

Lindbeck argues that before the advent of multireligious Western societies, it was easy to make harsh judgements about non-Christian peoples. In the contemporary world, however, in which globalisation has increased unity and effectively made the world smaller, non-Christians are neighbours, and therefore it is impossible to ignore them.[115] Hence, Lindbeck develops a futuristic eschatological theory, which offers salvation to non-Christians after death:

> Actually it would seem that Protestants should find a primarily futuristic eschatological theory more congenial to their own tradition. The Reformation emphasized the *fides ex auditu*. . . . It is only through explicit faith in Christ men and women are redeemed; and if this does not happen during life, then the beginning of salvation must be thought of as occurring through an encounter with the risen Lord in or after death.[116]

Lindbeck's futuristic theory not only emphasises the *fides ex auditu* – faith comes from hearing the Gospel – but also offers salvation to non-Christians as a post-mortem confrontation with Christ.

32   *Christian theology of religions*

Lindbeck applies his cultural-linguistic theory, and this shapes his post-mortem solution. The salvation of non-Christians is one of a future salvation. For Lindbeck, the scriptural account of *fides ex auditu* seems to have advantage, although it is not sufficiently decisive. According to the New Testament eschatological picture, there is neither salvation nor damnation for others; instead, it seems that they have no future. Only through the message of the Messiah and the coming kingdom, will the future of the world be made true, and thus people will be judged for final redemption or damnation. Following this account, Lindbeck claims, 'there is no damnation – just as there is no salvation – outside the church. One must, in other words learn the language of faith before one can know enough about its message knowingly to reject it thus be lost.'[117] Consequently, Lindbeck argues that non-Christians will have a second chance for salvation after this world.

Lindbeck's theory of the untranslatability of religions helps maintain the exclusivist claims of Christianity while simultaneously accepting the real otherness of other religions. The Christian claim for the uniqueness of Jesus or the Gospel and the requirement of *fide ex auditu* for salvation is retained, however, at the same time Lindbeck's approach also considers the salvific means of other religions as comprehensible in their own culture and language.

4.2 Other post-liberal theologies

Paul Griffiths follows Lindbeck's methodology but directs his theology of religions towards exclusivism. In other words he develops Lindbeck's cultural-linguistic theory at the same time as offering an exclusivist theology of religions. Like Lindbeck, he also believes that religious truths or claims are comprehensive within each religious tradition, thus making different religious truths incompatible. He discusses the *necessity of inter-religious apologetics* (the *NOIA* principle),[118] which suggests that the followers of each religion should challenge each other's religious truths in inter-religious practice. In other words, since the religious truths are comprehensive according to their respective believers, in inter-religious encounters they should make the case that their religion is more comprehensible than the others. His theology of religions neither attempts to seek a common ground nor places emphasis on differences; rather, in a similar way to Lindbeck, Griffiths calls for the challenging of religious truth claims.

DiNoia also takes post-liberalism's insistence on the differences as a starting point and offers his own type of theology of religions. In fact, DiNoia does not offer a theology of religions; rather, he aims to shift theology of religions towards comparative theology. As such, he urges 'theology in dialogue' rather than 'theology for dialogue'.[119] His theology attempts to remove the centrality of the salvation of non-Christians from the current discussion of theology of religions and go beyond that discussion. For DiNoia, the question of '[h]ow do the soteriological programs of other religious communities promote the pursuit and enjoyment of distinctive overall aims they propose for human life'[120] is more important than asking if non-Christians can attain salvation or if their religions aim at the same sort of salvation. From this perspective, 'theology in dialogue' promotes a closer reading of distinct religious traditions. In essence, the overall point is that different religious traditions have different aims. In terms of the salvation of members of non-Christian religions, DiNoia's theology offers a similar solution to Lindbeck's theology. For DiNoia, the doctrine of purgatory allows the salvation of non-Christians without underestimating the distinctive aims they have pursued in life.[121]

Mark Heim moves post-liberal theology in a different direction from his post-liberal counterparts. His theology of religions retains Christian orthodoxy; however, he also views non-Christian religions as equally valid compared with Christianity. He argues that religions should not be classified as true or false but may be seen as both true and alternative. Thus, the truths of different religions should not be viewed as if representing the same truth. In this respect, Heim rejects both pluralism's insistence on the sameness of religions and inclusivism's anonymous criterion. He contends that his approach does not necessarily lead to relativism, which views all religions as equally valid, rather his approach calls for respect for the integrity of other religions. For him, each religion has its own truth within its own context. Furthermore, he contends that like religious truths, salvation is also multifaceted; that is to say, each religion has its own ends.[122] Thus, Heim takes the incommensurability of religions seriously and rejects searching for common ground.

In the same way as Barth's theology came to life at a time when the influence of Enlightenment ideals was pervasive in Christian theology, post-liberal theology of religions has also emerged in opposition to pluralist theology of religions, which takes its root from liberalism. Although in recent decades, post-liberal theology has been appreciated by many theologians, some theologians remain critical.

4.3 Objections to Lindbeck's post-liberal theology of religions

Firstly, from an orthodox Christian perspective, Milbank and Hütter argue that Lindbeck dismisses the central doctrines and claims of Christianity. Milbank believes that the way Lindbeck interprets the narratives is problematic. More explicitly, he argues that Lindbeck converts the narratives and practices central to the Christian faith into a different set of narratives and practices, resulting in a denial of the main claims of Christianity.[123] Hütter finds Lindbeck's approach problematic due to the fact that by understanding religious dogma as a kind of grammar of religion, the ontological or universal truth claims of Christianity[124] are undermined, despite being the central themes of Christianity. Both Hütter and Milbank's criticism are raised against Lindbeck's cultural-linguistic theory, which can be extended to other post-liberal theologians who also use that theory. This criticism may not be an accurate summary of Lindbeck's aim as his approach focuses

34 *Christian theology of religions*

on offering a new method for interpreting religious texts; at no point does he deny or downplay the distinctness of Christianity among other religions. Nevertheless, it is also true that post-liberal theologies do to some extent restrict the universal truths of a particular religion. Most of the adherents of different religions would not be satisfied with the idea that their religious truths are limited only to themselves because, for almost all religious believers, the goals of life they outline are intended for all humanity.

Secondly, it is argued that the cultural-linguistic approach falls prey to relativism, in particular the argument that religions and languages are incommensurable and cannot be translated. D'Costa argues that this remains an unsolved problem for Lindbeck's theory.[125] Although the cultural-linguistic theory may entail some form of relativism, however, it is not as deep as the relativism employed by pluralists. Unlike most pluralists, post-liberals never argue that each religious claim can be equally true. Instead, they only place emphasis on the comprehensible nature of each religious claim within its own cultural-linguistic framework. Moreover, the cultural-post-liberal approach clearly maintains that all religions are fundamentally different, while pluralists insist on the underlying similarity of all religions. The post-liberal approach can thus be seen as an attempt both to preserve the trueness of Christianity and to 'protect the real differences between faiths'[126] while simultaneously accepting all religions as the comprehensible explanations of particular cultures and languages.

Thirdly, pluralist theologians criticise post-liberals because of their insistence on the differences among religions. Some argue that the insistence on differences prohibits making a link or connection among religions, which leads to the suppression of something that is common to all religions.[127] In terms of recognising the other, the insistence on differences is a requirement: post-liberal theologies offer, in Knitter's words, a 'good neighborhood' policy. For further engagement, however, insistence on the differences should not mean that members of different religions are imprisoned by those differences and unable to communicate across boundaries. In that context, Knitter argues that for there to be a real dialogue, there needs to be something common which religions share.[128] On this point there are two contrasting options: either the pluralist view that promises common ground or the post-liberal view that rejects common ground. The former promotes radical sameness, while the latter promises fundamental differences. Religions are neither as similar as pluralists describe nor as completely different as post-liberals believe. As Knitter states,

> the followers of the Mutuality Model (referring to pluralism) can be accused of imperialism when they impose their claim that all religions are really intending the same goal, so might the Acceptance Model (referring to post-liberal theology) be slipping into similar imperialism when it insists that the goals of religions are totally different.[129]

However, it should be noted that the interaction between particularists and pluralists seems to offer a new breath in Christian theology of religions.

Considering similarities and differences of religions, both positions seem to offer something consistent in certain aspects.

5 Race's threefold typology evaluated

Since Race produced his threefold typology, it has been both criticised and welcomed in the discussion of theology of religions. Some theologians have used his typology, others have offered alternatives, while others have criticised the usefulness of such typologies for categorising the different positions.

D'Costa, claiming 'that three dominant paradigms emerge from the recent history of theological reflection, usefully providing a conceptual matrix within which the theological issues are highlighted',[130] used Race's typology in *Theology and Religious Pluralism*. Unlike Race, however,[131] his typological order was pluralism, exclusivism and inclusivism, respectively. Since he followed the Rahnerian pattern, he started with the least tenable one and finished with the most defensible position. A decade later, D'Costa strongly objected to the threefold typology, arguing that all three are forms of exclusivism and thus the typology are redundant.[132] Despite his criticism of the typology, he utilises the typology by dividing each classification into either two or three categories.[133] He used typologies of unitary, pluriform and ethical forms for pluralists,[134] structural and restrictivist for inclusivists[135] and restrictive-access and universal-access for exclusivists.[136] Interestingly, this time his theological position shifts from inclusivism to universal-access exclusivism. Despite criticising the typology, he still thinks Race's typology has been useful as a starting point, 'like a raft crossing a river, to get to where we are now . . . [he then asks] But is the raft still useful?'[137] In terms of its continued utility, however, D'Costa maintains the typology is no longer useful[138] and as an alternative he offers seven 'centricisms': Trinity centred, Christ centred, Spirit centred, Church centred, theocentric, reality-centered and ethics-centered.[139]

Another alternative to Race's threefold typology comes from Knitter. Unlike D'Costa, however, he states that his typology does not reject Race's, rather it confirms the similarities. His early typology consists of: the Conservative Evangelical Model, a form of Barthian exclusivism; the Mainstream Protestant Model, Kraemer and Brunner's exclusivism; the Catholic Model, inclusivism; and the Theocentric Model, pluralism.[140] In 2001, however, with the publication of *Introducing Theologies of Religions*, Knitter revised his old model and offered a new one. In his new typology, he offers four main models and shows the diversity of theologies in each model. His first model is the Replacement Model, divided into two categories, either Total or Partial Replacement, which reiterates the first two models of his early classification. The second model is the Fulfilment Model, in which he shows the diverse responses to inclusivist theology, primarily from the Catholic tradition. In the third classification, the Mutuality Model, Knitter analyses different forms of pluralism. In this context, he not only considers his early Theocentric Model (Hick's early form of pluralism) but also presents

36 *Christian theology of religions*

the variety in the pluralist debate.[141] His final classification discusses post-liberal debates and offers post-liberal theology as the Acceptance Model. Like Knitter, Hedges also includes post-liberal theology of religions into his classification; unlike Knitter, however, he uses Race's threefold typology and adds post-liberal theology as particularism.[142] His emphasis on particularism differs from Knitter. While Knitter's emphasis on post-liberal theology focuses on post-liberal theology's 'acceptance' of the real differences of religions, Hedges's classification underlines the importance of the 'particularism' of each religious tradition.

Turning to criticisms of Race's typology, D'Costa argues that each position within the typology is a form of exclusivism. In contrast, Hick claims that in reality, religious exclusivism and pluralism are different logical forms. While exclusivism is based on the self-committing affirmation of faith, pluralism is a 'philosophical hypothesis'.[143] Consequently, Hick argues that pluralism is not just another form of exclusivist theology but a meta-theory about relations among the world religions. D'Costa also argues that pluralists attempt to place all the major world religions into the same 'pool' but exclude some quasi-religions, such as Nazism, from receiving recognition and thus demonstrate a form of exclusivism.[144] Hick's response to this charge is that to make an assertion, it is necessary to deny its opposite, and to propose a theory requires rejection of alternative views. Thus, Hick believes that it is justified to introduce a criterion of evaluation such as: 'whether a movement is a context of human transformation from natural self centeredness to a new orientation centered in the Transcendent, this salvific transformation being expressed in an inner peace and joy and in compassionate love for others'.[145] This point seems to offer a compelling counterargument to D'Costa's criticism. From an Aristotelian perspective,[146] D'Costa is right to see each typology as a form of exclusivism. Examining each position in the typology in more depth however, it becomes clear that the logic behind each one is different. Each position responds to the same proposition with totally different nuances. Schmidt-Leukel considers the fundamental question to be 'if the salvific knowledge of a transcendent reality is mediated by' other traditions or not.[147] For exclusivists the answer is only one tradition, while for pluralists it is more than one tradition. Thus, D'Costa's argument seems flawed.

Some theologians think that typology is '*too coarse or abstract. It does not do justice to the more complex and nuanced reality of real theologians*' (emphasis in original).[148] In response to this criticism, Schmidt-Leukel argues that this objection overlooks the significant difference between 'a kind of phenomenological typology' and 'a formal, logically comprehensive classification'.[149] He claims that if a theologians' theology does not fit any form of typology, it must be because that their theologies do not involve any answer to the precise problem which the typology focuses on. He further contends that theologians also might be ambiguous or inconsistent with their theological views. For example, on the one hand they might hold the pluralist view regarding soteriology; on the other hand they might claim exclusivist or inclusivist views on the epistemological level. For Schmidt-Leukel, however, this kind of situation would lead to inconsistent conclusions in their theological views.[150] Schmidt-Leukel's defence of typology in this level is not totally convincing. As will be seen in the next chapter, Rowan Williams's theology of religions does not entirely fit any settled typology. While Williams's views on Jesus Christ can sound exclusivist, his practice of interfaith dialogue shows radical openness towards the other. This is not because Williams offers an inconsistent theology of religions, but rather, each class in typology may not exactly correspond a certain theologian's theology.

Some theologians, like Markham, argue that their proposals do not fit into the threefold typology.[151] I will also have this difficulty when I attempt to locate Rowan Williams's theology of religions into the threefold typology. Rather than seeing Race's typology as the only standard arrangement of theology of religions, and thus rejecting it completely, it is better to engage with other theologians' typologies, which I will do in the next chapter. Race's typology provides a good overview of recent discussion in the Christian tradition, but it does not comment specifically on the nature of that discussion. It is for this reason that Knitter and Hedges have added a fourth classification to their typology, which I have also followed. Although Race himself thinks post-liberal theologians are either exclusivist or inclusivist,[152] Knitter and Hedges' judgement is helpful in distinguishing between their different logics. Consequently, unlike Markham, I do not reject the typology but rather find it useful with regard to picturing Christian theology of religions. Hedges rightly judges the typology, stating that

> the typology should be seen as descriptive (it tells us what positions have been taken, not what positions should be), heuristic (it gives guidelines to help understand the complexity of ideas and their relationships), multivalent (each category is not a single approach, but a spectrum of related approaches), and permeable (people may express ideas that spill over several of the categories), rather than as prescriptive, normative, defining, and closed.[153]

There are additional objections[154] to Race's typology; however, it is beyond the scope of this study to discuss them. I have only evaluated the objections that I find helpful. Aside from the critics mentioned of Race's typology, in recent decades comparative theologians have criticised the area of theology of religions. This requires a much more broad response. The next section will focus on comparative theology and its assessment.

6 Comparative theology

Comparative theology[155] in Christian theology is not a recent development. From the early eighteenth century, when Christians started to produce works on non-Christian religions, the term of 'comparative theology' has been used.[156] Later, the term was commonly used during the nineteenth

38 Christian theology of religions

century. However, the type of comparative theology that was developed in the eighteenth and nineteenth centuries is conceptually different from the contemporary comparative theology.[157]

Hedges describes the contemporary 'comparative theology' as '[referring] to a particular form of the theology of religions that seeks to engage in thinking about the Christian faith by comparison with, or in relation to, one or more religious traditions'.[158] However, some comparative theologians do not offer their theology as a fourth or fifth option in theology of religions; rather, they want to go beyond theology of religions. Recently, theologians like Francis Clooney and James Fredericks have offered comparative theology as an alternative to Race and others' theology of religions typologies. Unlike any theology of religions position offered in this chapter, comparative theology does not seek to theorise non-Christian religions before engaging with them. In other words comparative theologians suggest that rather than Christians examining non-Christian traditions in generic or abstract terms, or rather than asking whether non-Christian religions promise salvation, Christians should change their direction and engage deeply with non-Christian religions. Fredericks argues that 'all three options for a theology of religions [exclusivism, inclusivism, pluralism] inoculate Christians against the power and novelty of other traditions.'[159] Before theorising non-Christian religions, comparative theologians expect to learn about non-Christian traditions in dialogue. To sum up, comparative theology has two goals: to gain a better understanding of other religions by a close study and to understand their own religion through the eyes of others.

In the next section, I will offer Clooney's comparative theology as an example.

6.1 Clooney and his approach of comparative theology

Francis Clooney, a Roman Catholic Jesuit, is one of the prominent comparative theologians in the contemporary period. He has spent some time in India and Nepal, which influenced his later comparative theology which looks at Christianity and Hindu religions. He has produced many books and articles in which he presents his methodology of reading of Christian and Hindu scriptures. He offers side-by-side reading of scriptures, which he describes as 'a reflexive back-and-forth reading process, reading each hymn carefully, entering its world as far as possible, but later also rereading of it in light of other, similar but interestingly different hymns'.[160] He describes comparative theology as 'the practice of rethinking aspects of one's own faith tradition through the study of aspects of another faith tradition'.[161] More specifically comparative theology can be defined thus:

> *Comparative theology – comparative* and *theological* beginning to end – marks acts of faith seeking understanding which are rooted in a particular faith tradition but which, from that foundation, venture into

learning from one or more other faith traditions. This learning is sought for the sake of fresh theological insights that are indebted to the newly encountered tradition/s as well as the home tradition.[162]

From both descriptions, it is quite clear that unlike theology of religions, comparative theology does not seek to theorise non-Christian religions before encountering a specific tradition. It not only helps Christians learn about how their religious others understand themselves but also leads to a rethinking of their own tradition through this process of learning. From this perspective, comparative theology differs from theology of religions. Although Clooney thinks comparative theology is closely connected with other disciplines such as comparative religion and interfaith dialogue, together with theology of religions, he distinguishes comparative theology from these three disciplines.

Firstly, comparative theology differs from comparative religion as faith is a requirement for the former but not in the latter. However, it still needs to be connected since, to be able to do comparative theology, there is a need for in-depth and accurate study of a religious tradition.[163] Secondly, while comparative theology and inter-religious dialogue are connected in terms of engaging and practising dialogue, comparative theology is not only practical engagement but also academic theology which requires the theologization of what has been learnt from interaction.[164]

Thirdly, although both comparative theology and theology of religions involve theological reflection on other religion(s), they have different methodologies. While theology of religions 'reflects from the perspective of one's own religion on the meaning of other religions', comparative theology in contrast 'necessarily includes actually learning another religious tradition in significant detail. In brief, neither replaces the other. Neither is merely a prelude to the other; nor is defective because it does not perform the task of the other.'[165] Clooney further states that comparative theology can utilise theology of religions which 'can usefully make explicit the grounds for comparative study, uncovering and clarifying the framework within which comparative study takes place'.[166] Additionally, comparative theology '[can] help theology of religions to be more specific, fine-tuning their attitudes through closer attention to specific traditions'.[167] Thus it seems that Clooney considers these two disciplines to cover two distinct areas; neither replaces the other nor offers an alternative, but rather they are not totally separate from each other. Clooney does not reject the usefulness of theology of religions but suggests a particular theology of religions in harmony with his comparative theology. He states that '[my] comparative theology is in harmony with those inclusivist theologies, in the great tradition of Karl Rahner, SJ, and Jacques Dupuis, SJ, that balance claims to Christian uniqueness with a necessary openness to learning from other religions.'[168] Despite his claim that he benefits from inclusivist theologians' theology of religions, he does not offer a standard inclusivist vision which includes other religions within Christianity. He says that

40 *Christian theology of religions*

I do not theorize inclusion so as to imagine that Christianity subsumes all else, but prefer instead the act of including. I bring what I learn into my reconsideration of Christian identity. This is an "including theology," not a theory about religions; it draws what we learn from another tradition back into the realm of our own, highlighting and not erasing the fact of this borrowed wisdom.[169]

By having an inclusivist theology of religions, Clooney attempts to find God through Hindu texts and practice. His theological grounds for studying Hindu texts and practices are as follows:

1) God chooses to be known, encountered, and accessible through religious traditions as complex religious wholes, in fragile human ideas and words, images and actions.

2) That God is present, even fully, in one tradition does not preclude God's presence in other traditions; robust commitment to one tradition is compatible with still recognizing God at work outside that tradition's language, imagination, and doctrine.

3) God can speak to us in and through a tradition other than our own, even if we do not, cannot, embrace as our own the whole of that tradition. We are not compelled to affirm every aspect of other traditions, but neither does faith compel us to presume that what we know is always superior to what they know.

4) The intellectual and affective dimensions of a relationship to God are accessible through words, in language. Coming to know God in this richer way proceeds valuably through the study of our own tradition, but also in the study of other traditions.

5) How we learn from traditions other than our own cannot be predicted on the basis of our own tradition. There is no substitute for actually studying another tradition, and the trial-and-error progress that is made by trying to learn.[170]

So, unlike pluralist theologians who suggest that there are different salvific figures in other religions, or that those religions are different responses to the same reality, Clooney's theology remains inclusivist but is also particularist in the sense of realising differences and complexities. Clooney's comparative theological approach can 'help believers to unburden themselves of misconceptions they have about what other traditions believe or about the uniqueness of their own tradition's claims'.[171]

6.2 Assessment

While comparative theologians aim to go beyond the discussion of theology of religions, some theologians still consider their approach as another brand of theology of religions. For example, Knitter in *Introducing Theologies of Religions* approaches comparative theology under his Acceptance Model.

He thinks comparative theology is indebted to post-liberal theology and its cultural-linguistic theology of religion.[172] However, it seems that comparative theology and post-liberal theologies have different methodological and hermeneutical groundings. While cultural-linguistic theory,[173] with its insistence on the incommensurability of different religious worlds, occupies the central place in post-liberal theology of religions, comparative theology does emphasise difference to the same extent as it is founded on confidence in communication and learning. Clooney suggests that when a Christian learns about other religious traditions, he or she will sometimes find that some Christian beliefs and ways of doing theology are not totally unique. For the comparative theologians, just because religious traditions are different does not mean that there cannot be points of contact and perhaps even an exchange of ideas.

D'Costa, although appreciating the way comparative theologians emphasise 'the importance of particular and contextual engagement between religions', 'close textual and practical engagement' and 'the theological nature of their enterprise in contrast to the comparative religions' tradition,'[174] still finds some aspects of comparative theology to be problematic. He argues that Clooney and other comparative theologians dismiss judgement on the question of truth while engaging with others. He states:

> If there are no challenges and questionings of these other texts, but simply a self-referential transformation, can this be called "comparative," "dialogue," or even Christian? Mission, intrinsic to Christian witness, seems to have no place in the theological project except a deferred role.[175]

D'Costa makes a good point and comparative theologians like Clooney and Fredericks actually agree that there should be a role for seeking truth and making judgements in comparative theology. However, they do not want to make judgements prematurely, as was done by comparative theologians in the nineteenth century who generally concluded by vindicating Christian superiority. Mara Brecht suggests that D'Costa's critique is overstated because the comparative theologians want a theology that comes after comparison and that the stage of comparison is not necessarily the right time for making judgements about the beliefs of others.[176] This is an unresolved issue in contemporary comparative theology, but it is not necessarily a fatal flaw in the project.

Although Clooney claims that he utilises the inclusivist theologians' theories while doing comparative theology, Kenneth Rose considers him as a pluralist. He believes that Clooney does not include other religions within Christianity but rather approaches non-Christian religions as 'illumining' and 'enriching' his own tradition.[177] Rose argues that Clooney 'models a quasi pluralism that really wants (rightly, I think) to dispense with the unpleasant business of making judgments about the truths of other religions or seeing them as leading up to one's own'.[178] Rose is partly right. Clooney

42 *Christian theology of religions*

departs from the standard inclusivist approach which he affirms; however, his grounds for such a theological activity remain inclusivist grounded.

Comparative theologians want to move beyond theology of religions and offer their theology as an alternative to theology of religions. However, theology of religions is still important as the primary aim of theology of religions is to respond to a religious diversity to which Christians and Muslims need to respond. Clooney himself is aware of the importance of theology of religions while interacting with other religions as he utilises inclusivist theology. As comparative theologians move the discussion on religious pluralism another level, any approach in theology of religions can be consummated by the use of comparative theology. In the fifth chapter, I will recall this discussion, and I will argue that comparative theology should not be seen as an alternative to theology of religions but rather as something complementary.

As comparative theology postpones theorising other religions before encounters, this idea seems to be helpful for Muslim theologians' approaches towards others. Rather than the presuppositions of Muslims about Christianity, which have their origins in the Qur'an and the Sunnah, Muslims should engage with Christians and others and learn about their religion as the Islamic vision of Christianity lacks knowledge in certain respects. From this starting point I will make some limited use of the comparative theology approach to look at some specific notions, namely the concept of God and revelation in Islam and Christianity. I will do this in Chapter 5.

Conclusion

In the last century, Christian theologians have responded to religious diversity differently. I have presented each diverse response from the Christian world. I have attempted to show that none of the mentioned positions are perfect, nor are they invalid. Each represents a different theologian's perspective based on his or her beliefs and contextual understanding. Among them the exclusivist position is the least tenable for Christians and, as I shall demonstrate in the third chapter, also for Muslims.

The exclusivist position locates Christianity as a superior religion which holds the truth as a whole (revelation in Jesus) among world religions and thus dismisses the truth and goodness in non-Christian religions. Regarding the salvation of non-Christians, it also pictures Christianity (belief in Jesus Christ) as the only way to salvation. Inclusivism, in contrast, manages to extend the boundaries of truths and salvation but simultaneously locates Christianity or Christ as normative and thus still keeps the superior position of Christianity among world religions. However, the pluralist position solves this problem by showing radical openness to other religions, but it also leaves the problem of difference by equalising the truths of different religions. Post-liberal theology of religions solves this problem by accepting the real difference of other religions, but its insistence on the incommensurability of religions leaves less space for the universal claims of religions. The pluralist position's openness towards the truths of other religions and post-liberal theology's acceptance of the real difference of other religions seem to be fundamental insights of these positions. Comparative theology takes these two insights and carries them to another level via a deep engagement with non-Christian religions' texts and doctrines.

The discussion among pluralist and post-liberals has produced fruitful interfaith dialogue. On the one hand pluralism's openness to non-Christian religions and on the other hand post-liberal's acceptance of non-Christian traditions can be viewed as the overlap between these two positions. Furthermore, the current discussion between these two groups has also led the followers of each position to respond to critics and thus to strengthen their position. In my evaluation of Islamic responses to religious diversity, I will attempt to show that Muslim pluralists also need to be criticised from the post-liberal perspective of claiming difference.

I have shown that Race's typology has been both widely accepted and also widely criticised. In spite of some serious objections, I have claimed that Race's classification presents a good overview of current Christian theology of religions. However, the objection that Race's typology is too abstract and fails to do enough justice to complex theologies seems to be quite challenging. In the next chapter I will present Rowan Williams's theology of religions as a challenge to both Race's threefold typology specifically and theology of religions in general. The next chapter will focus on a specific theologian, Rowan Williams's theology, using the discussion I have supplied in this chapter.

Notes

1 For the nineteenth-century works, see: Max Müller, *Comparative Mythology* (London: Routledge, 1856) and *Introduction to the Science of Religion: Four Lectures Delivered at the Royal Institution in February and May (1870)* (London: Longmans, Green, 1899); J. Freeman Clarke, *Ten Great Religions: An Essay in Comparative Theology* (Boston: Houghton, 1881) and; F. Denison Maurice, *The Religions of the World and Their Relations to Christianity, Considered in Eight Lectures Founded by the Right Hon* (London: Robert Boyle, 1847). For twentieth-century works, see Mircea Eliade, *The Quest: History and Meaning of Religions* (Chicago: University of Chicago, 1984). For missionary works, see secondary sources on early missionaries such as Francis Xavier (1506–1552), Roberto de Nobili (1579–1656) and other Jesuit missionaries; see for example Francis Clooney, "Roberto de Nobili's Response to India and Hinduism, in Practice and Theory," *Third Millennium* 1/2 (Fall 1998): 72–80 and "A Charism for Dialogue: Advice from the Early Jesuit Missionaries in Our World of Religious Pluralism," *Studies in the Spirituality of Jesuits* (March 2002). See also John W. O'Malley and T. Frank Kennedy (eds.), *The Jesuits: Cultures, the Sciences, and the Arts 1540–1773* (Toronto: University of Toronto Press, 1999) and Christopher Chapple (ed.), *The Jesuit Tradition in Education and Missions: A 450-Year Perspective* (Scranton: Scranton University Press, 1993).
2 Race considers the particularist position as a form of either exclusivism or inclusivism. See Paul Hedges, *Controversies in Interreligious Dialogue and the Theology of Religions* (London: SCM Press, 2010), 161.
3 Hedges, *Controversies*, 1. His primary concern is to address 'the impasse between, what we may variously termed, liberal and postliberal, modern and postmodern, pluralist and particularist stances'.

44 *Christian theology of religions*

4 Paul Knitter, *Introducing Theologies of Religions* (Maryknoll, NY: Orbis Books, 2009), 19.
5 Alan Race, *Christians and Religious Pluralism* (London: SCM Press, 1983/1993), 10.
6 Gavin D'Costa, *Christianity and World Religions; Disputed Questions in Theology of Religions* (Oxford: Blackwell, 2009), 25–26.
7 Race, *Religious Pluralism*, 11.
8 Karl Barth, *Church Dogmatics vol. I/2* (Edinburgh: T&T Clark, 1956), 299–300.
9 Ibid., 300.
10 Ibid., 301.
11 Ibid., 307.
12 Ibid., 327.
13 Ibid., 339.
14 Colin Gunton, *The Barth Lectures* (London: T&T Clark, 2007), 18.
15 Ibid., 19.
16 Race, *Religious Pluralism*, 13.
17 Cited by Race, *Christians and Religious Pluralism*, 16, cited by H. Gerald Anderson, "Religion as a Problem for the Christian Mission," in *Christian Faith in a Religiously Plural World*, eds. D. Dawe and J. Carmen (Maryknoll, NY: Orbis Books, 1978), 114.
18 There are also some Muslims whose theology of religions shows a radical dependence on the authority of the Qur'an. I will also touch and criticise that kind of Islamic theology of religions in the third chapter.
19 Paul Knitter, *No Other Name? A Critical Survey of Christian Attitudes toward the World Religions* (Maryknoll, NY: Orbis Books, 1985), 91.
20 Acts 14:15, 17:22, and Romans 1:18.
21 Hendrik Kraemer, *Religion and the Christian Faith* (Cambridge: James Clarke, 1956), 358–359.
22 Hendrik Kraemer, *The Christian Message in a Non-Christian World* (New York: Harper, 1938), 125.
23 Ibid., 300.
24 Emil Brunner, *Revelation and Reason* (London: Student Christian Movement Press, 1947), 61.
25 Ibid., 62.
26 Ibid., 270.
27 Race, *Religious Pluralism*, 38.
28 For instance, Knitter in *No Other Name* argues that although the early Church fathers kept the exclusivist theory of uniqueness of Christ, they also thought that salvation was offered to all people. He gives Justin Martyr and Tertullian as examples whose thoughts assemble to inclusivism position. See Knitter, *No Other Name*, 121.
29 D'Costa, *World Religions*, 19.
30 Knitter, *No Other Name*, 125.
31 Molly T. Marshall, *No Salvation Outside the Church? A Critical Inquiry* (Lewiston, Lampeter: The Edwin Mellen Press, 1993), 115.
32 I will particularly look at Rahner's *Theological Investigations*, vols.5, 6 and 16.
33 Karl Rahner, "Christianity and Non-Christian Religions," in *Theological Investigations vol. 5* (London: Darton, Longman & Todd, 1966), 118.
34 Ibid., 121.
35 Karl Rahner, "Anonymous and Explicit Faith," in *Theological Investigations, vol. 16: Experience of the Spirit: Source of Theology* (London: Darton, Longman and Todd, 1979), 55.
36 Karl Rahner, "Anonymous Christians," in *Theological Investigations vol. 6: Concerning Vatican Council II* (London: Darton, Longman & Todd, 1969), 394.

37 Rahner, *Theological Investigations vol. 5*, 122.
38 Rahner comes to this conclusion by drawing the picture of Israel. According to Rahner, there were many true elements in Israel's religion at the same time there were some false and corrupt elements. Until the Gospel came, the Old Testament religion was always considered as lawful; thus, it provided salvation to many. He extends the concept of lawful religion to other non-Christian religions (*Theological Investigation vol. 5*, 125).
39 Ibid., 122.
40 Ibid., 131.
41 Ibid., 133.
42 While some theologians like D'Costa argue that the council does not approve the salvific will of the non-Christian religions, others, for example, Knitter, think that according to the council document, non-Christian religions are ways of salvation. See D'Costa, *The Meeting of Religions and the Trinity* (Edinburg: T&T Clark, 2000), 105 and Knitter, *Theologies of Religions*, 75–76. Considering the council documents as a whole, I think D'Costa's thought is more appropriate than Knitter.
43 In Nostra Aetate 2/2 it is stated: "The Catholic Church rejects nothing of what is true and holy in other religions. She has a high regard for the manner of life and conduct, the precepts and doctrines which often reflect a ray of that truth which enlightens all men."
44 See Lumen Gentium 16; 1 and Nostra Aetate 4; 1–4.
45 See Lumen Gentium 16; 1 and Nostra Aetate 3; 1.
46 For both Hindus and Buddhists, see Lumen Gentium 16; 1 and Nostra Aetate 2; 1.
47 Lumen Gentium, 14; 1.
48 Lumen Gentium, 16.
49 Hans Küng, *On Being a Christian* (London: Collins, 1977), 98.
50 Ibid., 123.
51 Ibid., 124.
52 John Hick, *God Has Many Names* (London: The Macmillan Press Ltd., 1980), 50.
53 Gavin D'Costa, *Theology and Religious Pluralism* (Oxford: Basil Blackwell Ltd., 1986), 89.
54 Maurice Boutin, "Anonymous Christianity: A Paradigm for Interreligious Encounter?" *Journal of Ecumenical Studies* 20/4 (Fall 1983): 602–629.
55 Karl Rahner, "The One Christ and the Universality of Salvation," in *Theological Investigations, vol. 16*, 219.
56 Race, *Religious Pluralism*, 62.
57 Knitter, *No Other Name*, 142.
58 Henri Maurier, "The Christian Theology of Non-Christian Religions," *Lumen Vitae* 21 (1976): 59, 66, 69, 70, cited in Knitter, *Introducing*, 142.
59 Hans Urs von Balthasar, *The Moment of Christian Witness* (San Francisco: Ignation Press, 1994), 101.
60 It is not only Rahner whose theology has been criticised as a product of Enlightenment philosophy, but contemporary liberal pluralist theologians' theologies have faced this criticism as well. In the next section, D'Costa's critique of pluralism will be explored more deeply.
61 Karen Kilby, "Balthasar and Rahner," in *The Cambridge Companion to Hans Urs von Balthasar*, ed. Edward T. Oakes (Cambridge: Cambridge University Press 2004), 118.
62 Gavin D'Costa, "Theology of Religions," in *The Modern Theologians*, ed. David Ford (Oxford: Blackwell, 1996), 626–644.
63 Knitter, *No Other Name*, 146–152.
64 Ibid., 44–47.
65 Knitter, *Introducing*, 112–113.

46 *Christian theology of religions*

66 In Race's classification, Panikkar is regarded as an inclusivist theologian. The form of theology that Panikkar has developed, however, is an example of pluralism. The reason why Race described him as inclusivist might be because he only evaluated Panikkar's book *The Unknown Christ of Hinduism* (London: Dorton, Longman & Todd, 1964), where he developed an inclusivist theory. In 1973, with the publication of *The Trinity and the Religious Experience of Man* (Maryknoll, NY: Orbis Books, 1973), Panikkar developed his own form of pluralism.

67 Raimon Panikkar, "Myth of Pluralism: The Tower of Babel—a Meditation on Non-Violence," *Cross Current* 29 (1979): 203.

68 Raimon Panikkar, "The Jordan, the Tiber, and the Ganges," in *The Myth of Christian Uniqueness: Toward a Pluralistic Theology of Religions*, eds. John Hick and Paul Knitter (London: SCM Press, 1987), 89–117.

69 John Hick, *God and the Universe of Faiths* (London: Macmillan, 19730), 120–131.

70 Ibid., 51–52.

71 Ibid., 52.

72 John Hick, *An Interpretation of Religion* (London: Macmillan, 1989), 241.

73 Ibid., 242.

74 Ibid., 252–277.

75 Ibid., 277–296.

76 Ibid., 235–236.

77 John Hick, *The Metaphor of God Incarnate* (London: SCM Press, 1993), 15–39.

78 For example, Hick contends that being called the Son of God has a long tradition in Jewish culture. He gives Psalm 2.7 and II Sam 7.14 as examples. John Hick, *The Myth of God Incarnate* (London: SCM Press, 1977), 167–185.

79 Ibid., 175.

80 Hick, *Metaphor*, 58.

81 Ibid., 181.

82 Paul Knitter, *No Other Name* and "Theocentric Christology," *Theology Today* 40/2 (July 1983): 130–149.

83 Knitter, *No Other Name*, 171.

84 Ibid., 172.

85 Ibid., 173.

86 Ibid.

87 Ibid., 174.

88 Ibid., 185.

89 Ibid., 182–184.

90 Paul Knitter, "Toward a Liberation Theology of Religions," in *The Myth of Christian Uniqueness: Toward a Pluralistic Theology of Religions*, eds. John Hick and Paul Knitter (London: SCM Press, 1987), 181.

91 Ibid., 185.

92 Ibid., 186.

93 Ibid., 187.

94 Knitter, "Liberation Theology," 192, see also *Jesus and Other Names*, 70–71.

95 Paul Knitter, *One Earth Many Religions: Multifaith Dialogue and Global Responsibility* (Maryknoll, NY: Orbis Books, 1995), 35.

96 Rosemary R. Ruether, "Feminism and Jewish-Christian Dialogue," in *The Myth of Christian Uniqueness: Toward a Pluralistic Theology of Religions*, eds. John Hick and Paul Knitter (London: SCM Press, 1987), 141.

97 D'Costa, *Meeting of Religions*, 39.

98 Hedges, *Controversies*, 27.

99 Panikkar, "The Jordon, the Tiber, the Ganges," 110.

100 Gavin D'Costa, "The Impossibility of a Pluralist View of Religions," *Religious Studies* 32 (June 1996): 223–232.

Christian theology of religions 47

101 Gavin D'Costa, "Other Faiths and Christians," in *The Cambridge Companion to Christian Ethics*, ed. Robin Gill (Cambridge: Cambridge University Press, 2001), 159.

102 Ethical truth for Kant can be known by reason alone, and reason is able to judge and evaluate religions according to their conformity. As a philosopher Kant saw himself in this capacity, but he also argued that Christianity was helpful for those who could not use their reason to arrive at the truth since Christianity was the highest embodiment. D'Costa argues that the only difference between Kant and Knitter is that while Kant saw Christianity as the highest embodiment, Knitter considers other religions as equal to Christianity, thus he extends Kant's Golden Rules (D'Costa, "Other Faiths and Christians," 159).

103 D'Costa, *Meeting of Religions*, 39.

104 S. Mark Heim, *Salvation: Truths and Difference in Religion* (Maryknoll, NY: Orbis Books, 1997), chapter 3.

105 Hans Küng, *A Global Ethic* (Munich: SCM Press, 1993).

106 William C. Placher, "Postliberal Theology," in *An Introduction to Christian Theology in Twentieth Century*, eds. David Ford and Rachel Muers (Cambridge: Blackwell Publishers, 1997), 343–356.

107 Ibid., 343–345.

108 George Lindbeck, *Nature of Doctrine: Religion and Theology in Postliberal Age* (London: SPCK, 1984), 23.

109 Ibid., 47.

110 Jeffrey C. K. Goh, *Christian Tradition Today: A Postliberal Vision of Church and World* (Louvain: Peeters, 2000), 362–363.

111 Lindbeck, *Nature of Doctrine*, 47–48.

112 Ibid., 49.

113 Ibid., 53–54.

114 Ibid., 55.

115 George Lindbeck, "Fides Ex Auditu," in *The Gospel and the Ambiguity of the Church*, ed. Vilmas Vajta (Minneapolis: Fortress Press, 1974), 91–123.

116 George Lindbeck, *The Church in a Postliberal Age* (London: SCM Press, 2002), 80.

117 Lindbeck, *Nature of Doctrine*, 59.

118 Paul Griffiths, *An Apology for Apologetics; a Study in the Logic of Interreligious Dialogue* (Maryknoll, NY: Orbis Books, 1991).

119 Joseph A. DiNoia, *The Diversity of Religions: A Christian Perspective* (Washington, DC: The Catholic University of America Press, 1992), 111.

120 Ibid., 55.

121 Ibid., 104–107.

122 Heim, *Salvations*, chapter 8.

123 John Milbank, *Theology and Social Theory: Beyond Secular Reason* (Malden, Oxford: Blackwell Publisher, 2006), 382–388.

124 Essentially, Hütter attacks Lindbeck's cognitive-linguistic understanding of truth. As mentioned, Lindbeck's cultural-linguistic approach is primarily concerned with coherency rather than correspondence, something with which Hütter disagrees. For Hütter, Christian doctrines and dogmas should be a matter of propositional truth. Reinhard Hütter, *Suffering Divine Things: Theology as Church Practice* (Grand Rapids: William B. Eerdmans Publishing Company, 1997), 51–54.

125 D'Costa, *World Religions*, 30.

126 Knitter, *Theologies of Religions*, 182.

127 Ibid., 230.

128 Ibid.

129 Ibid., 213.

130 D'Costa, *Theology and Religious Pluralism*, 6.

131 Race used the typology to demonstrate the shift from exclusivism to pluralism.

132 D'Costa, "Impossibility."

48 Christian theology of religions

133 He expanded the typology firstly in "Theology of Religions," in *Modern Theologians: An Introduction to Christian Theology since 1918*, ed. David Ford (Malden, Oxford: Oxford Blackwell Publishing, 2005), 636–644.

134 Hick's, Panikkar's and Knitter's forms of pluralism, respectively.

135 I explained these terms in the section on inclusivism.

136 Restrictive-access exclusivists are those who emphasise the necessity of Jesus Christ for salvation as they believe God has chosen some for salvation and others for damnation, whereas universal-access exclusivists highlight the universal salvific will of God. According to this group, Jesus died for all humanity, not for a limited number of people. There is still a need for belief in Jesus; however, they find some solutions for those who have never heard the Gospel or heard but do not believe it. D'Costa places post-liberal theologians mainly within universal-access exclusivism, although he puts Heim into the category of pluriform pluralism (D'Costa, *World Religions*, 7).

137 D'Costa, *World Religions*, 34.

138 Jenny Daggers, similar to D'Costa, also argues that the utility of threefold typology is ended as, for her, the approach taken in threefold typology is 'to present exclusivist and inclusivist positions through the lens of pluralist critique, to enable a critical consideration of pluralist approaches that seek to supersede these options'. *Postcolonial Theology of Religions: Particularity and Pluralism in World Christianity* (Abingdon, Oxon: Routledge, 2013), 90.

139 Ibid., 35.

140 Knitter, *No Other Name*, xvi.

141 I have used Knitter's models in the pluralism section.

142 Hedges, *Controversies*, 1. He offers the pluralist position as 'radical openness' (chapter 3) and particularist position as 'radical difference' (chapter 4).

143 Hick, "The Possibility of Religious Pluralism: A Reply to Gavin D'Costa," *Religious Studies* 33/2 (June 1997): 161–166.

144 Ibid.

145 Ibid.

146 The logic behind D'Costa's argument probably operates in that way. A) Exclusivists hold an exclusive criterion. B) Pluralists hold an exclusive criterion. C) Pluralists are exclusivists.

147 Perry Schmidt-Leukel, "Exclusivism, Inclusivism and Pluralism," in *The Myth of Religious Superiority*, ed. Paul Knitter (Maryknoll, NY: Orbis Books, 2005), 13–27. In that book chapter, Schmidt-Leukel addresses most objections against Race's threefold typology and tries to eliminate each objection and then reaffirms that the typology is still useful and applicable.

148 Ibid., 16. For example, see Wesley Ariarajah, "The Need for a New Debate," in *The Uniqueness of Jesus: Dialogue with Paul Knitter*, eds. Paul Knitter, Lenard Swindler and Paul Mojzes (Maryknoll, NY: Orbis Books, 1997), 29–34, 30.

149 Schmidt-Leukel, "Exclusivism, Inclusivism and Pluralism," 25.

150 Ibid., 25–26.

151 Ian Markham, "Creating Options: Shattering the 'Exclusivist, Inclusivist, and Pluralist' Paradigm," *New Blackfriars* (January 1993): 33–41 and Michael Barnes, *Christian Identity and Religious Pluralism: Religions in Conversation* (London: SPCK, 1989).

152 Race has suggested that to Hedges on a number of occasions. Hedges, *Controversies*, 161.

153 Paul Hedges, "A Reflection on Typologies: Negotiating a Fast-Moving Discussion," in *Christian Approaches to Other Faiths*, eds. Paul Hedges and Alan Race (London: SCM Press, 2008), 27.

154 For a good overview of the objections to Race's classification, see Schmidt-Leukel, "Exclusivism, Inclusivism, Pluralism."

Christian theology of religions 49

155 See recent works by Francis Clooney, *Comparative Theology: Deep Learning across Religious Borders* (Chichester: Wiley-Blackwell, 2010), *Theology after Vedanta: An Experiment in Comparative Theology* (Albany: State University of New York, 1993), "Reading the World in Christ," in *Christian Uniqueness Reconsidered: The Myth of Pluralistic Theology of Religions*, ed. Gavin D'Costa (Maryknoll, NY: Orbis Books, 1990), 63–80, "Comparative Theology," in *The Oxford Handbook to Systematic Theology*, eds. John Webster, Kathryn Tanner and Iain Torrance (Oxford: Oxford University Press, 2007), 653–669, *Divine Mother, Blessed Mother: Hindu Goddess and Virgin Mary* (Oxford: Oxford University Press, 2005), *Theology after Vedanta: An Experiment in Comparative Theology* (Albany, New York: State University of New York Press, 1993), *Beyond Compare: Francis de Sales and Sri Vedanta Desika on Loving Surrender to God* (Washington, DC: Georgetown University Press, 2008), James Fredericks, *Faith among Faiths: Christian Theology and Non-Christian Religions* (New York: Paulist Press, 1999), "A Universal Religious Experience? Comparative Theology as an Alternative to a Theology of Religions," *Horizons* 22 (1995): 67–87, Keith Ward, *Religion and Revelation* (Oxford: Oxford University Press, 1994).
156 See, Clooney, *Deep Learning*, 31. James Garden (1645–1726) published a book named *Comparative Theology; or True and Solid Grounds of Pure and Peaceable Theology: A Subject Very Necessary, tho Hitherto almost Wholly Neglected.*
157 Frederick D. Maurice and James F. Clarke have been seen as the pioneers of nineteenth-century comparative theology. For a good overview of their works see Tomoko Masuzawa, *The Invention of World Religions* (Chicago, London: University of Chicago, 2005), 72–95.
158 Hedges, *Controversies in Interreligious Dialogue*, 52.
159 Fredericks, *Faith among Faiths*, 167.
160 Clooney, *Divine Mother*, 23.
161 Clooney, "Comparative Theology," 654.
162 Clooney, *Deep Learning*, 10.
163 Ibid., 12.
164 Ibid., 13.
165 Ibid., 14.
166 Ibid.
167 Ibid.
168 Ibid., 16.
169 Ibid.
170 Ibid., 115.
171 Ibid., 113.
172 Knitter, *Theologies of Religions*, 177.
173 For further discussion see, Marianne Moyaert, "Comparative Theology in a Search of Hermeneutical Framework," in *Inter-Religious Hermeneutics in Pluralistic Europe: Between Text and People*, eds. David Cheltenham, Ulrich Winkler Oddbjørn Leirvik and Judith Gruber (Amsterdam, New York: Radopi, 2011), 161–186.
174 D'Costa, *World Religions*, 40.
175 Ibid., 40.
176 Mara Brecht, *Virtue in Dialogue: Belief, Religious Diversity and Women's Interreligious Encounter* (Eugene: Pickwick Publications, 2014), 25–26.
177 Kenneth Rose, *Pluralism: The Future of Religion* (London: Bloomsbury Publishing, 2013), 47.
178 Ibid., 48.

50 *Christian theology of religions*

Bibliography

Anderson, H. Gerald. "Religion as a Problem for the Christian Mission." In *Christian Faith in a Religiously Plural World*, edited by D. Dawe and J. Carmen, 114. Maryknoll, NY: Orbis Books, 1978.

Barnes, Micheal. *Christian Identity and Religious Pluralism: Religions in Conversation*. London: SPCK, 1989.

Barth, Karl. *Church Dogmatics Vol. I/2*. Edinburgh: T&T Clark, 1956.

Boutin, Maurice. "Anonymous Christianity: A Paradigm for Interreligious Encounter?" *Journal of Ecumenical Studies* 20/4 (Fall 1983): 602–629.

Brecht, Mara. *Virtue in Dialogue: Belief, Religious Diversity and Women's Interreligious Encounter*. Eugene: Pickwick Publications, 2014.

Brunner, Emil. *Revelation and Reason*. London: Student Christian Movement Press, 1947.

Chapple, Christopher, ed. *The Jesuit Tradition in Education and Missions: A 450-Year Perspective*. Scranton: Scranton University Press, 1993.

Clarke, J. Freeman. *Ten Great Religions: An Essay in Comparative Theology*. Boston: Houghton, 1881.

Clooney, Francis. *Beyond Compare: Francis de Sales and Sri Vedanta Desika on Loving Surrender to God*. Washington, DC: Georgetown University Press, 2008.

———. "A Charism for Dialogue: Advice from the Early Jesuit Missionaries in Our World of Religious Pluralism." *Studies in the Spirituality of Jesuits* 34/2 (March 2002): 1–39.

———. "Comparative Theology." In *The Oxford Handbook to Systematic Theology*, edited by John Webster, Kathryn Tanner and Iain Torrance, 653–669. Oxford: Oxford University Press, 2007.

———. *Comparative Theology: Deep Learning across Religious Borders*. Chichester: Wiley-Blackwell, 2010.

———. *Comparative Theology: Meaning and Practice*. Chichester: Wiley-Blackwell, 2010.

———. *Divine Mother, Blessed Mother: Hindu Goddess and Virgin Mary*. Oxford: Oxford University Press, 2005.

———. "Reading the World in Christ." In *Christian Uniqueness Reconsidered: The Myth of Pluralistic Theology of Religions*, edited by Gavin D'Costa, 63–80. Maryknoll, NY: Orbis Books, 1990.

———. "Roberto de Nobili's Response to India and Hinduism, in Practice and Theory." *Third Millennium* 1/2 (Fall 1998): 72–80.

———. *Theology after Vedanta: An Experiment in Comparative Theology*. Albany: State University of New York, 1998.

Daggers, Jenny. *Postcolonial Theology of Religions: Particularity and Pluralism in World Christianity*. Abingdon, Oxon: Routledge, 2013.

D'Costa, Gavin, ed. *Christianity and World Religions: Disputed Questions in the Theology of Religions*. Oxford: Wiley-Blackwell, 2009.

———. *Christian Uniqeness Reconsidered: The Myth of a Pluralistic Theology of Religions*. Maryknoll, NY: Orbis Books, 1990.

———. "The Impossibility of a Pluralist View of Religions." *Religious Studies* 32 (June 1996): 223–232.

———. *The Meeting of Religions and the Trinity*. Edinburg: T&T Clark, 2000.

———. "Other Faiths and Christians." In *The Cambridge Companion to Christian Ethics*, edited by Robin Gill, 154–168. Cambridge: Cambridge University Press, 2001.

Christian theology of religions 51

————. *Theology and Religious Pluralism: The Challenge of Other Religions.* Oxford, New York: Basil, Blackwell, 1986.

————. "Theology of Religions." In *The Modern Theologians*, edited by David Ford, 626–644. Oxford: Blackwell, 1996.

DiNoia, Joseph A. *The Diversity of Religions: A Christian Perspective.* Washington, DC: Catholic University of America Press, 1992.

Eliade, Mircea. *The Quest: History and Meaning of Religions.* Chicago: University of Chicago, 1984.

Frederiks, James. *Faith among Faiths: Christian Theology and Non-Christian Religions.* New York: Paulist Press, 1999.

————. "A Universal Religious Experience? Comparative Theology as an Alternative to a Theology of Religions." *Horizons* 22 (1995): 67–87.

Goh, Jeffrey C.K. *Christian Tradition Today: A Postliberal Vision of Church and World.* Louvain: Peeters, 2000.

Griffiths, Paul. *An Apology for Apologetics; a Study in the Logic of Interreligious Dialogue.* Maryknoll, NY: Orbis Books, 1991.

Gunton, Colin. *The Barth Lectures.* London: T&T Clark, 2007.

Hedges, Paul. *Controversies in Interreligious Dialogue and the Theology of Religions.* London: SCM Press, 2010.

————. "A Reflection on Typologies: Negotiating a Fast-Moving Discussion." In *Christian Approaches to Other Faiths*, edited by Paul Hedges and Alan Race, 17–35. London: SCM Press, 2008.

Heim, S. Mark. *Salvation: Truths and Difference in Religion.* Maryknoll, NY: Orbis Books, 1997.

Hick, John. *God and the Universe of Faith.* London: Macmillan, 1973.

————. *God Has Many Names.* London: Macmillan, 1980.

————. *An Interpretation of Religion.* London: Macmillan, 1989.

————. *The Metaphor of God Incarnate.* London: SCM Press, 1993.

————. *The Myth of God Incarnate.* London: SCM Press, 1977.

————. "The Possibility of Religious Pluralism: A Reply to Gavin D'Costa." *Religious Studies* 33/2 (June 1997): 161–166.

Hick, John and Paul Knitter, eds. *The Myth of Christian Uniqueness: Toward a Pluralistic Theology of Religions.* Maryknoll, NY: Orbis Books, 1987.

Hütter, Reinhard. *Suffering Divine Things: Theology as Church Practice.* Grand Rapis: William B. Eerdmans Publishing Company, 1997.

Kilby, Karen. "Balthasar and Rahner." In *The Cambridge Companion to Hans Urs von Balthasar*, edited by Edward T. Oakes, 256–268. Cambridge: Cambdridge University Press, 2004.

Knitter, Paul. *Introducing Theologies of Religions.* Maryknoll, NY: Orbis Books, 2009.

————. *Jesus and Other Names: Christian Mission and Global Responsibility.* Oxford: Oneworld, 1996.

————. *No Other Name? A Critical Survey of Christian Attitudes toward the World Religions.* Maryknoll, NY: Orbis Books, 1985.

————. *One Earth, Many Religions: Multifaith Dialogue and Global Responsibility.* Maryknoll, NY: Orbis Books, 1995.

————. "Theocentric Christology." *Theology Today* 40/2 (July 1983): 130–149.

————. "Toward a Liberation Theology of Religions." In *The Myth of Christian Uniqueness: Toward a Pluralistic Theology of Religions*, edited by Jonh Hick and Paul Knitter, 178–202. London: SCM Press, 1987.

52 Christian theology of religions

Kraemer, Hendrik. *The Christian Message in a Non-Christian World*. New York: Harper, 1938.

———. *Religion and the Christian Faith*. Cambridge: James Clark, 1956.

Küng, Hans. *Global Responsibility: In Search of a New World Ethic*. London: SCM, 1991.

———. *On Being a Christian*. London: Collins, 1977.

Lindbeck, George. *The Church in a Postliberal Age*. London: SCM Press, 2002.

———. "Fides Ex Auditu." In *The Gospel and the Ambiguity of the Church*, edited by Vilmos Vajta, 91–123. Philadelphia: Fortress Press, 1974.

———. *Nature of Doctrine: Religion and Theology in Postliberal Age*. London: SPCK, 1984.

Markham, Ian. "Creating Options: Shattering the 'Exclusivist, Inclusivist, and Pluralist' Paradigm." *New Blackfriars* 74/867 (January 1993): 33–41.

Marshall, Molly T. *No Salvation Outside the Church? A Critical Inquiry*. Lewiston, Lampeter: The Edwin Mellen Press, 1993.

Maurice, Denison F. *The Religions of the World and Their Relations to Christianity, Considered in Eight Lectures Founded by the Right Hon*. London: Robert Boyle, 1847.

Milbank, John. *Theology and Social Theory: Beyond Secular Reason*. Oxford: Blackwell, 2006.

Moyaert, Marianne. "Comparative Theology in a Search of Hermeneutical Framework." In *Inter-Religious Hermeneutics in Pluralistic Europe: Between Text and People*, edited by Ulrich Winkler Oddbjørn Leirvik and Judith Gruber David Cheltenham, 161–186. Amsterdam, New York: Radopi, 2011.

Müller, Max. *Comparative Mythology*. London: Routledge, 1856.

———. *Introduction to the Science of Religion: Four Lectures Delivered at the Royal Institution in February and May (1870)*. London: Longsman, Green, 1899.

O'Malley, John W., and T. Frank Kennedy, eds. *The Jesuits: Cultures, the Sciences, and the Arts 1540–1773*. Toronto: University of Toronto Press, 1999.

Panikkar, Raimundo. "The Jordan, the Tiber, and the Ganges." In *The Myth of Christian Uniqueness: Toward a Pluralistic Theology of Religions*, edited by John Hick and Paul Knitter, 89–117. London: SCM Press, 1987.

———. "Myth of Pluralism: The Tower of Babel- a Meditation on Non-Violence." *Cross Current* 29 (1979): 197–230.

———. *The Trinity and the Religious Experience of Man*. New York: Orbis Books, 1973.

———. *The Unknown Christ of Hinduism: Towards an Ecumenical Christophany*. London: Darton, Longman & Todd, 1981.

Placher, William C. "Postliberal Theology." In *The Modern Theologians: An Introduction to Christian Theology in Twentieth Century*, edited by David Ford and Rachel Muers, 343–356. Cambridge: Blackwell Publishers, 1997.

Race, Alan. *Christians and Religious Pluralism*. London: SCM Press, 1983/1993.

Rahner, Karl. *Theological Investigations Vol.5*. London: Darton, Longman & Todd, 1966.

———. *Theological Investigations Vol.6: Concerning Vatican Council II*. London: Darton, Longman & Todd, 1969.

———. *Theological Investigations Vol.16: Experience of the Spirit: Source of Theology*. London: Darton, Longman & Todd, 1979.

Rose, Kenneth. *Pluralism: The Future of Religion*. London: Bloomsbury Publishing, 2013.

Ruether, Rosemary R. "Feminism and Jewish-Christian Dialogue." In *The Myth of Christian Uniqueness: Toward a Pluralistic Theology of Religions*, edited by Paul Knitter and John Hick, 137–148. London: London SCM Press, 1987.

Schmidt-Leukel, Perry. "Exclusivism, Inclusivism and Pluralism." In *The Myth of Religious Superiority*, edited by Paul Knitter, 13–27. Marknoll, NY: Orbis Books, 2005.

Urs von Balthasar, Hans. *The Moment of Christian Witness*. San Francisco: Ignation Press, 1994.

Wesley, Ariarajah. "The Need for a New Debate." In *The Uniqeness of Jesus: Dialogue with Paul Knitter*, edited by Paul Knitter, Leonard Swidler and Paul Mojzes, 29–34. Maryknoll, NY: Orbis Books, 1997.

2 Rowan Williams's theology of religions

Introduction

Rowan Douglas Williams was born in 1950 in Swansea, Wales. He went to a state school, Dynevor School in Swansea, and then took an undergraduate degree at Christ's College, University of Cambridge, in the field of theology. He received his doctorate in 1975 at Wadham College, University of Oxford for a thesis titled 'The Theology of Vladimir Nikolaevich Lossky: an Exposition and Critique'. After finishing his doctoral study, he was employed in well-known UK universities such as the University of Cambridge as a lecturer and appointed to the Lady Margaret Professorship at Oxford University. He served as bishop of Monmouth in the Church of Wales from 1991 to 1999, when he was elected as archbishop of Wales. He was enthroned on the 27 February 2003 as the 104th archbishop of Canterbury, remaining in this position until December 2012.

Williams is recognised as one of the greatest theologians and scholars of the contemporary period. He has shown a keen interest in several fields of theology. He is also one of the most difficult theologians in terms of locating his precise position among Christian theologians; indeed, he is often described both as liberal and orthodox.[1] On the one hand, he is progressive in terms of matters such as sexuality, gender and social issues, but on the other hand, he challenges liberalism in terms of its tendency towards relativism.

His deep knowledge of the literature of other religions, especially Islam and Judaism, makes his speeches and writings on other religions very easy for members of other religions to comprehend. His speech in Pakistan on 'What Is Christianity'[2] is one clear example of this ability. In this speech, he used Islamic literature and terminology to explain Christianity as his main audience was Muslims. If this speech is read by a Muslim, the language used might be enough to convince them that the writer is actually a Muslim. In this chapter I will argue that his theology of religion does not perfectly fit into any of the established approaches provided by Race's threefold paradigm. His position seems distinctive and complex. Knitter describes Williams as an exclusivist in theology and a pluralist in practice.[3] Williams's theology of religions challenges the idea that the pluralist position theoretically is the best way to engagement with the believers of other faiths. Although his early writings provide an exclusivist or particularist theology, while putting them in practice, his theology shows a profound openness towards other religions. That is why he is, I think, one of the best choices through which to analyse the theological background of interfaith dialogue.

Says Moulasion in her review of Williams's theology ('The Theological Vision of Rowan Williams'):

> To attempt to summarize the work of Rowan Williams, the present Archbishop of Canterbury, is the height of folly, or perhaps hubris. His writings are numerous, his contributions vast, his tastes eclectic. A public figure, a Patristics scholar, a polyglot, and an occasional poet, he is not easily summarized.[4]

While I am aware of this difficulty, my aim remains to summarise, as far as possible, Williams's theology of religions and his inter-religious practice. In doing this, I will mostly look at the sermons, speeches and lectures he has given during his period of service as the archbishop of Canterbury. I will also address some of his writings in the field of the theology of religions and inter-religious practice (up till the end of his time as archbishop). To do so, firstly, I will try to locate Williams's theology of religions in the landscape of theology of religions I provided in the first chapter. Then I will move on to consider his model of the theology of religions. Finally, I will conclude this chapter by arguing that Williams's theology of religions, which is based on Trinitarian theology, shows a radical openness towards other religions.

It is difficult to place Williams's thoughts precisely on the theology map I outlined in the first chapter due to three factors. Firstly, Williams's language is a bit difficult to understand, and the complexity inherent in his writings makes it difficult to determine his exact thinking. Secondly, he does not seek to develop a specific form of theology of religions. In other words, he does not strictly promote or oppose any specific label of theology of religions. This is unusual when, in the contemporary period, most theologians who are writing in the field of theology of religions are either promoting or criticising a specific theological view. Thirdly, Williams has not produced any book focused particularly on the field of theology of religions,[5] rather his theological works mostly focus on Christian theology more broadly. Despite such an orthodox approach, his experience of serving as the archbishop of Wales and the archbishop of Canterbury means that Williams has actively engaged in inter-religious dialogue with many non-Christian faith groups in the UK. Indeed, he has offered great support to many frameworks for interfaith dialogue and has himself been involved with many dialogues with many different traditions.

Williams's personal commitment to inter-religious dialogue was perhaps illustrated most clearly when he was a bishop in the southeast of Wales and was involved with many discussions with Muslims. The type of dialogue conducted, however, mostly concerned social issues, such as family

56 Rowan Williams's theology of religions

break-ups, antisocial behaviour and the problems of crime and drugs. As the archbishop of Wales, Williams started to meet with faith leaders, mostly Muslims, to discuss both theological and social issues,[6] but after his enthroning as the archbishop of Canterbury, he became one of the leading advocates and proponents for inter-religious dialogue. For instance, he improved the Building Bridges Seminars,[7] which brings together Muslims and Christians from across the world annually to speak, read the scriptures of both traditions and have discussion on theological issues. He has further supported such frameworks in the UK as the Muslim-Christian Forum[8] and the Hindu-Christian Forum. Moreover, he developed close relations with the chief rabbi and the Jewish community through the Council of Christians and Jews.[9] Apart from these major initiatives, Williams continued to pursue more general inter-religious and multireligious dialogue with many other religions, such as Buddhism, Sikhism, Jainism, Zoroastrianism and Baha'ism.[10]

1 Locating Williams's theology of religions on the map

When we try to locate Williams's position on a theological map, it is not easy to say whether he should be considered as an exclusivist or an inclusivist or pluralist. From his theological view on locating Jesus into the discussion of salvation, according to Race's classification, it might seem that his theology of religion can be classified as an exclusivist theology. Like in exclusivist theologies, as will be presented, Williams also thinks that salvation is possible only through Jesus Christ. But as pointed out in the previous chapter, Race's classification only gives an outline for any theological point. It does not exactly give the whole picture of a theologian's theological view. However, it should be noted that sometimes there are parallels between his Trinitarian theology of religions and inclusivist theology. Despite this, his inclusivist statements differ from mainstream inclusivist theology on many points. I will touch on this issue while discussing his theology of religions. In general, considering Race's threefold typology, as will be shown, it would not be totally wrong to suggest that Williams's theology of religions is an example of exclusivism. Thus, since there are many different types of exclusivism, it would be better to describe exactly what kind of exclusivism Williams's theology depends on. From this perspective, it would be better to examine some other theologians' classification of exclusivism and see how they fit.

First of all, if the problem of salvation of non-Christians is taken into consideration, D'Costa's classification of exclusivism is relevant to the discussion. As has been presented previously, according to D'Costa there are two types of exclusivism: restrictive-access and universal-access exclusivism. According to D'Costa, restrictive-access exclusivists are those who emphasise the necessity of Jesus Christ for salvation as they believe God has chosen some for salvation and others for damnation, whereas universal-access exclusivists highlight the universal salvific will of God. According to this group, Jesus died for all humanity, not for a limited number of people. There is still a need for belief in Jesus; however, they find some solutions for those who have never heard the Gospel or heard but do not believe it.[11] Thus the only difference between these groups is that while universal-access exclusivists underline the importance of the salvific will of God, restrictive-access exclusivists highlight the necessity of Christ for salvation.[12] Yet, considering Williams's theological concerns on soteriological problems, the term 'exclusivist' does not seem an exact fit with Williams's theology or practice. In this respect, it may be better to consider him as belonging with universal-access exclusivist theologians. I will show that like universal-access exclusivist theologies, Williams's theology also underlines the importance of the universal salvific will of God.

Secondly, when the emphasis on religious differences is taken into consideration, Hedges's use of 'particularism' may help us to define Williams's theology. Hedges basically argues that there are two mainstream theological positions on the discussion of theology of religions: pluralism and particularism.[13] He contends that despite certain differences within mainstream particularist theology, there are six core points on which particularist theologians come to a consensus: firstly, particularists stress the differences of religions, denying the possibility that there can be a common ground among religions. Secondly, they accept that it is only possible to speak from the perspective of a specific tradition and that therefore a pluralist interpretation of religions is untenable. Thirdly, the Holy Spirit is recognised as having the power to work in other religions. Fourthly, the salvific efficacy of non-Christian religions is denied, although this does not mean that non-Christians are excluded from God's plan. Fifthly, the post-liberal theological tradition has a large influence and sixthly, their position is shaped by an orthodox reading of Christ and the doctrine of Trinity.[14]

Based on the points Hedges has made concerning particularism, I will show that it is possible to see most of these aspects of particularism as present in Williams's model of theology of religions. However, to simply say that Williams's theology of religions is one of the examples of universal-access exclusivism or particularism would not be fair when considering the whole theme of Williams's theology of religions. I do not mean that both Hedges's and D'Costa's classifications are not adequate, but rather they only stress certain specific aspects of exclusivist theology. While D'Costa constructs his classification by taking the problem of salvation as the standpoint, Hedges uses the term 'particularism' to define theologians' dependence on the idea that religions are different and that they cannot have a common ground. Due to the drawbacks, I think that Knitter's classification offers a more suitable alternative in the term 'Acceptance Model', which helps us better identify the central theme of Williams's theology. Knitter uses this term in particular to underline the importance of theologians' acceptance of other religions as they define themselves.[15] Considering Williams's position towards other religions, especially in terms of inter-religious dialogue practice, the terms of the Acceptance Model seem to fit neatly with Williams's practical theology.

58 Rowan Williams's theology of religions

I will address this issue in more detail when discussing Williams's Trinitarian theology of religions.

In fact, D'Costa's description of universal-access exclusivism, Hedges's particularism and Knitter's Acceptance Model could potentially all apply to the same theologian's work insofar as they highlight different aspects or emphases. This is suggested by the fact that in outlining these classifications D'Costa, Hedges and Knitter address more or less the same theologians, although the stress is on different aspects of theological position. Thus, it can be said that Williams's theology could be recognised as one based on universal-access exclusivism, particularism and the Acceptance Model. Apart from these models, Williams's practice of interfaith dialogue also shows that he is using the tools of comparative theology while engaging with a particular faith.

2 Williams's theology of religions

Williams's theology can be seen as representative of mainstream Christian orthodoxy. Jesus Christ, the doctrine of the Trinity and Christian identity are quite central in his theology, and all three shape his theology of religions. In this section, I will investigate his theology of religions. In this respect, firstly I will examine his approach to the theology of religions, secondly the issues concerning the place of Jesus and salvation will be discussed, and then I will present his Trinitarian-based theology of religions.

Williams in his early writings provided some background for his theology of religions, though he did not intend to build his own model of theology of religions. However, when he started in his role as archbishop of Canterbury, he found an environment in which he could put his ideas into practice. There are some concerns that appear in his works before he became archbishop. Four conclusions can be drawn from his both early writings and later development: firstly, Williams strongly opposes the relativism which is encouraged by pluralist theologians, specifically by Hick. As a result of his objection to relativism, secondly, Williams emphasises the post-liberal notion of the difference of religions. Thirdly, Williams's theology of religions takes its roots from his orthodox reading of such doctrines of Christianity as incarnation and Trinity. Finally, as a result of these three conclusions, his theology offers a Trinitarian-based theology of religions.

To gain an understanding of his theology of religions, it is important to consider the kind of theology which Williams is engaging in. In the prologue of *On Christian Theology*, Williams offers three types of theological activity: celebratory, communicative and critical.[16] Celebratory phenomena is where theology begins. It seeks to outline and show the connections between thought and image to display the fullest possible range of importance in the language which is used in the hymnody and preaching. Communicative theology 'experiments with the rhetoric of its uncommitted environment';[17] it tries to put the theologians in an environment in which they can communicate with the surrounding culture. Critical theology is alert to inner tensions and irresolution, might consider issues in agnosticism or nihilism and move towards a revaluation of dogmatic language, or alternatively 'it may move towards a rediscovery of the celebratory by hinting at the gratuitous mysteriousness of what theology deals with.'[18] In terms of developing Christian theology, Williams has made a variety of efforts. Ford claims that Williams's basic activity is one of continuing conversation, learning and involvement in the practical demands of history. If theology is to stay healthy, these three types have to be in constant interaction with each other. Williams's theology does not depend on one system; it represents the coherence of all three.[19] Similarly, in terms of the relation of Christian theology to other faiths, Williams applies all three types of theology. In fact, the kind of theology he uses depends on the audience he communicates with. For example, when he talks to non-Christian communities, such as Muslims or Jews, he uses communicative theology. However, when he writes on Christian theology or gives a speech to a Christian community, he tends to apply the other two types of theologies. Hence, in his lecture on 'Christian Theology and Other Faiths', Williams defines theology as:

> [trying] to work out what the implications are of seeing everything in relation to a holy reality that is never absent. It is not about advice as to what we should do when in the territory marked off as religious, where we do business with invisible rather than visible things; it is about what lives should look like when they find their meaning as a whole in relation to holy reality. To put it a bit differently, theology tries to make connections between the stories told about the holy or the fundamentally real and the words and actions people use in order to let those stories take hold of their lives and give them shape in every detail and aspect.[20]

By describing theology in this way, Williams is trying to say that all religious practices 'go along with . . . disciplined thinking, exploring interrelated ideas and metaphors, making connections and searching for consistencies'.[21] He further argues that differences and disagreements among religions tend to be about the universe we inhabit and what that universe makes possible for human beings.[22] Thus, for him, religious disagreements cannot be reduced through recourse to relativism as he regards this as offering a limited perspective.

From his perspective on the nature of theology, it can be seen that Williams is suggesting that the world religions offer different types of theology. In *The Myth of Christian Uniqueness*[23] some pluralist theologians have offered different forms of pluralism, in Knitter's terminology, historical-cultural, theologico-mystical and ethico-practical bridges. However, three years later, some Christian theologians from the orthodox wing came up with the edited book called *Christian Uniqueness Reconsidered: The Myth of a Pluralistic Theology of Religions*.[24] Williams was one of the contributors to this book, which had the main purpose of making counterarguments to

60 Rowan Williams's theology of religions

pluralist theologians' theologies. Williams, in this particular work, applauds Panikkar's contribution to the *The Myth of Christian Uniqueness* because Panikkar's pluralistic theology takes a Trinitarian perspective as starting point rather than the theocentric form of pluralism. Williams argues that

> [t]o affirm the plurality of religions in the way Panikkar does is actually the opposite of being a relativist and holding that all religious positions are so conditioned by their context that they are equally valid and invalid. That would be to take up a position outside of all historical standing points and real traditions, and Panikkar in effect denies that this can be done.[25]

In contrast to the notion that all religions are in some way the same, Williams's theology gives more emphasis to the differences. Difference for Williams is not something which can exclude the existence of the other, nor can it be reduced to sameness. Williams describes difference as '*neither* (at any moment) final, a matter of mutual exclusion, nor simply reducible, a matter of misperception to be resolved by either a return to the same or a cancellation of one term before the Other'.[26] Although Williams does not express this view in the context of religious diversity, his apprehension of difference reflects his views on the religious difference.

During his time as archbishop of Canterbury, Williams on several occasions has reiterated his early thoughts on religious difference. In one of his speeches addressing a Muslim and Christian audience, he strongly criticised the Hickian model of the pluralist approach because of Hick's theory's dependence on a form of relativism and an idea of shared common reality (the idea of the sameness of religions is also shared by Hans Küng who was the chief advocator of 'Global Ethic'). Williams criticises the relativistic approach of Hick and Küng since, for him, relativism depends on the idea that no religion can claim to possess ultimate truth. He says that

> when I see some of the great classics of comparative religion of a certain kind, whether it's the work of Professor John Hick, or Fr. Hans Küng, my worry is that these are people who are eager to persuade everybody that their differences don't really matter in the way they thought they did, that everyone is really asking the same questions, and that it ought to be possible to find the same answers.[27]

In contrast to Hick or other pluralists and inclusivists, who place more emphasis on a shared common ground, Williams thinks that religious relativism reduces narratives and beliefs into a 'basic common vision'.[28] When he argued against this idea, he addressed the famous parable of the blind men and an elephant[29] (which Hick used to support his pluralist hypothesis[30]) and argued that 'the one thing the parable isn't really about is a distinction between what everyone can see and what some people unreasonably argue about.'[31]

Williams argues that it is thus wrong to say that different religious traditions are in fact seeking to give an answer to the same questions. In particular, he contends that if we claim that different religions all answer the same question, the consequence for the relations among religions would be 'simple rivalry, systematic mutual exclusion'.[32] Thus, for him, the different religious traditions actually do provide different explanations for creation and humanity.[33] Applying an approach similar to comparative theology to Islam and Christianity, Williams uses the concept of revelation in both traditions as an example to expresses how for Muslims, who see Muhammad as the seal of the prophets, all prophetic revelation, including Jesus, comes together in a single pattern. If we ask questions like 'What is the climax of prophecy? Where in divine word and human example is the will of God most completely made known?', Muslims would answer in light of the Qur'an and the Prophet.[34] Thus from such an answer, Christians would struggle to discover any unique relationship identified between Jesus and God. As a result, for Williams, the revelation traditions in these two religions and the narratives they offer are different. Hence, they need different questions and different narrative structures to be understood and investigated properly. In Williams's approach then the core of the Christian and Islamic concepts of revelation is recognised as being different. Therefore, the fundamental subject of the religions, if it is to be understood, needs to be approached through its theology and practice rather than through external presuppositions.[35]

It is quite clear that Williams takes the distinctiveness and differences among religions very seriously. According to him, each religion represents a different worldview, and as such there cannot be an all-encompassing common ground among them. He describes the world of religion as 'one area of human experience or human aspiration or language'.[36] For Williams, universal truths cannot be recognised by a relativistic approach: since all truths 'are represented as connected with moments in history and language, their credibility and intelligibility is bound up with history and language, and their expression is determined by these stories of encounter and enlightenment'. This idea echoes Lindbeck's cultural-linguistic theory. As has been pointed out previously, Lindbeck, in his cultural-linguistic theory, introduced the idea of the incommensurability of religions. According to his theory, religions should be considered as different idioms for constructing reality, expressing experience and ordering life.[37]

Even though Williams has some reservation about some aspects of Lindbeck's methodology of intratextuality, it seems that he applies in practice a similar concept of the incommensurability of religions. However, it would not be wrong to say that Williams's use of the incommensurability of religions is a softer version of Lindbeck's. Yet, while Williams appreciates Lindbeck's challenges to the typical liberal assumptions, he is also critical of Lindbeck's use of intratextual theology. Williams thinks that when narratives confront people, they can lead to personal transformation and that it

62 Rowan Williams's theology of religions

is the Church's duty to confront and transform the world. The Church is interpreting the world within its own foundational narratives, and at the same time the act of the interpretation also affects those same narratives as well as the experienced world. During the process of interpretation, there may be a new discovery of what a primal text has become as well as a new discovery of the world.[38] He argues that

> the interpretation of the world "within the scriptural framework" is intrinsic to the *Church's* critical self-discovery/ In judging the world, by its confrontation of the world with its own dramatic script, the Church also judges itself: in attempting to show the world a critical truth, it shows itself to itself as Church also.[39]

While Lindbeck's theory of the untranslatability of religions helps maintain the exclusivist claims of Christianity and simultaneously accept the real otherness of other religions, Williams adopts these two conclusions without engaging so deeply with the concept of the untranslatability of religions. Furthermore, as the example discussed of the concept of revelation in Islam and Christianity indicates, Williams accepts the idea of incommensurability in certain respects. Lindbeck explicitly argues that the religious doctrines of non-Christian religions are comprehensible within their culture and language, but he also notes that being comprehensible does not necessarily mean that they are truthful.[40] By saying so, Lindbeck's approach thus accepts the salvific means of other religions as comprehensible in their own culture and language. On the other hand, Williams never comments on whether the religious truths of non-Christian religions are really true or comprehensible within their culture or language. Thus, he also does not explicitly accept other religions as possible ways to salvation. Instead, his main concern is to accept and respect non-Christian religions in the way they express themselves and have a fruitful dialogue with them. Hence, considering Williams's emphasis on difference of religions and rejection of pluralist interpretation of religions, Hedges's first two points of particularism have been proved. Additionally, we could also find some elements of Knitter's Acceptance Model if Williams's stress on acceptance and respect to other religions' differences are taken into account. The next section will focus on Jesus Christ's place in Williams's theology of religions. In this part of Williams's theology of religions, we could see elements of D'Costa's universal-access exclusivism and Hedges's points relating to soteriological issue.

2.1 Christ's uniqueness and the problem of salvation

Concerning theology of religions, the concept of salvation and Jesus's uniqueness are two clearly important concepts in the Christian tradition. In other words, theologians' theological positions depend on how they consider the problem of salvation of non-Christians and how they approach Jesus in discussions. While pluralist theologians accept the existence of other salvific figures in non-Christian religions, exclusivist or particularist theologians attempt to retain the necessity of belief in Christ for salvation, and thus they object to the suggestion of salvific means through other religions. Williams's views on Jesus Christ can be seen as an example of exclusivism. Like many exclusivist theologians, Williams also thinks salvation can only achieved through Jesus Christ. However, he does not contend that those who do not believe in Jesus will not be saved. For him, Jesus is a universal figure, and the promise of salvation is for everyone. Thus, in D'Costa's terminology Williams's ideas with regard to Jesus and his place among diverse religions can be categorised as a type of universal-access exclusivist theology.

Before and after Williams became archbishop of Canterbury, Christ has been a robust figure in his theology. While in his written works, he seems to be intellectually more sophisticated, in his public speech referring to the issue of salvation and centrality of Christ, he presents his ideas in a more accessible way.

Being aware of discussion going on in theology of religions, Williams in *Finality of Christ*[41] wants to escape from the settled exclusivist theory, which maintains that Christ is the only revelation. He refers to Jesus as the 'meaning of meaning', an approach which was originally formulated by Cornelius Ernst.[42] Thus, his approach is seeking to answer the question of how to understand Jesus by suggesting that he is the meaning of human meanings. While doing this, he does not want to follow any of three common classifications used in the field of theology of religions, namely exclusivism, inclusivism and pluralism.[43] Williams discusses possible statements representing these three options and dismisses them, arguing that firstly, an exclusive statement would argue that all meaning can only be found explicitly and solely in the person of Jesus. Williams thinks, this statement 'rules it out in principle'.[44] Secondly, an inclusive statement would be that all human meaning can be found 'ontologically in the Logos and virtually in Jesus'. This idea for Williams 'makes a bid for ownership'[45] of what is acceptable and tolerable in non-Christian faiths. Thirdly, the pluralist idea would present human meaning as 'accessible through a multitude of equally valid but culturally incommensurable symbol systems, among which the story of Jesus has its place'.[46] According to Williams, this statement does not enable a questioning of coexistence. Instead, he seeks to move beyond these distinctions as it is evident that he feels the claims made by these three options fail to serve as a concrete basis for dialogue.

For Williams, then, Jesus is not the goal and source of all religious traditions, nor is he at work unrecognizably. The meaning of Jesus, for Williams, is not as a container for all other meanings but their test, judgement and catalyst.[47] In this respect, Williams does not explicitly comment on the problem of salvation, but rather he wants to shift the focus. To strengthen this approach Williams tries to read the early Christians within an ancient Jewish context and attempts to show how the finality of Christ became a crucial point in the Church's history. He contends that the statement of the finality of Jesus is the Church's aspiration made on behalf of Jesus. Thus, he

64 *Rowan Williams's theology of religions*

is attempting to illustrate Christ as 'the definitive and critical embodiment of God in Israel's history'.[48] Furthermore, he contends that the events of the Jesus's life, death and resurrection have created a different kind of relation between human beings and God, with the outcome that each believer is now growing into 'a Christ-shaped' future; in other words, the history of human beings is now 'the story of the discovery and realisation of Jesus Christ in the faces of all the women and men.'[49] Thus, Williams comes to the conclusion that

> Jesus 'uniquely' reveals the God whose nature is not to make the claim of unique revelation as total and authoritative meaning. . . . This does seem to break through, to some extent, the option of exclusivism, inclusivism and pluralism. Jesus is not dehistoricized [exclusivism] or absolutized [inclusivism] as an icon of significance, but neither [is] he depicted as the teacher of one among several possible ways of salvation [pluralism]. He is presented as the revelation of God: as God's question, no more, no less.[50]

From the explanation I have given, while Williams attempts to escape from the threefold typology, his emphasis on the finality of Christ creates another form of exclusivism (or universal-access exclusivism, with D'Costa's terminology). Thus, in this form, belief in Jesus Christ remains necessary for achieving salvation (like in exclusivism). However, unlike exclusivist theories, Williams intends to give the main emphasis to the universality of Jesus Christ. Thus, Jesus Christ is for Williams not something to be understood only in a Christian context, but rather he is the main tool for Williams for the interpretation of the whole universe. In other words, Christ is not only restricted in the life and practice of Christians, but also he is something universal, reflected in every human being.

In his speech *The Finality of Christ in a Pluralist World*, Williams engages in a discussion of salvation and of the uniqueness of Jesus in light of John (14:5–6) and Acts (4:8–13). Here, as a preacher, he does not engage with the sophisticated arguments presenting Jesus Christ as the 'meaning of meaning', but rather he wants to present the ideas surrounding the issue in a simple way. In this particular speech, he also makes a connection between Jesus's finality and the fate of the believers of other faiths. Firstly, he introduces three categories of objections to the exclusivist claim of Jesus's finality, namely 'moral, political and philosophical objections', which are commonly raised by pluralist theologians, and then aims to show how John (14:5–6) and Acts (4:813) should be understood.

Beginning with the moral objections, a number of common questions are raised: what happens to those who never have a chance to hear Jesus or the Gospel, those who heard the Gospel but could not understand or those who lived before the coming of Jesus? In response, pluralist theologians, who oppose the perspective that Jesus is unique and offers the only means to attain salvation, argue that God should be seen as the God of all humanity, and thus other religions should not be excluded from having access to salvation. As Hick states:

> [I]n the light of our accumulated knowledge of the other great world faiths [Christian exclusivism] has become unacceptable to all except a minority of dogmatic diehards. For it conflicts with our concept of God, which we have received from Jesus, as the loving heavenly Father of all mankind; could such a Being have restricted the possibility of salvation to those who happen to have been born in certain countries in certain periods of history?[51]

Williams tries to eliminate this objection by emphasising the universality of the claims made in the New Testament. He argues that in the New Testament 'there's something about human beings which is true universally; an orientation, a magnetic "drawing-towards" the source of all things, and a capacity to relate to the source of all things.'[52] He further claims that for Christians, it is certainly clear that God has revealed himself in Jesus, but what we (Christians) cannot know (and 'better pretend not to know') is how those who have not shared in the Mystery of Christianity are related to Jesus and the Father. For Williams the unfairness in this interpretation would be 'in saying that there is no access for some at all, or in saying that we don't have to bother to share'.[53]

The second objection comes from a political perspective. This objection is based on the idea that if Jesus represents the final truth about God, it legitimises the crusades and colonialism and can also be used as a legitimate reason to justify any suppression of claims that differ from Christianity. An example of this objection is provided by the feminist theologian Ruether, who argues that the uniqueness of Christian beliefs led to the crusades, religious violence and the chauvinist history of Christianity.[54] Williams's answer to this particular objection is related to how he understands the act of revelation. According to him, the New Testament is speaking about a specific relationship between the persons of Trinity, not about any claim of political protection. He says that

> this mystery of growing into human fulfillment and fruition through the Son and the Spirit is not something that can be enforced by human power. It belongs to the act of God. The more you believe that God really is God, the less you believe God needs to be protected by human beings from the consequences of his own recklessness.[55]

The third objection is based on philosophy. According to this objection, being an adherent of any religion is based on the place or the time in which you live, so every truth can only be spoken in the terms of its own contemporary time and culture. Thus, it is not possible to apply a truth which was expressed 2,000 years ago to all people everywhere. We can also recognise this objection in Hick's philosophy as he recognised that all of the world

66 *Rowan Williams's theology of religions*

religious traditions are culturally conditioned. Williams strongly opposes this relativistic approach. More specifically, he contends that the New Testament states that it is impossible to become what you are made to be, nor can you live up to the fullness of your human destiny without a relationship with Jesus.[56] However, this approach does not contend that there is no possibility of a fulfilled life or of an afterlife without belief in the finality of Jesus Christ.

Williams goes beyond the objections presented here and presents arguments for why Christians believe in the uniqueness and finality of Jesus Christ. He argues that Christians believe in the uniqueness and finality of Jesus because they think that Jesus has opened a new phase in human history, creating a new community, new creation and a restored humanity. He explains that Jesus is unique 'in the sense that this "turning of a historical epoch", this induction of a new historical moment, can only happen because of the one event and the narratives around it'.[57] He is final; he has changed the relationship between human beings and God; for Williams, 'to affirm the uniqueness and the finality of Jesus Christ is actually to affirm something about the universal reconcilability of human beings: the possibility of a universal fellowship.'[58] For Williams, the uniqueness and finality of Christ is not a problem for the project of inter-religious dialogue. However, he contends that even if Christians accept this perspective, it does not necessarily mean that they will be intolerant or make the claim that everybody except for them will go to hell. Williams instead argues that the value of dialogue is in its ability to help us learn something rather than expecting it to lead people to change their minds.[59]

Williams believes that the means through which someone is directed to heaven lie only in Jesus; that is to say, salvation is possible only through Jesus, and only Jesus can give unity to the world: 'The path to heaven lies solely through Jesus Christ our Savior and the unity he gives, and the only use and integrity of the instruments of unity is when they serve that.'[60] However, this does not mean that Williams argues for the exclusion of others from salvation. Instead, Williams argues that the law of God, as revealed in the Old Testament, promises salvation to the whole community of God; no one is forgotten or invisible in the kingdom of God. However, he also argues that with the life, death and resurrection of Jesus, the life of human beings was reshaped, and God's final purpose was uncovered thorough these events. For Williams, then, Jesus has reshaped and redefined what it means to be a part of God's community, and thus every person can find meaning relating to their destiny or their freedom:

> Jesus is where the history of the world comes to a crisis; comes to a point of finality and new decision; and where Jesus is the future, the end is around him and, unlikely as it may sound, we who gather around Jesus are part of the end of the world.[61]

The promise of salvation being reserved only for those who believe in Jesus is not what Williams intended in this quote. Instead, his point is that the Church is not only reserved for those who believed this promise but also for those 'who do not believe', 'might believe', 'could believe' or 'will believe'. He says that we cannot know with certainty what the status of those who do not believe will be, but we know that the promise is for them.[62]

Thus like many particularist theologians, Williams's theology includes non-Christians for the universal plan of salvation. But, unlike many particularists, he does not seek to develop a theology in which the salvation of non-Christians is discussed since his primary concern is not soteriological issues. More recently particularist theologians have found alternative solutions to open the gates of salvation of non-Christians without dismissing the uniqueness of Christ. For example, Lindbeck develops a futuristic eschatological theory which offers salvation to non-Christians after death in a post-mortem state.[63] DiNoia also offers a similar solution. For him the doctrine of purgatory allows the salvation of non-Christians without underestimating the distinctive aims they have pursued in life.[64] Having been influenced by post-liberal theology, Williams also thinks that the promise of salvation includes non-Christians. However, unlike post-liberal theologians, Williams does not promote a post-mortem solution. In his theology, the salvation offered to non-Christians is in terms of hope.

Yet, while Williams tries to escape from the problems of exclusivism, he develops his own particularist or exclusivist theology based on Christ. In particular, his primary concern is not whether Jesus has any meaning for non-Christians, but rather he is concerned for the development of a comprehensive theology about Jesus within Christian theology. Yet, while he attempts to deal with the objections outlined, it seems the explanations he offers are not fully convincing. The problem is not why non-Christians will not be saved but why the salvation of non-Christians is related to Christian doctrines. As has been previously argued, Williams's theology of religions regarding the question of salvation can be an example of exclusivism (in Race's typology). But his stress on universality of Jesus makes him a more universal-access exclusivist and a particularist who does not question the salvific efficacy of non-Christian religions but also believes that non-Christians are not excluded from the universal plan of salvation. In spite of his particularist positions relating to Jesus's place in the discussion of religious pluralism, how he still maintains openness to non-Christians relies on his Trinitarian theology of religions. The next section will explore Williams's Trinitarian theology.

2.2 Trinitarian theology of religions

Williams's understanding of the doctrine of Trinity shapes his theology of religions. In other words, his understanding of the place of Jesus and his views on religious differences are related to his understanding of Trinitarian revelation. His theology of religions is one of the great examples of Trinitarian-based theology of religions, which in a certain way leads him to direct to interfaith practice. In *Trinity and Pluralism* Williams makes use of

68 *Rowan Williams's theology of religions*

Panikkar's Trinitarian language and proposes his own Trinitarian theology. He states:

> Being Christian . . . is believing the doctrine of Trinity to be true, and true in a way that converts and heals the human world. It is not to claim a *totality* of truth about God or about the human world, or even a monopoly of the means of bringing divine absolution or grace to men and women. The Christian says, 'Our religious history shows us that God is *thus*: a God who can only be known and witnessed comprehensively in a human form of life in which Logos and Spirit are held balance with each other. . . . What it *will* finally be is not something theory will tell us, but something only discoverable in the expanding circles of encounter with what is not the Church.' This not only enables but impels dialogue, and, more significantly, practical work together; it also recognizes the inescapability of conflict, even judgment, when there are different perceptions of the nature of human unity at work.[65]

It is quite clear from this quote that Williams's theology of religions neither aims to replace other religions (like exclusivist theories) nor imposes the truths of Christianity on non-Christian religions.

While I outlined Williams's views on Jesus Christ, I have already mentioned that for Williams, human history is reshaped in Jesus Christ. The incarnation, life and resurrection of Jesus need to be discovered since Jesus 'turns his face' to all men and women. This means that the fullness of Jesus is found in the process of discovery, and hence everything about Jesus will never be capable of being predicted or explained. Thus, the process of 'discovery' leads Christians to turn their face to others.[66] Elsewhere Williams presents the Christian understating of God as mystery, arguing that

> [a] very significant part of the Christian tradition, especially the Christian mystical tradition, is the conviction that you will never have said enough about God. If God is infinite then you will never run out of things to say. And you'll never come to a place where you can say, 'all that has to be said about God has now been said'. Our speech about God brings us constantly to the edge of a mystery which is at one and the same time dark and even alarming, because it throws out all our preconceptions, and yet is also inviting, because we know it is a mystery of endless love and invitation and welcome. So the process of talking about faith, for Christians who've inherited that particular strand of Christian reflection, is always a process of coming to the point where you look into a mystery.[67]

Thus as a result of this Mystery, the goal of interfaith dialogue for Christians is

> to invite the world of faiths to find here, in the narrative and practice of Jesus and his community, that which anchors and connects their human

hopefulness- not necessarily in the form of "fulfilling their aspiration" or "perfecting their highest ideals," but as something which might unify a whole diverse range of struggles for human integrity without denying or "colonizing" their own history and expression.[68]

Through this idea it seems that Williams is employing the language of inclusivism. Although he tries to escape from the restraints of inclusivist or exclusivist language, this only serves to make the issue more complicated. On the one hand, he includes the non-Christian religions in the Mystery of God, incorporating them in a Christian narrative, but on the other hand he accepts that they have their own history and expression. Put differently, one part of the proposition promotes an inclusivist perspective, but another emphasises the distinctive features and particularity of non-Christian religions. Williams never questions the truths of non-Christian religions. He is silent about non-Christian religions' doctrines, narratives and ethics, and as such he employs the language of tolerance and respect more effectively. This prevents him to categorise non-Christian religions in a single line. In other words, he does not label religions as true which contain true beliefs and false which consist of false elements. He uses similar language in a speech referring to the Christian aim in interfaith dialogue. He states:

> The language that the other person uses about God may not be the language you use; you may disagree and find areas of enormous strangeness between you. And yet you will still want to say, 'In that attention to the other, I will discover something of God'. The image I've repeatedly used in speaking about dialogue at its best is that it is a process where I try and 'look at another person's face turned towards God': not a face turned towards me in a rapid, perhaps adversarial, relationship, but to look at their face as they pray and absorb the reality of God, and then to speak and listen with them.[69]

When trying to interpret this particular statement, it may seem that Williams is making recourse to the notion of 'anonymous Christianity'. The question then can be asked as to whether non-Christians are unconsciously turning their face towards God or whether what Williams sees is the same as what the non-Christians see. However, Williams contends that his viewpoint is not the equivalent of anonymous Christianity, which he regards as having many problems.[70] He argues that

> [t]he language of 'anonymous Christianity' is now not much in fashion – and it had all kinds of problems about it. Yet who that has been involved in dialogue with other faiths has not had the sense of an echo, a reflection, of the kind of life Christians seek to live? St Paul says that God did not leave himself without witnesses in the ages before the Messiah; in those places where that name is not named, God may yet give himself to be seen.[71]

70 Rowan Williams's theology of religions

Although the position taken here sounds like inclusivism, this does not necessarily mean that Williams's theology takes the standard inclusivist stance. As has been noted, Williams's theology does not seek to find common shared ground among other faiths, but rather it is based on the conviction of difference.

Williams's Trinitarian theology resonates with the document *Generous Love: The Truth of the Gospel and the Call to Dialogue: an Anglican Theology of Interfaith Relations*, which was issued by the NIFCON in 2008. This document is a product of a long time of engagement between Anglicans and non-Christians faiths, but Williams's Trinitarian theology of interfaith dialogue seems to influence the nature of document.[72] Although the document does not have any magisterial authority, the document was formed for providing theological guidance for Anglicans. In the foreword of *Generous Love*, Williams states:

> With great foresight, the Roman Catholic Church at the Second Vatican Council set out some of the theological perspectives that might help shape a faithful and generous approach to other faiths. But the situation has moved on, both in theology and in practical relations between communities, so that there is a need to draw together some of the rich reflection that has been going on more recently.[73]

The document has eight sections, each section aiming to offer a basis for interfaith dialogue. The first section starts with *Beginning with God*, in which Trinitarian belief is reiterated and offered as the basis of Christian understanding of dialogue. It says:

> We believe that through the life, death and resurrection of Jesus of Nazareth the One God has made known his triune reality as Father, Son and Holy Spirit. . . . As members of the Church of the Triune God, we are to abide among our neighbours of different faiths as signs of God's presence with them.[74]

The second section presents the contemporary context and Anglican heritage together and offers an Anglican approach to religious diversity (both diversity within Christianity and other religions). Thus it states:

> [An] Anglican approach dismisses nothing as outside God's concern, but attends to the world in its manifold differences in the expectation that it ultimately coheres, having one source and one goal in God. This is a discipline against sectarianism, and a resource for living with plurality.[75]

The third section encourages Christians, alongside their study of the Bible, to read the Scriptures of other faiths ('Scriptural Reasoning').[76] The fourth section presents tradition and reason as sources of Anglican insight, while the remaining sections stress why and how the interfaith dialogue should be conducted.

From our consideration of *Generous Love*, we see that on the one hand, it acknowledges religious differences, while on the other hand it presents them in terms of a unity with God. Sudworth claims that

> Generous Love offers a brief perspective of what is distinctively Anglican in a Trinitarian theology of religions, recognizing the plurality in unity, characteristic of Anglicanism, underpinning the affirmation of God's work in the world, but also a Christian unity that avoids sectarianism.[77]

Overall, in the interfaith practice of Williams, there is reflection of both his Trinitarian theology of religions and his post-liberal conviction of the importance of difference. The first part offers a vision of human unity with God, while the second part accepts the real differences of other religions. Thus, using Knitter's term, post-liberals encourage what Williams would regard as a 'good neighborhood'[78] policy. This is based on the conviction that the more people know the distinctness and differences among themselves and other groups, the more likely they are to be able to understand each other. For Williams, the terms 'mutual understanding', 'mutual respect' and 'mutual trust' are quite central for inter-religious dialogue, and his approach reflects this trend. This approach accepts the real differences of others, but it also manages to preserve the distinct features of Christian identity.

For Williams, one can only understand another's religious beliefs by delving deeply into their religions. It requires seeing others not from your own specific religion but trying to see them in the way that they see and describe themselves. Thus, Williams describes inter-religious dialogue in this way:

> Dialogue is not debate; dialogue is not proselytism; dialogue is not the attempt to persuade; dialogue is not negotiation. When I enter dialogue with someone of another religious tradition. . . . I am not out to secure agreement, but to secure understanding. An honest and constructive dialogue leads us to go away thinking 'Now I begin to see a little better what it is like to hold those views, pray those prayers and to live those lives.'[79]

Williams's interfaith practice gives more emphasis to relating different religions' different perspectives on theological and practical issues. The important thing is not to recognise how people of other faiths share the same story or to use their teachings to learn more about God. To him, through dialogue a person can relate someone else's questions to their own questions, and that process may lead them to discover something much deeper than suspected or expected.[80] In addition, he makes no attempt to argue that other faiths should have the same goals as Christians but rather emphasises that the

72   Rowan Williams's theology of religions

believers of other faiths can have goals which are comparable in distinctiveness and importance.[81] In the process of inter-religious engagement, all participants will obviously be changed, but this does not mean that they will adopt the religions or aspects of the religions of those they are debating with. Instead, Williams's emphasises that they can learn something about their own tradition by discovering new ways of thinking about their own religion. In this respect, inter-religious engagement presents mutual benefits for all those involved, according to Williams. Instead of a pluralistic reading of religions, or a relativistic approach, Williams is a supporter of religious pluralism. He thinks that to gain social cohesion in society, debate and disagreement among different religions play major roles.[82]

Although Williams stresses religious difference, unlike most post-liberals he is not so strict on the rejection of common ground. While he rejects the relativistic approach to religions, in his practice he acted together with other religious leaders on many social issues, including poverty, social justice and ecological issues. In other words, while talking about such problems, he cross-references other religious teachings. To give a solid example, while Williams spoke on *Ecology and Economy*, he made some general claims which most world religions would agree on. He stated that all 'the great religious traditions, in their several ways, insist that personal wealth is not to be seen in terms of reducing the world to what the individual can control and manipulate for whatever exclusively human purposes may be most pressing.'[83] After presenting a general idea, he presented Jewish and Islamic perspectives ecology to indicate that the religions have something to say in common but which can also be complementary. His demonstration of other religions' accounts of the issue is as follows:

> Judaism's teachings about the 'jubilee' principle stress that the land is lent not given to human cultivators: it requires 'sabbatical' years, and its value is to be seen not in terms of absolute possession but as a source of a limited number of harvests between the sabbatical years (Lev.25). The assumption is that the environment that is given, the land bestowed by God, has to be set free regularly from our assumption that it belongs to us; it has to be left to be itself, to be in relation simply to the God who has given it. A year of uncultivation, wildness, is not a lot, but it speaks eloquently of our willingness to organise economy around ecology, to 'keep house' within the limits of a world where we are guests more than owners. Similarly, Christianity not only has its challenges in the Sermon on the Mount to anxiety about controlling the environment, prohibiting us from identifying wealth with possession; it also has its sacramental tradition which presents the material order as raw material for the communication of God's love – the Eucharist as the effective symbol of God's action in creating a radically different human society, not characterised by rivalry and struggle for resources. At the centre of Christian practice is a rite in which all are equally fed by one gift, and in which material things are identified symbolically with the self-offering

of Christ. Islam also underlines the partnership of humanity and the rest of the natural order – and, in a passing observation in the Qur'an (Sura 16.8) reminds us that some of the purposes of the animal creation are unknown to us. And a twentieth century Iranian scholar (Muhammad Husayn Tabatabai) quotes both Muhammad and the fifth of the Shi'a Imams as commending farming because it is beneficial for humans and for the animal world as well. Examples could be multiplied from these and other faiths; but what I have quoted makes it abundantly clear that religious faith assumes that our humanity grows into maturity by allowing the material environment its own integrity. While the detail of this is inescapably complex, the point is plain.[84]

What I am trying to show is that although Williams on several occasions puts stress on the different narratives and religious teaching, he does not entirely reject any common points or purposes among religions. This is because his Trinitarian theology on the one hand sees the whole of humanity or the universe in unity with Trinitarian God and, on the other hand, enables him to see the difference of other faiths.

Overall Williams's theology of religions offers quite an open approach towards other religions while simultaneously committed to his own Christian belief. I started my overview of his theology of religions with his view on difference. This part of Williams's theology of religions presents the particularist vision of his theology. Then I moved on to present his view on Jesus Christ and salvation, which show the universal-access exclusivist aspect. Then I presented his Trinitarian theology and interfaith practice, which has some overlap with the inclusivist vision. Despite taking the account of Christian orthodoxy seriously, his theological account does not aim to hold the totality of truths. Practically, his theology promotes a 'good neighborhood' policy and radical openness towards other. Hedges, quoting one of Williams's speeches,[85] argues that 'others within the churches, including those in senior positions, are led by their experience of dialogue *towards a radical openness* [emphasis added] in relation to religious Others, even if their expressed theology is inclusivist or particularist.'[86] However, from my point of view, Williams's openness towards other religions does not come in spite of his theology but rather as a result of his theology.

We can see how Williams challenges the theology of religions classifications outlined in the previous chapter. His position seems to combine elements of universal-access exclusivism and inclusivism, whilst also retaining the emphasis on difference characteristics of the particularist vision. In addition, his theology is oriented towards the practical context of dialogue and cooperation among the religions.

A strong point of Williams's inter-religious dialogue practice is that it has significant coherence given the situation in modern society. In the modern age, there is almost no longer any homogenous society in terms of ethnicity and religion. As a result, people need to know and understand each other more than at any time in the past. Williams's approach may offer people a

74 Rowan Williams's theology of religions

good way to start addressing and recognising their differences but also does not close off the possibility of finding common ground.

Conclusion

Williams has shown us how a particularist or universal-access exclusivist theological approach can involve a surprising level of openness to inter-religious engagement. His theology is not one which excludes other religions, but in spite of that he still contends that Jesus is the only means for salvation. Yet, he also believes that God's promise of salvation covers everyone. Williams maintains that ultimately, in regard to discussions concerning how people can reach salvation, this matter should be left to God as no one else really has the right to make final judgements on this topic.

He is also a prominent supporter of the perspective that different religions can live together in the same society, but he deemphasises the relativist perspective of pluralism. To him the unique relationship between Jesus and God has established a new community across the world, and this should not be denied by relativisation.

Williams suggests that in the modern world, to discover more about God requires 'turning to see the faces of others'. In this sense, he believes that theological dialogue conducted with this goal in mind would actually help to increase awareness of Christianity because people would start to ask new question about their religion. This Trinitarian theology is the fundamental reason why he encourages interfaith dialogue. Furthermore, it is now a reality of the globalised world that almost all communities contain different religions living together within the same society. Based on the common aims found in the diverse religions, social cohesion will be enhanced through interfaith dialogue as a diverse range of people will be better able to work collaboratively to address the same issues. Mutual benefits thus seem possible through the means of interfaith dialogue.

Notes

1 Rupert Short, Rowan Williams, *An Introduction* (London: Dortan, Longman and Todd, 2003), 1.
2 Rowan Williams, *What Is Christianity* (23 November 2005), available at: http://rowan williams.archbishopofcanterbury.org/articles.php/1087/what-is-christianity (accessed in 10 January 2013).
3 He told me in a private conservation.
4 Jane Barter Moulaison, "The 'Secret Fire at the Heart of Earthly': The Theological Vision of Rowan Williams," *Touchstone* (January 2010): 53–62.
5 While contemporary theologians produce books which primarily focus on discussions of a Christian theology of religions. For example, look at Gavin D'Costa, *Christianity and World Religions: Disputed Questions in the Theology of Religions* (Oxford: Willey-Blackwell, 2009), Paul Knitter, *Introducing Theology of Religions* (New York: Orbis Books, 2009), and Jacques Dupuis, *Towards a Christian Theology of Religious Pluralism* (New York: Orbis Books, 1998).
6 Rowan Williams, "Muslim Christian Dialogue in Britain," *Islam and Christian-Muslim Relations* 19/3 (2008): 33–338.

Rowan Williams's theology of religions 75

7 The Building Bridges Seminars were founded by the previous archbishop of Canterbury George Carey to develop Muslim-Christian relations a year after the event of September 11 in 2002. Each seminar lasts three days, during which the participants try to explore the significant themes in the interface between Islam and Christianity. All information can be found at: http://berkleycenter.george town.edu/resources/networks/building_bridges (accessed in 10 January 2013).
Williams's contribution to Building Bridges Seminars has been important. Since he became an archbishop of Canterbury, he has attended and contributed all the meetings. At his first seminar as an archbishop, for the first time, the process of 'Scriptural Reasoning' was applied in practice and throughout ten years of his experience, Christian and Muslims scholars have discovered certain topics in the light of both traditions' scriptures.
8 The forum was founded in 1997 and aims to bring Christians and Muslims together to develop an open and honest relationship and to build a public platform so as to strengthen Christian and Muslim cooperation in working for the common good. All documents and events can be found at: http://www.christian muslimforum.org (accessed in 10 January 2013).
9 The council was founded in 1949 and aims to conduct inter-religious dialogue between Christians and Jews on a variety of issues. All related information can be found at: http://www.ccj.org.uk/Groups/172742/Council_of_Christians.aspx (accessed in 10 January 2013).
10 For more information, see the website: http://rowan williams.archbishopof-canterbury.org/pages/dialogues-categorised-by-faith.html (accessed in 10 January 2013).
11 D'Costa, *World Religions*, 7.
12 Ibid., 26–30.
13 See Paul Hedges, "Particularities: Tradition-Specific Post-Modern Perspectives," in *Christian Approaches to Other Faiths*, eds. Alan Race and Paul Hedges (London: SCM Press, 2008), 112–113.
14 Paul Hedges, *Controversies in Interreligious Dialogue and Theology of Religions* (London: SCM Press, 2010), 28–29.
15 Paul Knitter, *Introducing Theology of Religions* (Maryknoll, NY: Orbis Books, 2002), 173.
16 Rowan Williams, *On Christian Theology* (Oxford: Blackwell Publisher, 2000), xiii.
17 Ibid., xiv.
18 Ibid., xv.
19 David Ford, "Theological System: British Style," *The Christian Century* (5 April 2000): 388–391, available at: http://www.religion-online.org/showarticle. asp?title=1976 (accessed in 10 January 2013).
20 Rowan Williams, *Christian Theology and Other Faiths* (11 June 2003), available at: http://rowanwilliams.archbishopofcanterbury.org/articles.php/1825/christian-theology-and-other-faiths (accessed in 10 January 2013), later published at Scriptures in Dialogue Christians and Muslims Studying: the Bible and the Qur'an together: A Record of the Seminar 'Building Bridge' held at Doha, Qatar, 7–9 April 2003, ed. Michael Ipgrave (London: Church House Publishing, 2004), 131–143.
21 Williams, *Christian Theology and Other Faiths*.
22 Ibid.
23 John Hick and Paul Knitter (eds.), *The Myth of Christian Uniqueness: Toward a Pluralistic Theology of Religions* (Maryknoll, NY: Orbis Books, 1987).
24 Gavin D'Costa (ed.), *Christian Uniqueness Reconsidered: The Myth of a Pluralistic Theology of Religions* (Maryknoll, NY: Orbis Books, 1990).
25 Rowan Williams, "Trinity and Pluralism," in *Christian Uniqueness Reconsidered: The Myth of a Pluralistic Theology of Religions*, ed. Gavin D'Costa (Maryknoll, NY: Orbis Books, 1990), 4.

26 Rowan Williams, "Between Politics and Metaphysics: Reflections in the Wake of Gillian Rose," in *Wrestling with Angels: Conversation in Modern Theology*, ed. Mike Highton (London: SCM Press, 2007), 71. This work was originally published in *Modern Theology* II (January 1991): 3–22.

27 Williams, *Dialogue Is Means of 'God's Given Discovery'* (22 March 2010), available at: http://rowanwilliams.archbishopofcanterbury.org/articles.php/926/archbishop-dialogue-is-a-means-of-god-given-discovery (accessed in 10 January 2013).

28 Rowan Williams, *Archbishop's Chevening Lecture at the British Council* (15 October 2010), New Delhi, available at: http://rowanwilliams.archbishopofcanterbury.org/articles.php/569/archbishops-chevening-lecture-at-the-british-council-new-delhi#sthash.UYlmY9Yr.dpuf (accessed in 10 January 2013). This speech is published with the title "Pluralism-Public and Religion," in Williams' *Faith in the Public Square* (London: Bloomsbury Publishing, 2012), 126–136.

29 The blind men and an elephant parable is said to have been narrated by many religious traditions: Jain, Hindu, Buddhist and Sufi. According to the parable, an elephant has been brought to a group of blind men who never have encountered such an animal before. Each one has touched a different part of the elephant and identified it differently: a leg as a tree, the trunk as a great snake, a tusk as a sharp ploughshare and so on. When they came together each man claimed that their description was true and the others were false. In fact each was true, but they were only referring to a particular part of the same reality. This parable is used by pluralist theologians to illustrate the idea that each religious tradition represents a particular aspect of divine reality.

30 See John Hick, *God and Universe of Faiths*, 140, and *Problems of Religious Pluralism* (London: The MacMillan Press, 1985), 37.

31 Williams, *Christian Theology and Other Faiths*.

32 Ibid.

33 Ibid.

34 Ibid.

35 Ibid.

36 Rowan Williams, *Archbishop keynote address at Methodist Church* (28 June 2004), available at: http://rowanwilliams.archbishopofcanterbury.org/articles.php/1636/archbishop-keynote-address-at-the-methodist-conference (accessed in 10 January 2013).

37 George Lindbeck, *Nature of Doctrine* (London: SPCK, 1984), 47–48.

38 Rowan Williams, "Postmodern Theology and Judgment of the World," in *Postmodern Theology: Christian Faith in a Pluralist World*, ed. F. B. Burnham (New York: Harper & Row, 1989), 94.

39 Ibid., 95.

40 Lindbeck argues, 'There is nothing in the cultural-linguistic approach that requires the rejection (or the acceptance) of the epistemological realism and correspondence theory of truth' (*Nature of Doctrine*, 68–69).

41 Rowan Williams, "Finality of Christ," in *On Christian Theology* (Oxford: Blackwell Publishing, 2000), 93–107. This work was originally published in Marry Kelly (ed.), *Christianity and Religious Pluralism* (London: The Sisters of Our Lady Sion, 1990), 21–38.

42 For Williams's explanation of Ernst theory and the two possible meanings of 'the meaning of meaning', see Williams, "Finality of Christ," 93–94. Cornelius Ernst, *Multiple Echo, Exploration in Theology*, eds. Fergus Kerr and Timothy Radcliff (London: Darton, Longman Todd, 1979), 85.

43 Williams, "Finality of Christ," 95.

44 Ibid.

45 Ibid.

46 Ibid.

47 Ibid., 94.

Rowan Williams's theology of religions   77

48 Ibid., 103.
49 Rowan Williams, "Trinity and Pluralism," in *Christian Uniqueness Reconsidered: The Myth of a Pluralistic Theology of Religions*, ed. Gavin D'Costa (Maryknoll, NY: Orbis Books, 1990), 3–15.
50 Ibid., 105.
51 John Hick, *God Has Many Names*, 27.
52 Rowan Williams, *The Finality of Christ in a Pluralist World* (2 March 2010), available at: http://rowanwilliams.archbishopofcanterbury.org/articles.php/585/the-finality-of-christ-in-a-pluralist-world (accessed in 10 January 2013).
53 Ibid.
54 Rosemary R. Ruether, "Feminism and Jewish-Christian Dialogue," in *The Myth of Christian Uniqueness: Toward a Pluralistic Theology of Religions*, eds. John Hick and Paul Knitter (London: SCM Press, 1987), 141.
55 Williams, *The Finality of Christ in a Pluralist World*.
56 Here, his view echoes his early development (in *On Christian Theology*) on Jesus's finality. In fact, he is trying to explain the meaning and the life of Jesus and what the events of death and resurrection mean for Christians; hence, he is not trying to present a connection between the fate of non-Christians and the finality of Jesus. In his Larkin-Stuart lecture, Williams builds his argument in nearly the same way. He contends that on the basis of two particular verses (John 14:5–6) and (Acts 4:8–13), Christians should not attempt to find the fate of non-Christians, but they should think 'how the disciples are to understand the death of Jesus as the necessary clearing of the way which they are to walk'. *The Bible Today: Reading and Hearing* (16 April 2007), available at: http://rowanwilliams.archbishopofcanterbury.org/articles.php/2112/the-bible-today-reading-hearing-the-larkin-stuart-lecture (accessed in 10 January 2013).
57 Williams, *The Finality of Christ in a Pluralist World*.
58 Ibid.
59 Ibid.
60 Rowan Williams, *One Holy Catholic and Apostolic Church* (28 October 2005), avaliable at: http://rowanwilliams.archbishopofcanterbury.org/articles.php/1675/one-holy-catholic-and-apostolic-church (accesed in 10 January 2013).
61 Rowan Williams, *No One Can Be Forgotten in God's Kingdom* (9 March 2007), avaliable at: http://rowanwilliams.archbishopofcanterbury.org/articles.php/1436/no-one-can-be-forgotten-in-gods-kingdom-team-conference-south-africa (accessed in 10 January 2013).
62 Ibid.
63 Lindbeck, *Nature of Doctrine*, 55–63.
64 Joseph A. Dinoia, *The Diversity of Religions: A Christian Perspective* (Washington, DC: The Catholic University Press 1992), 104–107.
65 Williams, *Trinity and Pluralism*, 14–15.
66 Ibid., 8.
67 Rowan Williams, *Dialogue Is Means of 'God's Given Discovery'* (22 March 2010), available at: http://rowanwilliams.archbishopofcanterbury.org/articles.php/926/archbishop-dialogue-is-a-means-of-god-given-discovery (accessed in 10 January 2013).
68 Williams, *Trinity and Pluralism*, 10.
69 Williams, *Dialogue Is Means of 'God's Given Discovery'*.
70 Rowan Williams, *What We Mean by Christian Identity* (17 February 2006), World Council of Churches, available at: http://rowanwilliams.archbishopof canterbury.org/articles.php/1781/what-we-mean-by-christian-identity-world-council-of-churches-address (accessed in 10 January 2013).
71 Ibid.
72 For a good overview Williams's influence on the document, see Philip W. D. Ind, "Rowan Williams, Archbishop of Canterbury, February 2003–December 2012, and His Relation with Islam" (MPhil diss., Heythrop College, 2013), 85–94.

78 *Rowan Williams's theology of religions*

73 *Generous Love, v.*
74 Ibid., 1.
75 Ibid., 4.
76 'Scriptural Reasoning' is 'a practice of group reading of the scriptures of Judaism, Christianity, and Islam that seeks to build sociality among its practitioners and release sources of wisdom and compassion for healing our separate communities and for repair of the world'. Steven Kepnes, "A Handbook for Scriptural Reasoning," in *The Promise of Scriptural Reasoning*, eds. David F. Ford and C.C. Pecknold (Oxford: Blackwell, 2006), 23; also posted on the *Journal of Scriptural Reasoning* website: http://etext.lib.virginia.edu/journals/jsrforum/). The practice has its origins in dialogue between Jewish and Christian scholars.' Cited in *Genereous Love*, 17.
77 Richard J. Sudworth, *Anglicanism and Islam: The Ecclesial-Turn in Interfaith Relations, Living Stones Yearbook* (London: Melisende, 2012), 87.
78 Knitter, *Theologies of Religions*, 183.
79 Williams, "Muslim Christian Dialogue."
80 Williams, *Dialogue Is Means of 'God's Given Discovery'.*
81 Williams, *Trinity and Pluralism*, 10.
82 Rowan Williams, *Why Social Cohesion Needs Religion* (6 December 2007), available at: http://rowanwilliams.archbishopofcanterbury.org/articles.php/1144/why-social-cohesion-needs-religion (accessed in 10 January 2013).
83 Rowan Williams, *Ecology and Economy* (8 March 2005), available at: http://rowanwilliams.archbishopofcanterbury.org/articles.php/1550/ecology-.and-economy-archbishop-calls-for-action-on-environment-to-head-off-social-crisis (accessed in 10 January 2013).
84 Ibid.
85 'When others appear to have arrived at a place where forgiveness and adoption are sensed and valued, even when these things are not directly spoken of in the language of another faith's mainstream reflection, are we to say that God has not found a path for himself?' Rowan Williams, *Christian Identity and Religious Pluralism* (17 February 2006), Plenary Session Paper from World Council of the Churches Assembly, Porto Alegre, available at: https://www.oikoumene.org/en/resources/documents/assembly/2006-porto-alegre/2-plenary-presenta tions/christian-identity-religious-plurality/rowan-williams-presentation?set_language=en (accessed in 20 August 2015).
86 Hedges, *Controversies*, 112.

Bibliography

D'Costa, Gavin. *Christianity and World Religions: Disputed Questions in The Theology of Religions.* Oxford: Wiley-Blackwell, 2009.
———, ed. *Christian Uniqeness Reconsidered: The Myth of a Pluralistic Theology of Religions.* Maryknoll, NY: Orbis Books, 1990.
DiNoia, Joseph A. *The Diversity of Religions: A Christian Perspective.* Washington, DC: Catholic University of America Press, 1992.
Dupuis, Jacques. *Towards a Christian Theology of Religious Pluralism.* New York: Orbis Books, 1998.
Ernst, Cornelius. *Multiple Echo, Exploration in Theology*, edited by Fergus Kerr and Timothy Radcliff. London: Darton, Longman & Todd, 1979.
Ford, David. "Theological System: British Style." *The Christian Century* (5 April 2000): 388–391. www.religion-online.org/showarticle.asp?title=1976 (accessed January 10, 2013).

Hedges, Paul. *Controversies in Interreligious Dialogue and the Theology of Religions*. London: SCM Press, 2010.

———. "Particularities: Tradition Specific Post-Modern Perspectives." In *Christian Approaches to Other Faiths*, edited by Alan Race and Paul Hedges, 112–135. London: SCM Press, 2008.

Hick, John. *God and the Universe of Faiths*. London: Macmillan, 1973.

———. *Problems of Religious Pluralism*. London: Macmillan, 1985.

Hick, John and Paul Knitter, eds. *The Myth of Christian Uniqueness: Toward a Pluralistic Theology of Religions*. Maryknoll, NY: Orbis Books, 1987.

Ind, Philip W.D. "Rowan Williams, Archbishop of Canterbury, February 2003 – December 2012, and His Relation with Islam." MPhil diss., Heythrop College, 2013.

Kepnes, Steven. "A Handbook for Scriptural Reasining." In *The Promise of Scriptural Reasining*, edited by David Ford and C. C. Pecknold, 23–40. Oxford: Blackwell, 2006.

Knitter, Paul. *Introducing Theologies of Religions*. Maryknoll, NY: Orbis Books, 2009.

Lindbeck, George. *Nature of Doctrine: Religion and Theology in Postliberal Age*. London: SPCK, 1984.

Moulaison, Jane Barter. "The 'Secret Fire at the Heart of Earthly': The Theological Vision of Rowan Williams." *Touchstone* (January 2010): 53–62.

Ruether, Rosemary R. "Feminism and Jewish-Christian Dialogue." In *The Myth of Christian Uniqueness: Toward a Pluralistic Theology of Religions*, edited by Paul Knitter and John Hick, 137–148. London: London SCM Press, 1987.

Short, Rupert. *Rowan Williams: An Introduction*. London: Dortan, Longman & Todd, 2003.

Sudworth, Richard J. *Anglicanism and Islam: The Ecclesial-Turn in Interfaith Relations, Living Stones Yearbook*. London: Melisende, 2012.

Williams, Rowan. *Archbishop's Address at al-Azhar al-Sharif, Cairo*. 11 September 2004. http://rowanwilliams.archbishopofcanterbury.org/articles.php/1299/archbishops-address-at-al-azhar-al-sharif-cairo (accessed January 10, 2013).

———. *Archbishop's Address to Faith Leaders in Birmingham*. 16 November 2008. http://rowanwilliams.archbishopofcanterbury.org/articles.php/1158/archbishops-address-to-faith-leaders-in-birmingham (accessed January 10, 2013).

———. *Archbishop's Chevening Lecture at the British Council, New Delhi*. 15 October 2010. http://rowanwilliams.archbishopofcanterbury.org/articles.php/569/archbishops-chevening-lecture-at-the-british-council-new-delhi (accessed January 10, 2013).

———. *Archbishop's Lecture – Civil and Religious Law in England: A Religious Perspective*. 7 February 2008. http://rowanwilliams.archbishopofcanterbury.org/articles.php/1137/archbishops-lecture-civil-and-religious-law-in-england-a-religious-perspective (accessed January 10, 2013).

———. *Archbishop's Lecture – Religious Hatred and Religious Offence*. 29 January 2008. http://rowanwilliams.archbishopofcanterbury.org/articles.php/1328/archbishops-lecture-religious-hatred-and-religious-offence (accessed January 10, 2013).

———. "Between Politics and Metaphysics: Reflections in the Wake of Gillian Rose." In *Wrestling with Angels: Conversation in Modern Theology*, edited by Mike Highton, 53–77. London: SCM Press, 2007.

80   *Rowan Williams's theology of religions*

———. *The Bible Today: Reading and Hearing.* 16 April 2007. http://rowanwil liams.archbishopofcanterbury.org/articles.php/2112/the-bible-today-reading-hearing-the-larkin-stuart-lecture (accessed January 10, 2013).

———. "Christian Identity and Religious Pluralism." Plenary Session Paper from World Council of the Churches Assembly. 17 February 2006. https://www.oikou mene.org/en/resources/documents/assembly/2006-porto-alegre/2-plenary-presen tations/christian-identity-religious-plurality/rowan-williams-presentation?set_ language=en (accessed August 20, 2015).

———. *Christian Theology and Other Faiths.* 11 June 2003. http://rowanwilliams. archbishopofcanterbury.org/articles.php/1825/christian-theology-and-other-faiths (accessed January 10, 2013).

———. *Christianity, Islam and the Challenge of Poverty – Archbishop Calls for Co-Operation on Global Poverty.* 18 May 2005. http://rowanwilliams.archbish opofcanterbury.org/articles.php/1296/christianity-islam-and-the-challenge-of-poverty-archbishop-calls-for-co-operation-on-global-poverty (accessed January 10, 2013).

———. *Christianity: Public Religion and the Common Good.* 12 May 2007. http:// rowanwilliams.archbishopofcanterbury.org/articles.php/1165/christianity-public-religion-and-the-common-good (accessed January 10, 2013).

———. *Climate Change Action a Moral Imperative for Justice.* 19 December 2007. http://rowanwilliams.archbishopofcanterbury.org/articles.php/1706/climate-change-action-a-moral-imperative-for-justice (accessed January 10, 2013).

———. *A Common Word for the Common Good.* 15 July 2008. http://rowanwil liams.archbishopofcanterbury.org/articles.php/1107/a-common-word-for-the-common-good (accessed April 30, 2015).

———. "Dialogue Is a Means of 'God-Given Discovery'." The Christian Muslim Forum at Lambeth Palace. 22 March 2010. http://rowanwilliams.archbishopof canterbury.org/articles.php/926/archbishop-dialogue-is-a-means-of-god-given-discovery (accessed January 10, 2013).

———. *Ecology and Economy.* 8 March 2005. http://rowanwilliams.archbishop-ofcanterbury.org/articles.php/1550/ecology-.and-economy-archbishop-calls-for-action-on-environment-to-head-off-social-crisis (accessed January 10).

———. *Faith and Climate Change.* 29 October 2009. http://rowanwilliams.arch-bishopofcanterbury.org/articles.php/770/faith-and-climate-change (accessed January 10, 2013).

———. *Faith, Poverty and Justice – Lambeth Palace Inter-Faith Event with DFID.* 26 June 2012. http://rowanwilliams.archbishopofcanterbury.org/articles.php/2539/ faith-poverty-and-justice-lambeth-palace-inter-faith-event-with-dfid (accessed January 10, 2013).

———. *Faith in the Public Square, Lecture at Leicester Cathedral.* 22 March 2009. http://rowanwilliams.archbishopofcanterbury.org/articles.php/817/faith-in-the-public-square-lecture-at-leicester-cathedral (accessed January 10, 2013).

———. "Finality of Christ." In *On Christian Theology*, 93–107. Oxford: Blackwell Publishing, 2000.

———. *The Finality of Christ in a Pluralist World.* 2 March 2010. http://rowan williams.archbishopofcanterbury.org/articles.php/585/the-finality-of-christ-in-a-pluralist-world (accessed January 10, 2013).

———. "Justice and Rights." Fifth Building Bridges Seminar, Opening Remarks. 28 March 2006. http://rowanwilliams.archbishopofcanterbury.org/articles.php/ 1275/justice-and-rights-fifth-building-bridges-seminar-opening-remarks (accessed January 10, 2013).

Rowan Williams's theology of religions 81

————. "Long Life to the Diversity of Communities." The Archbishop of Canterbury at the Launch of Inter Faith Week. 21 November 2011. http://rowanwilliams.archbishopofcanterbury.org/articles.php/2254/ (accessed January 10, 2013).

————. "Muslim – Christian Dialogue in Britain and Beyond- a Lecture Given at Al-Hamra Hall, Lahore 23 November 2005." *Islam and Christian – Muslim Relations* 19/3 (July 2008): 333–338.

————. *New Perspectives on Faith and Development.* 12 November 2009. http://rowanwilliams.archbishopofcanterbury.org/articles.php/768/new-perspectives-on-faith-and-development (accessed January 10, 2013).

————. *No One Can Be Forgotten in God's Kingdom.* 9 March 2007. http://rowanwilliams.archbishopofcanterbury.org/articles.php/1436/no-one-can-be-forgotten-in-gods-kingdom-team-conference-south-africa (accessed in 10 January 2013).

————. *On Christian Theology.* Oxford: Blackwell Publishers, 2000.

————. *One Holy Catholic and Apostolic Church.* 28 October 2005. http://rowanwilliams.archbishopofcanterbury.org/articles.php/1675/one-holy-catholic-and-apostolic-church (accesed in 10 January 2013).

————. "Pluralism-Public and Religion." In *Faith in the Public Square*, edited by Rowan Williams, 126–136. London: Bloomsbury Publishing, 2012.

————. "Postmodern Theology and Judgment of the World." In *Postmodern Theology: Christian Faith in a Pluralist World*, edited by F.B. Burnham. New York: Harper & Row, 1989.

————. *Relations between the Church and State Today: What Is the Role of the Christian Citizen?* 1 March 2011. http://rowanwilliams.archbishopofcanterbury.org/articles.php/2009/relations-between-the-church-and-state-today-what-is-the-role-of-the-christian-citizen (accessed January 10, 2013).

————. *Religion Culture Diversity and Tolerance – Shaping the New Europe: Address at the European Policy Centre.* 7 November 2005. http://rowanwilliams.archbishopofcanterbury.org/articles.php/1179/religion-culture-diversity-and-tolerance-shaping-the-new-europe-address-at-the-european-policy-centr (accessed January 10, 2013).

————. "Sharing the Story." Archbishop's Sermon at Evening Prayer, Hereford Diocesan Conference. Thursday, 5 June 2008. http://rowanwilliams.archbishopofcanterbury.org/articles.php/1341/archbishops-sermon-at-evening-prayer-hereford-diocesan-conference (accessed January 10, 2013).

————. "Trinity and Pluralism." In *Christian Uniqueness Reconsidered: The Myth of a Pluralistic Theology of Religions*, edited by Gavin D'Costa, 1–15. Maryknoll, NY: Orbis Books, 1990.

————. "What We Mean By Christian Identity." World Council of Churches Address. 17 February 2006. http://rowanwilliams.archbishopofcanterbury.org/articles.php/1781/what-we-mean-by-christian-identity-world-council-of-churches-address (accessed January 10, 2013).

————. "Why Social Cohesion Needs Religion." Building Bridges Conference, Singapore. 6 December 2007. http://rowanwilliams.archbishopofcanterbury.org/articles.php/1144/why-social-cohesion-needs-religion-building-bridges-conference-singapore (accessed January 10, 2013).

3 Islamic theology of religions

Introduction

In the first chapter I have presented a Christian-based discussion of theology of religions. Christian theologians began to develop different types of theology of religions in response to increasing encounters with non-Christian religions. Islam was born and developed in a plural society, and the Qur'an itself refers to non-Islamic religions in an open and explicit way. The Prophet's sayings also mention non-Islamic traditions in both a positive and negative way.

From the early ages of Islam, Muslim scholars have placed Islam among world religions. The status of non-Islamic religions has not only been a theological problem but has also created a legal question. Islamic countries have used the status of *dhimmi*, in which non-Muslims were legally protected and required to pay a special tax to the Islamic authorities. In this chapter, I will not only present theological approaches of Muslims to non-Muslims but will also refer to legalistic issues if necessary.

Waardenburg, in *Muslim Perceptions of Other Religions*,[1] presents the Muslim study of non-Islamic traditions in four different eras: the early period, the mediaeval period, the modern period and the contemporary period. He uses these four eras as a way to differentiate between the political and theological confrontations between Muslims and non-Muslims, which changed in each period. In this chapter, since the focus of my research is on the contemporary period, I will only evaluate the contemporary period. I will argue that contemporary Muslim approaches to non-Islamic religions do not follow Christian understandings. While Christian approaches deal mostly with theological considerations, apart from intellectual theology, contemporary Islamic approaches also deal with contemporary political situations. In other words, the sociopolitical situations in Muslim countries, the relationship between Muslim countries and the Western world, and the situation of Muslim communities in Western countries affect Muslim understanding of non-Muslims.

The academic discipline of theology of religions originated in Christianity, specifically Western Christianity. The main questions of theology of religions in Christian circles include how Christianity is related to non-Christian

Islamic theology of religions 83

religions, if non-Christian religions lead to salvation, if Jesus Christ the only saviour and so on. The different responses to these questions have led Christians to adopt diverse theological approaches. These discussions have led to a new area within Christian theology, namely theology of religions. In the contemporary era, Muslims have not studied this area systematically. However, contemporary Christians proposals, especially those made by liberal pluralist theologians, have had an effect on the development of Islamic pluralist approaches by liberal Muslim theologians, who in the last five or four decades have produced a number of important and systematic works on the subject.

Despite valuable efforts to transpose Christian theology of religions concepts, like Race's threefold typology, to Islamic theology, Islamic theology of religions is not preoccupied with the same questions as its Christian counterpart. The problem of salvation is not the first issue in Islamic theology of religions; rather, the main issues are whether Islam accepts religious diversity as willed by God, whether Islam allows cooperation with non-Muslims and whether Islam is superior to other religions. Diverse responses to these questions generate different approaches among contemporary Muslims in academic circles.

Race's typology has been widely used outside of Christian tradition, although it has been constructed in the light of epistemological and soteriological concerns raised by Christian approaches towards other religions. Even though the Christian and Islamic theologies of religions are generated by different questions, Muslim and non-Muslim scholars have used Race's classification while presenting Islamic theology of religions. I will present and claim that the question of salvation has never been a central issue in Islamic theology of religions. In this chapter, I will argue that Race's threefold classification is not fully applicable to the Islamic theology of religions. The inclusivist position in the Islamic theology of religions (or its application to the Islamic theology of religions) seems the most problematic issue. This is not because no inclusivist theology exists in the Islamic theology of religions, but rather because some scholars give more emphasis to soteriology when applying Race's inclusivism to Islamic theology of religions, whilst others take epistemological concerns into account. Unlike these scholars, I will use only exclusivism and pluralism to present Islamic theology of religions. My application of these two theories focuses on religious epistemology instead of soteriology. Thus, I will use supersessionist theory (Islam is the only true religion which supersedes other religions) to distinguish between exclusivism and pluralism. I will consider this theory as a form of exclusivism, which according to Knitter's classification would be seen as the Replacement Model.[2] As will be seen, contemporary discourse on Islamic response to religious pluralism is between exclusivists who hold the belief that Islam is the only religion which has superseded other religions and pluralists who think the opposite. Although both positions occupy the central place in Islamic discourse, such aspects of exclusivist and pluralist positions have significant parallels with the inclusivist stance. I will touch

84 *Islamic theology of religions*

on this issue while evaluating both positions. In this respect, the main subject of this chapter will be exclusivism and pluralism in Islamic theology of religions. Firstly, I will analyse the usages of Race's threefold typology in the context of the Islamic theology of religions. Then I will evaluate the Qur'anic position on non-Islamic religions as the Qur'an and its interpretation play a central role in the Islamic theology of religions. Finally, I will evaluate exclusivist and pluralist positions and then assess and criticise each, after which I will provide a conclusion.

1 Race's threefold typology and its application to Islamic theology of religions

Race's typology defines inclusivism as a dialectical 'yes' and 'no' with reference to non-Christian religions.[3] On the one hand, they accept the spiritual power of non-Christian religions; on the other hand they see non-Christian religions as insufficient to lead to salvation apart from Jesus. I have also outlined D'Costa's interpretation of Race's classification in the first chapter. In brief, D'Costa divided inclusivism and exclusivism into two types: structural and restrictivist inclusivists and restrictive-access and universal-access exclusivists, respectively.[4] After discussing how Muslim scholars have used that classification, I will return to this issue.

Since Race announced his threefold classification, it has been used by both Christian and non-Christian theologians. Even though his classification is relatively Christian oriented, some non-Christian theologians have adapted his classification into their own traditions. For example, Muhammad Khalil in *Islam and the Fate of Others*[5] has interpreted Race's classification in a different way from its original use.

He firstly describes exclusivism as the position that there is only religious tradition or interpretation of that tradition that leads to salvation, while followers of other beliefs will be punished in hell.[6] Secondly, inclusivism is the position that only one religion leads to heaven, but the 'sincere outsiders who would not have recognized it as such will be saved.'[7] Finally, with regard to pluralism he thinks that it is to affirm that 'regardless of circumstances, there are several religious traditions or interpretations that are equally effective salvifically.'[8] Unlike Race, Khalil is not concerned with religious epistemology, although he takes soteriology seriously, and this shapes his interpretation of the question of whether salvation is possible outside of one specific religion. In fact, D'Costa also interpreted Race's threefold typology in this way. He also placed the question of salvation at the centre.[9]

Another Muslim theologian, Rifat Atay, also uses Race's classification to picture Islamic theology of religions. In his doctoral thesis,[10] Atay firstly examines Race's threefold classification in Christian context[11] and then applies it to Islamic theology of religions. Firstly, he identifies exclusivism, in Islamic context, as the idea that 'Islam is the final and full religion for humanity as put forward in the Qur'an as a way of life.'[12] For the exclusivist form of theology of religions, he uses Imam Abu Mansur al-Maturidi[13] as an

Islamic theology of religions   85

example theologian. The main reasons why he chooses Maturidi are because he believes that Maturidi's exclusivist views have been widely accepted by Muslim communities and he also thinks that several contemporary scholars offer almost the same exclusivist theory as Maturidi's.[14]

Secondly, Atay portrays inclusivism as the theory that 'there is one surest way to salvation, which is Islam in Muslims' case, others may lead to salvation but not as good as one's own, i.e. Islam.'[15] In this case, he uses a Turkish Qur'anic commentator Süleyman Ateş as an advocator of inclusivist theory. Even though Ateş's ideas are ones commonly shared by pluralist theologians, and despite the fact that Ateş does not classify himself as an inclusivist, Atay still classifies Ateş as an inclusivist for two reasons. Firstly, for Atay, Ateş has a limited understanding of the concept of the People of the Book. He does not include mainstream orthodox Christians who take Christian doctrines seriously such as the Trinity. Secondly, Atay believes that Ateş's pluralist- sounding theology of religions does not take non-theistic religions into account.[16] Considering Race's threefold typology, Atay's judgements seem consistent with the original use. However, as we will see in the section on pluralism, so-called Muslim pluralist theologians' ideas sometimes overlap with inclusivism. Thus it is not only Ateş who takes mainly monotheistic religions seriously, but also so-called pluralist Muslims either dismiss theistic religions other than Islam, Christianity and Judaism, together with non-theistic religions, or make abstract claims regarding non-theistic religions.

Thirdly, as for pluralism, Atay utilises Hick's form of pluralism as a definition. Pluralism is thus the theory that 'the great world religions are each equally efficient ways of perceiving the Real.'[17] In his section on pluralism, he classes Arkoun's theology of religions as a model of an Islamic pluralism. Atay's justification for each class in the typology seems to be following the original threefold typology introduced by Race. However, I still think that in contemporary discourse, there are mainly two general trends: exclusivism and pluralism. Atay himself, while evaluating exclusivism and inclusivism, uses two Turkish theologians, Koçyiğit and Ateş, to represent opposing positions. While scholars attempt to apply Race's classification in Islamic theology of religions, they either interpret each position on the typology differently from the original or spend extra effort to place certain theologians of theology of religions in the inclusivist class.

Though he is not a Muslim, Lewis Winkler also uses Race's classification in his evaluation of Muslim theologians' responses to religious pluralism. He defines exclusivism in an Islamic context as the position which refuses to grant salvific and epistemic legitimacy to non-Islamic religions.[18] Inclusivism 'is usually expressed in the Islamic terminology of ethical "submission" and "obedience" to the commandments of God'.[19] In addition, he sees pluralism as the position that accepts the salvific and epistemological validity of all world religions.[20] In fact Winkler also seems to be aware of the difficulty of differentiating inclusivist and pluralist positions in Islamic discourse. He uses Turkish scholar Mahmut Aydin as a representative of both inclusivism

86 *Islamic theology of religions*

and pluralism, though he uses different articles to illustrate each position.[21] Moreover, in the section on inclusivism, he cites another Turkish scholar Aslan[22] as promoting inclusivism. However, the arguments that Aslan uses are mostly arguments the so-called pluralists also use. The reason why he uses Aslan and Aydin as representatives of inclusivism might not be because both scholars believe they are inclusivists[23] but because their pluralistic arguments are essentially consistent with some inclusivist ideas.

From the evaluation of these three applications of Race's typology, it is clear that Atay's and Winkler's interpretations differ from Khalil's. While the first two scholars consider religious epistemology with soteriological concerns (like Race does), Khalil does not take religious epistemology into account. Atay's and Winkler's interpretations seem to follow original typology, but it also appears that they have difficulty in locating inclusivist theology on the map of the threefold typology. This inconvenience derives from the fact that there is no sharp distinction between what they would describe as inclusivist and pluralistic theology in the Islamic theology of religions, unlike in the Christian one. However, in their presentation the difference between exclusivist and inclusivist/pluralist theology is quite apparent. Thus rather than applying Race's three distinct types to Islamic theology of religions, it appears to be more convenient to present exclusivist theology on one hand and pluralist theology on the other hand and their overlap with inclusivist theology.

Turning to Khalil's interpretation of the threefold classification, it seems his interpretation is different from both Race's interpretation and D'Costa's. As noted, Race deals with epistemological problems. His definition of inclusivism is broader than Khalil's. Khalil's definition of inclusivism is similar to D'Costa's universal-access exclusivism. Actually, D'Costa believes that universal-access exclusivism and restrictive inclusivism refer to the same theology.[24] Looking at Khalil's interpretation, he divides inclusivism into two categories: limited inclusivists and liberal inclusivists. Limited inclusivists argue that among non-Muslims, only the unreached will be saved, while liberal inclusivists maintain that 'the category of sincere non-Muslims includes individuals who have been exposed to the message in its true form yet are in no way convinced.'[25] The criterion here is whether the message of Islam has reached a non-Muslim or not. If it has not, it is the first category. If it has reached and a non-Muslim is not convinced and does not accept the message, then it is the second category. As can be seen from both theologians' interpretations, Khalil's liberal inclusivism equates with D'Costa's universal-access exclusivism. I am not arguing that Khalil's justification is wrong; however, from my perspective the main criterion to justify a position as inclusivist or exclusivist is whether or not the position accepts the salvific means of the non-Islamic tradition – with the Islamic term, whether it accepts Islam as the only true religions which supersede other religions (exclusivism) or it accepts non-Islamic religions as valid but not as true as Islam (inclusivism).

One of the main arguments of this chapter is that the discussion in Islamic theology of religions is mainly between exclusivists and pluralists.

Islamic theology of religions 87

I have indicated that Islamic theologians who have adapted Race's three-fold typology tend to find the category of inclusivism problematic and so include within it theologians who do not identify themselves as inclusivists or who have significant overlap with the exclusivist or pluralist positions. I will demonstrate this later in the chapter when I look at exclusivist and pluralist theologians. I consider acceptance of other religious traditions as salvific means to be a distinguishing mark of inclusivism. However, those who accept the salvific means of non-Islamic traditions mostly describe themselves or are described by others as pluralists. However, from my point of view, some aspects of their theology seem more inclusivist than pluralist. I will present how Muslim theologians' so-called pluralist theologies overlap with inclusivism when I evaluate pluralism in Islamic theology of religions. The next section will evaluate the Qur'anic account of non-Islamic religions with the special attention to supersessionist theory.

2 The Qur'anic approach to non-Islamic religions

The Quran is believed by Muslims to be the revealed word of God to the Prophet Muhammad via the angel Gabriel over the period of twenty-three years between the years 610 and 623. Muslims regard the Qur'an as 'being a firm speech of Allah (*kalam Allah*), uncorrupted by human experience, and viewed as one revelation in a chain of revelations from God'.[26] There is a connection between the early Muslims' problems and the Qur'anic verses; thus it is a response to people's needs during the time of the Prophet. The Qur'anic verses mainly focus on belief in God, the belief system, the ordering of social life, religious practices, morality, and the stories of old prophets. Whilst its focus is on these subjects, the Qur'an sometimes refers to non-Islamic traditions and makes some claims which suggest exclusivist or, occasionally, inclusivist or pluralist claims. The Qur'anic view of Islam and non-Islamic religions can be divided into four sections: Qur'anic verses which suggest inclusivist/pluralist ideas without singling out a specific religion; verses which speak positively about non-Islamic religions, mainly Abrahamic religions; verses which make exclusivist (epistemologically) claims without mentioning specific religions; and verses which speak negatively about non-Islamic traditions, generally Abrahamic religions.

2.1 Inclusivist/pluralist verses in general

There are some verses in the Qur'an which are used by pluralist theologians as sources for the Qur'anic acceptance of pluralist view. In these verses, the emphasis is either on diversity (racial, ethnic or religious) or commonality between Islamic faith and other faiths. These verses are as follows:

> To thee We sent the Scripture in truth, confirming the scripture that came before it, and guarding it's in safety: so judge between them by what God hath revealed, and follow not their vain desires, diverging

88   *Islamic theology of religions*

from the truth that hath come to thee. To each among you have We prescribed a law and an open way. If God had so willed. He would have made you a single People, but (His plan is) to test you in what He hath given you: so strive as in a race in all virtues. The goal of you all is to God; it is He that will show you the truth of the matters in which ye dispute.[27]

O men! Behold, We have created you all out of a male and a female, and have made you into nations and tribes, so that you might come to know one another. Verily, the noblest of you in the sight of God is the one who is most deeply conscious of Him. Behold, God is all-knowing, all-aware.[28]

THERE SHALL BE no coercion in matters of faith. Distinct has now become the right way from [the way of] error: hence, he who rejects the powers of evil and believes in God has indeed taken hold of a support most unfailing, which shall never give way: for God is all-hearing, all-knowing.[29]

O you who have attained to faith! Offend not against the symbols set up by God, nor against the sacred month [of pilgrimage], nor against the garlanded offerings, nor against those who flock to the Inviolable Temple, seeking favour with their Sustainer and His goodly acceptance; and [only] after your pilgrimage is over are you free to hunt. And never let your hatred of people who would bar you from the Inviolable House of Worship lead you into the sin of aggression: but rather help one another in furthering virtue and God-consciousness, and do not help one another in furthering evil and enmity; and remain conscious of God: for, behold, God is severe in retribution![30]

O YOU who have attained to faith! Be ever steadfast in your devotion to God, bearing witness to the truth in all equity; and never let hatred of any-one lead you into the sin of deviating from justice. Be just: this is closest to being God-conscious. And remain conscious of God: verily, God is aware of all that you do.[31]

Say: "O followers of earlier revelation! Come unto that tenet which we and you hold in common: that we shall worship none but God, and that we shall not ascribe divinity to aught beside Him, and that we shall not take human beings for our lords beside God." And if they turn away, then say: "Bear witness that it is we who have surrendered ourselves unto Him."[32]

2.2 Inclusivist/pluralist verses on the People of the Book

One of the pluralist theologians' most cited verses is as follows. In this verse, the Qur'an explicitly accepts that, like Muslims who follow God, People of the Book will also attain salvation. This verse is cited twice in the Qur'an.

VERILY, those who have attained to faith [in this divine writ], as well as those who follow the Jewish faith, and the Christians, and the

Sabians – all who believe in God and the Last Day and do righteous deeds-shall have their reward with their Sustainer; and no fear need they have, and neither shall they grieve.[33]

2.3 Exclusivist verses in general

The Qur'an makes some statements that see Islam as the only true religion. Because of these Qur'anic verses, exclusivist theologians use these statements as justification of the exclusivist theology.

> Behold, the only [true] religion in the sight of God is Islam (submission to His will); and those who were vouchsafed revelation aforetime took, out of mutual jealousy, to divergent views [on this point] only after knowledge [thereof] had come unto them. But as for him who denies the truth of God's messages – behold, God is swift in reckoning![34]
>
> For, if one goes in search of a religion other than Islam, it will never be accepted from him, and in the life to come he shall be among the lost.[35]
>
> [And] fight against those who – despite having been vouchsafed revelation [aforetime] – do not [truly] believe either in God or the Last Day, and do not consider forbidden that which God and His Apostle have forbidden, and do not follow the religion of truth [which God has enjoined upon them] till they [agree to] pay the exemption tax with a willing hand, after having been humbled [in war].[36]

2.4 Exclusivist verses on the People of the Book

The Qur'an sometimes criticises or rejects the belief systems of the other two Abrahamic religions while on some occasions advise Muslims not to be friends with or follow Christians and Jews.

> Abraham was neither a "Jew" nor a "Christian", but was one who turned away from all that is false, having surrendered himself unto God; and he was not of those who ascribe divinity to aught beside Him. Behold, the people who have the best claim to Abraham are surely those who follow him – as does this Prophet and all who believe [in him] – and God is near unto the believers.[37]
>
> AND THEY claim, "None shall ever enter paradise unless he be a Jew" – or, "a Christian". Such are their wishful beliefs! Say: "Produce an evidence for what you are claiming, if what you say is true!" Yea, indeed: everyone who surrenders his whole being unto God, and is a doer of good withal, shall have his reward with his Sustainer; and all such need have no fear, and neither shall they grieve. Furthermore, the Jews assert, "The Christians have no valid ground for their beliefs," while the Christians assert, "The Jews have no valid ground for their beliefs" – and both quote the divine writ! Even thus, like unto what they

90   *Islamic theology of religions*

say, have [always] spoken those who were devoid of knowledge;" but it is God who will judge between them on Resurrection Day with regard to all on which they were wont to differ.[38]

O YOU who have attained to faith! Do not take the Jews and the Christians for your allies: they are but allies of one another and whoever of you allies himself with them becomes, verily, one of them; behold, God does not guide such evildoers.[39]

For, never will the Jews be pleased with thee. nor yet the Christians, unless thou follow their own creeds. Say: "Behold, God's guidance is the only true guidance." And, indeed, if thou shouldst follow their errant views after all the knowledge that has come unto thee. thou wouldst have none to protect thee from God, and none to bring thee succor.[40]

AND THE JEWS say, "Ezra is God's son," while the Christians say, "The Christ is God's son." Such are the sayings, which they utter with their mouths, following in spirit assertions made in earlier times by people who denied the truth! [They deserve the imprecation:] "May God destroy them!" How perverted are their minds![41] O followers of earlier revelation! Why do you deny the truth of God's messages to which you yourselves bear witness? O followers of earlier revelation! Why do you cloak the truth with falsehood and conceal the truth of which you are [so well] aware?[42]

Thou wilt surely find that, of all people, the most hostile to those who believe [in this divine writ] are the Jews as well as those who are bent on ascribing divinity to aught beside God; and thou wilt surely find that, of all people, they who say, "Behold, we are Christians," come closest to feeling affection for those who believe [in this divine writ]: this is so because there are priests and monks among them, and because these are not given to arrogance.[43]

As can be seen from these verses, the Qur'anic position towards non-Islamic traditions is complex. On the one hand the Qur'an states exclusivist claims on non-Islamic traditions; on the other hand it states positive or more pluralist statements. Unlike Christians,[44] Muslim scholars not only need to address exclusivist claims in the Qur'an; they also need to address the polemical verses in the Qur'an that focus on the other two Abrahamic religions, namely Judaism and Christianity. As will be seen in the following sections, Muslim theologians have developed different theologies with regard to other religions. While some Muslim scholars overemphasise the negative statements in the Qur'an to strengthen their exclusivist position, pluralist Muslims overcome these exclusivist statements by using a different methodology of Qur'anic exegesis. Before moving on to present exclusivism and pluralism in Islamic theology of religions, a few hermeneutical considerations need to be addressed.

From the early time of Islam, Muslim scholars have addressed these verses and constructed a doctrine which considers Islam the only true religion. In spite of the Qur'anic affirmation of non-Islamic traditions' certain values, early scholars developed a supersessionist theory which assumed that other religions were superseded by Islam. The doctrine of supersessionism in Islamic studies has been discussed in the literature of Islamic jurisprudence (*uṣūl al-fiqh*). The Islamic term for supersessionism is *naskh*, which literally means 'to abrogate'. The Qur'an states, 'For every verse We abrogate (*naskh*) or cause to be forgotten, We bring down one better or similar.'[45] Muslim scholars later developed the theory of abrogation to address which verses are abrogated.[46]

In response to the abrogation of non-Islamic religions, there have been two different views. The first view argues that the law (*shari'a*) given a prophet would keep its validity until there is a sign of its abrogation, while the second presupposes that unless the latter announces its continuity, the validity of a law given a certain prophet is terminated by the mission of his successor.[47] Regardless of these views, Muslim scholars have used the Qur'anic verses 3:85 and 3:19 to claim that Islam has superseded other religions.[48] The classic, mediaeval and contemporary form of exclusivism has been shaped in the light of supersessionist theory. Thus, the positive affirmation of non-Islamic traditions in the Qur'an has been regarded as abrogated. In other words, the Qur'anic verses which value the Christian and Jewish traditions have been considered to be part of this supersessionism process. In summary, despite its varieties and its different nuances, the application of legal principle of abrogation to non-Islamic traditions has shaped Islamic exclusivism, which still finds supporters in contemporary Islamic discourse.

Abdulaziz Sachedina argues that supersessionism theory in Islam is not based on the Qur'an and hadith traditions. He claims that 'the Muslim jurists were involved in the routinization of the qur'anic message about *"islam"* (submission) being "the only true religion with God" (Q. 3:19) in the context of the political and social position of the community.'[49] He further argues that this notion of supersessionism has provided a justification to expand the notion of jihad. Essentially, he argues that the state-power relations have led Muslim jurists to claim the superiority of Islam over other religions. While it is beyond the scope of this study to investigate the relations between the early conception of supersessionist theory and its application to the notion of jihad, Sachedina's criticism of supersessionist theory remains important because it shows that the development of supersessionist theory has not simply been an intellectual activity and that political motivation has played an important part in the shaping of this theory.

Modernist Muslims have overcome the exclusivist claims of the Qur'an by utilising a contextual hermeneutical methodology.[50] Fazlur Rahman introduced contextual reading of the Qur'an into Islamic studies. In his reading, Rahman offered two historical movements for understanding of the Qur'an which are different from traditional methodological approaches. The first movement is 'from the present situation to Quranic times' and the second one is 'back to the present day'. To fulfil this first movement, he mentions two important steps. The first step is to look at the historical situation or problem, which was answered by the Qur'an, to understand the meaning

92 *Islamic theology of religions*

of its statement; therefore, this step provides us with an 'understanding' process. The second step is to generalise the specific answers that are indicated in the Qur'an and then deduce general moral-social objectives while considering the socio-historical background of the Qur'an; thus this stage may be considered as a process of interpretation and implementation. While some have remained critical to Rahman's contextual reading of the Qur'an, his method has been applied by various Muslim scholars in addressing the Islamic approach to non-Muslims. From this perspective, as the section on pluralism will show, the negative verses on non-Muslims generally have been regarded as part of the historical-political environment of early Muslims' confrontation with the Qur'an. While Modernist Muslims somehow successfully achieve to present a more positive picture of non-Islamic traditions, their achievement remains limited, and it will be discussed in the section on pluralism.

The next section will explore exclusivism in Islamic theology of religions.

3 Exclusivism

The exclusivist position in the Islamic tradition is not a modern concept. From the early ages of Islam, Muslims tried to investigate non-Islamic traditions. In the first years of Islam since Muslims believed that Islam superseded other religions, they demonstrated little interest in learning about other traditions.[51] When Islamic states expanded their territories, they were confronted by more converts and non-Muslims.[52] As a result of confronting non-Muslim traditions, Muslim scholars started to learn more about the theology, religious practice and doctrines of non-Muslims, which in most cases were learnt to refute them.[53] Eventually, the mainstream Islamic belief was that Islam was the original religion, taught by all the prophets and confirmed by the Qur'an, whose verses provide knowledge about non-Islamic traditions. The theory of supersessionism[54] was also constituted during the first centuries of Islam. In terms of salvation, the Islamic view was that salvation is possible only by following Islamic beliefs since the Qur'an confirms the old revelations and supersedes them.

However, when we come to the modern or contemporary period, with the development of new ideologies, Islamic exclusivism has taken a different form. The global sociopolitical environment has caused some Muslims to develop another type of exclusivist approach to non-Islamic traditions. This is not to say that there is a monolithic exclusivist position among Muslim scholars; on the contrary in the contemporary period there are a considerable number of Muslims who still follow the mediaeval form of Islamic exclusivism – in other words they still follow a traditional exclusivist approach. What is new in the modern period is that new methodologies of Qur'anic exegesis became an alternative to traditional methodologies. From this perspective, the proponents of the so-called sociopolitical reading of the Qur'an offered an alternative exclusivist approach. In that approach the sociopolitical exclusion of non-Muslims is more apparent than theological refutation. This does not mean that there is no theological background for that type of exclusivism; rather it is primarily social and political conditions that shape the theological standpoint.

After the demise of the Ottoman Empire, which covered almost the entire Muslim world and included the institution of Caliphate, the territory was divided by the intervention of Western powers during the First World War.[55] In the nineteenth century, almost all successor Muslim states were either colonised by the West or taken under the control of a Western state through commercial and military agreements.[56] Moreover, the establishment of a Jewish state in Palestinian land has further complicated relations between Muslims and non-Muslims.[57] During that period, Muslims began to think about the reasons why Muslim civilization had regressed. In this context, the revivalist Muslim scholars have offered a new approach to interpreting the Qur'an. The primary aim was to make the Qur'an accessible for the younger generation who were influenced by Western civilization. In the meanwhile, because of its complexity, the traditional form of the Qur'anic interpretation was alien to the younger generation.[58] The sociopolitical reading of the Qur'an came to light in that environment. Regarding Islamic positions towards non-Islamic traditions, this type of reading not only rejects non-Islamic traditions theologically, but it also rejects the social, political and economic values of non-Islamic traditions, especially Christianity and Judaism. In the next section as a representative of the sociopolitical reading of the Qur'an, I will firstly present Sayyid Qutb's exclusivist views and then move on to theological exclusivism. I will then present a critique of both theologies.

3.1 Sayyid Qutb's sociopolitical exclusivism

In the late nineteenth century Jamaluddin Afghani and Muhammad Abduh had highlighted the importance of the rationality of Islam and supported the reinterpretation of the Quran, while Hasan al-Banna[59] refused modernist interpretations since he was suspicious about reason and thought that Muslims needed to be under the continuous guidance of God. For both Banna and Qutb, the Qur'an, which is the final arbiter on historical, social and scientific matters, is the only source of true knowledge. Sayyid Qutb pursued al-Banna's way, and he constituted his *tafsir* (Qur'anic exegesis) in light of his personal theological and political thought.[60] Qutb is one of the representatives of the sociopolitical form of exegesis, which has had repercussions in the twentieth century. Along with other Islamic revivalists,[61] Qutb introduced a new approach to Qur'anic interpretation with a sociopolitical reading of the Qur'an. In his *fi Zilal al-Qur'an*, his reflections on the political and economic situations are quite obvious. Saeed maintains that 'Qutb's work, a good example of tafsir of a personal reflective nature, is somewhat divorced from standard exegetical tradition in its more free-floating ideas: it draws in the modern world and challenges, and refuses to follow dogmatically early approaches to the Quran.'[62]

94 *Islamic theology of religions*

His new development in Qur'anic exegesis is to interpret the Qur'an using modern concepts such as imperialism, communism, capitalism, democracy and others and to attempt to construct a Qur'anic argument against these concepts. He divides the world into two groups: Islamic[63] societies and ignorant/*jahiliyyah* societies (*jahiliyyah* is a term referring to pre-Islamic Arabia), and he believes that Islam is the perfect system on the grounds that it is created by God; in contrast other systems are imperfect because they are created by man. Dividing the world into two groups, namely jahiliyyah and Islamic, does not mean that Qutb was suggesting that Islamic countries in his time embody real Islamic values, but rather for him these countries were also part of the jahiliyyah category. From this perspective, Qutb's rejection of non-Islamic traditions does not only include non-Muslims but also Muslims.

Qutb reads negative verses on non-Islamic traditions in a radical way and positive verses in an exclusivist way. Firstly, I will evaluate how Qutb interprets religious diversity, and then I will move onto his approach to non-Islamic faiths. In fact because of the Qur'anic statements on Judaism and Christianity, most Muslim scholars who comment on non-Islamic traditions mainly comment on other Abrahamic faiths. Like other Muslim scholars, Qutb also generally comments on Judaism and Christianity when he writes about non-Muslims.

In Qutb's evaluation of the verse 49:13, which is the foundational verse of the arguments of pluralists, there are reflections of his ideological reading of the Qur'an. The verse itself clearly declares that God has created his creatures differently for them to know each other better. However, while Qutb emphasises that fact, he also goes beyond this and uses his rhetoric of dual systems: Islamic and jahiliyyah. He states:

> In their place, an important and distinctly clear reason for friendship and cooperation looms large: that is, God's lordship of all and the fact that He has created all mankind from the same origin. A single banner is raised so that all compete to line up under it. That is the banner of fearing God alone. This is the banner raised by Islam in order to save humanity from the evil consequences of fanatic bonds of race, homeland, tribe, clan, family, etc. All these belong to the world of ignorance, or Jahiliyya, although they make take up different names, colours and fashions. In essence, though, they are ties of ignorance that have nothing to do with Islam.[64]

As can be seen from this quote, Qutb does not interpret Islam as just another religion among the world's religions, but rather it is a system under God's sovereignty. Consequently, there are two competing systems: the Islamic and non-Islamic (ignorance or *jahilliyya*) systems. What belongs to the non-Islamic system is the source of all evil things, and the role of Islam in this world is that 'Islam has fought ignorant fanaticism in all its forms and shapes so as to establish its world system under God's banner alone.'[65]

Thus, Islam is not only the system that offers the complete life system that God wants for the well-being of humanity, but it is also the system which should fight against rival systems. From this viewpoint, Qutb relies on the concept of 'jihad' (literally meaning 'effort' or 'struggle' but often used with reference to holy war). Jihad, for Qutb, is 'a positive movement that aims to liberate man throughout the world, employing appropriate means to face every situation at every stage'.[66] Since the Islamic faith liberates humankind from servitude to creatures, the Islamic rules, or Shari'a, should be applied to humanity as a whole, not only to Muslims.

Qutb does not advocate jihad to make non-Muslims convert to Islam, rather he aims to offer a theology which depends on the rule of God. As such the Qur'anic verse of 2:256, which states that there is no coercion in Islam, becomes important. Qutb contends that unlike Christian empires, Islamic states have not pushed their community to believe or convert to only one single religion. This is the primary rule which should be applied to non-Muslims. Qutb argues that freedom of belief is the most basic right which identifies man as a human being and to deny this right is to deny humanity.[67] According to Qutb's interpretation, the Islamic system accepts man's most basic right, in contrast to 'man-made systems and regimes which, despite all their inherent shortcomings, impose their beliefs and policies by the force of the state and deny their opponents the right to dissent or even live'.[68] Thus both Muslims and non-Muslims' rights are protected under the Islamic system. Qutb seems to embrace two conflicting ideas together. On the one hand he accepts the Qur'anic statement of no compulsion in religion; on the other hand he believes that Islam should fight against non-Islamic systems.[69] In his opinion, these two statements are not two conflicting ideas. The basic idea that lies behind these statements is the legalistic framework for non-Muslims in Islamic states. According to Islamic law non-Muslims are protected by the Islamic states. The main principle is that 'submission to God alone is a universal message which all mankind must either accept or be at peace with.'[70] As a result, jihad is applicable in situations where the message of Islam is impeded: 'anyone who puts such impediments in the face of the message of complete submission to God, must be resisted and fought by Islam.'[71] Thus, it is reasonable to argue that, for Qutb, the main justification for jihad is the need for the Islamization of the world but a rejection of any Muslimization of people through coercion. To summarise, Qutb locates Islam among world religions in three stages. Firstly, Qutb does not accept that any other system than Islam is valid. Secondly, he believes Islam not only liberates humankind in the next world but also in this world. Finally, to accomplish liberation of humans, the concept of jihad should be applied.

Qutb's theology of religions offers an extreme form of exclusivism. Having presented how he approaches Islam in the world, I will now discuss how he evaluates non-Islamic religions and his views on such religions, specifically Judaism and Christianity. He reiterates negative views on Christianity and Judaism whenever he comments on both traditions. There is a parallelism between his views on the other two Abrahamic faiths and his dualist

96 *Islamic theology of religions*

system. Since non-Islamic systems are unacceptable, both traditions are also part of jahiliyyah. His approach to the related verses is a literal reading, and he draws a universal conclusion from the negative verses related to Christianity and Judaism. Looking at both traditions, for instance, when Qutb interprets the verses 2:62 and 5:69, which confirm the salvation of Christians, Jews and Sabians, he also confirms the content of the verse. In his exegesis, he understands 'Jews' to refer to the followers of Moses and 'Christians' to followers of Jesus. However, what he understands by Christians and Jews is not derived from historical versions of the Christian and Jewish traditions.

According to Qutb, and he is not alone in his ideas, the true Christians and Jews would believe in Prophet Muhammad's message.[72] If they have not confirmed the message of Muhammad, then they cannot be called true Christians and Jews. He further argues that from this verse we cannot claim that God accepts these faiths as valid religions. He states that Muslims 'cannot try to reduce the pressure of ignorance by coming to terms with the followers of other creeds or doctrines, giving them the privilege of having "a faith" acceptable to God and constituting grounds for mutual support'.[73] This statement makes Qutb's view on pluralism rather obvious. Not only does he reject the pluralistic view of religions, since he believes the only true religion is Islam, but he also criticises Christianity and Judaism. For example, when he comments on Jews, he states:

> No other nation in history has shown more intransigence and obstinacy than the Jews. They viciously and mercilessly killed and mutilated a number of prophets and messengers. They have over the centuries displayed the most extreme attitudes towards God, and towards their own religion and people. . . . Nevertheless, they have always boasted of their virtue and made the implausible claims of being the most rightly-guided nation, the chosen people of God and the only people that shall be saved.[74]

Qutb also makes similar comments on Christians. In fact his comments on both traditions cannot be separated from the Qur'anic objections to these traditions. Qutb considers the literal meaning of the Qur'anic condemnations of Christianity and Judaism, and he extends these condemnations, providing further details. For instance, the Qur'an objects to Christian doctrines but does not provide details of the historical institutionalisation of Christian beliefs. On the other hand, when Qutb comments on verses related to Christians, he provides many details and offers them as if these things had occurred in history. For example, when he interprets the Qur'anic rejection of Jesus's divinity, he claims that due to their doctrine of divinity, Christian popes and emperors have used that metaphor for themselves. However, when Christians conquered Islamic lands during the crusades, they received ideas and influences which became the seeds of rebellion against such notions of divine right.[75] Thus in the Reformation Movement both

Islamic theology of religions 97

Calvin and Luther were influenced by the Islamic concept of denial of any attribution of divinity or special holiness to human persons.[76] Regardless of whether this reading of history is right or not, Qutb explains that he does not support any source which accepts the idea. Although Lutheranism and Calvinism strongly objected to papal claims, they still believe in the doctrine of Trinity and incarnation, which undermines Qutb's point.

Qutb's exclusivism does not only exclude non-Islamic traditions theologically; it also subordinates them in social, historical, economic and cultural contexts. There is another type of exclusivism in contemporary Islamic discourse which mainly focuses on the traditional theological view of Islam's position with regard to other religious traditions. In these cases, rather than Qutb's vision of the social subordination and/or exclusion of non-Islamic religions, the traditional form of exclusivism is apparent. Yasir Qadhi' and Tim Winter's theology of religions matches perfectly with this traditional form of exclusivism.

3.2 Yasir Qadhi's and Tim Winter's theological exclusivism

Although the traditional form of exclusivism is the oldest Islamic position towards non-Muslims, recently some scholars have revised traditional exclusivism more sophistically in the contemporary period. Yasir Qadhi, an America-based Muslim theologian, is among these theological exclusivists. Having examined discussions of the salvation of non-Muslims from the classical and mediaeval period, Qadhi has come to the conclusion that the shared belief of mediaeval Muslim scholars is that Islam is the only path to God; thus other religions, including Christianity and Judaism, are not acceptable in the eyes of God.[77] In other words, he reiterates the theory of supersessionism. He believes that the main reasons for the rejection of the salvific means of non-Islamic traditions are given in numerous Qur'anic verses. He classifies these verses into three categories.

The first group of verses[78] indicates that Islam is the only religion acceptable to God. According to Qadhi, the term 'Islam' cannot be reduced to such an abstract meaning as submission alone. He contends that the context is clear and apparent that Islam is used to refer to the religion of Islam and that surrounding verses criticise aspects of the Christian and Jewish faiths. The second group of verses indicates that rejection of the message of the Prophet and his Prophethood is tantamount to a rejection of God. He uses verses 2:285, 38:14, 34:45, 68:9, 57:7, 7:156–158, 4:115, 4:65 and 48:13 as examples and argues that 'true belief in God goes hand in hand with belief in His Prophet and His final revelation.'[79] The final group of verses criticise the beliefs of other faiths. Qadhi states that although the Qur'an acknowledges the authenticity of the Torah, Psalms and Gospel, it presents Christians and Jews as having concealed and deviated from the true teaching of their prophets.[80] As for Christians, he uses verses 9:30–31 as an example of Christians' commitment to unbelief. Qadi argues that these

98   *Islamic theology of religions*

three groups of verses provide the context for interpreting any Qur'anic verses which seem to accept a more pluralistic vision.[81]

Apart from the Qur'anic account, the hadiths of Prophet Muhammad also show that the pluralist interpretation is not acceptable in Islam. In addition, there is a consensus (*ijma*) among Muslim scholars on the issue that more than one religion cannot be simultaneously valid; it is illogical as each religion has its own tenets.[82] As a result, using all the Islamic sources, Qadhi believes that the only path that leads to God is Islam. However, this neither means that all Muslims will go to heaven nor that all non-Muslims will be damned. For Muslims, the requirement to earn God's mercy is both orthodoxy and orthopraxy.[83] Regarding non-Muslims, God's punishment will be for those who understand the message of God and willingly reject it. Rather than judging who is going to be saved, it is better to leave it to God since God knows and therefore is the best judge.

Like Qadhi, Tim Winter, a British convert to Islam, relies on traditional theological *kalam*, mainly Al-Ghazali's thought, to construct his own approach. His approach can be explained using two principles. Firstly, he reiterates the classical Islamic theory of supersessionism. He states that 'not only paganism but the earlier monotheism, were distorted remnants of an original pristine teaching and had therefore been superseded by the new revelation of Islam.'[84] He argues that if the early traditions had not decayed, the Prophet would not have written letters to the Christian emperors, Heraclius and Chosroes. In addition, if Islam only came to light to refute the heretical extremes of the earlier faiths, the Qur'an would not have indicated its message as a new religion.[85] Secondly, he regards the doctrine of intercession as an Islamic Copernican revolution.[86] He quotes some hadiths and reiterates the classic explanation of intercession in three stages: the prophet would intercede; God would accept his intercession and that intercession would be prior and superior to all other intercessors.[87] Applying the Copernican revolution as an analogy, he states:

> Islamic theology has proposed a cyclical and universal history that constructs the Prophet as the sun, and other religions' founders as other celestial bodies, which, like planets, revolve around it. The light of the Prophet (*al-nūr al-Muḥammadī*), which is the basis of their own light, is not his own but is the reflection of the divine glory: the Prophet is the ultimate and most inclusive manifestation of all the divine names.[88]

By intercession theory, Winter allows non-Muslims access to salvation. Both Qadhi and Winter see Islam as the only true religion that leads to salvation. On the other hand salvation is not closed to non-Muslims: Qadhi uses divine justice for those who do not understand the message of God correctly, while Winter uses the theory of intercession to decide whether non-Muslims would attain salvation or not. Both Qadhi's and Winter's positions show the orthodox position of Muslims towards others. They use tradition as justification for exclusivism.

3.3 Assessment and criticism

I have discussed two broad exclusivist responses. Both positions find support from theologians, although Qutb's position has become mainly a position of extreme Muslims. Both positions have some methodological, theological and social problems. Before discussing these problems, it is better to touch on the issue of how Khalil's distinction between exclusivism and inclusivism finds a place in my discussion. In the introduction of this chapter, I claimed that Khalil's interpretation of inclusivism has some theoretical problems. After demonstrating how a traditional form of exclusivism plays a part in contemporary theology of religions, it is better to recall Khalil's interpretation and show that his interpretation is flawed.

In his book[89] Khalil assesses the theology of four different theologians, a Sunni theologian Al-Ghazali, a Sufi theologian Ibn al-Arabi, a Salafi theologian Ibn Taymiyya and a modernist theologian Rashid Rida. He argues that each represents a different type of inclusivism.[90] According to Khalil's criteria all four can be seen as inclusivist, but in reality none would deny supersession theory, and all would regard Islam as the only path to salvation. Among them, he presents Ghazali as the theologian who constructs the theory of excuse,[91] Ibn al-Arabi as a quasi-universalist, Ibn Taymiyya as a universalist and Rida as an ultimate universalist. It is beyond the scope of this book to examine these different theologians and discover whether their positions are consistent with Khalil's interpretation. But Khalil takes a different perspective from mine in this project. Apart from these four theologians, at the end of his book, Khalil also labels Winter as an inclusivist theologian of the contemporary period,[92] which I disagree with. The reason why Khalil places him among inclusivist theologians resides in his reading of Ghazali's and other mediaeval theologians' theology of religions. The problems raised with regard to Khalil's reading of the four theologians can be easily applied to his characterization of Winter's theology of religions. As has been noted, Winter's and Qadhi's theology of religions allows non-Muslims to be saved while strongly claiming the supersessionism of Islam. For them, non-Islamic religions are not valid in the eye of God, and they do not attribute any good or positive values to non-Islamic religious traditions.

Khalil's main questions are whether the theology of these theologians allows non-Muslims to access salvation and whether they believe in eternal damnation. For instance, since Ibn Taymiyya does not believe in the eternal damnation of non-Muslims, Khalil considers Ibn Taymiyya as a universalist. The degree to which a theologian can be considered universalist and whether or not his or her theology of religion can be characterised as inclusivist are two different matters. Karl Barth, who has been regarded as the most influential exclusivist Christian theologian in the modern period, has also been seen by some as a universalist. In addition, the theory of excuse cannot be considered a justification for inclusivism. The main characteristic of inclusivism is whether God is present in other religions and whether there are still good and true elements in other religions or not. If the answer is

100 *Islamic theology of religions*

affirmative, then inclusivists develop a different kind of interpretation of the presence of God. For instance, Rahner distinguishes between Christianity and lawful religions. In the exclusivist Islamic theology the presupposition is that God's message is present in non-Islamic religions, specifically in Christianity and Judaism, although they somehow destroyed or changed the original message of God, thus these religions no longer represent an authentic religion of God. From this point of view, the category of 'the excused' cannot be used as a legitimation of inclusivism.

The category of the excused finds echo in the theory of 'invincible ignorance' within Christian theology. According to D'Costa, the theory of invincible ignorance is based on scripture[93] and later sophistically formulated by the mediaeval theologian Thomas Aquinas.[94] For D'Costa, in the documents of Vatican II, for the salvation of non-Christians, the category of invincible ignorance has been reiterated. According to his reading of the council documents, non-Christian religions 'operate under the condition of invincible ignorance', and those who are in the category of invincible ignorance might be saved, but the council documents do not mention how they will be saved.[95] It is beyond the scope of this book to question whether or not the council documents consider non-Christians as being in the invincible ignorance category. However, previously, I have labelled the Second Vatican's position as restrictive inclusivism. The counter question might be asked, why I do not consider the category of excused as an implication of inclusivism. As I have argued before, some parts of the Muslim exclusivist theologians' theologies might sound as inclusivist, if especially the question of salvation is taken into account. However, when religious epistemology is taken into consideration, their theology does not accept the spiritual powers and truths of other faiths. Thus, certain aspects of their theology might be considered as restrictivist inclusivism or universal-access exclusivism (as for D'Costa, they refer to the same type of theology), but overall their theology of religions has more in common with exclusivism than inclusivism.

If we now turn to a critical analysis of Islamic exclusivist theories, there are some important issues, including methodological, theological and social ones, that both kinds of exclusivist theologians should consider. Firstly, looking at the first type of exclusivism (sociopolitical), their methodology has many flaws. Methodologically, the first problem is that the first group's reading of the sources is literal and selective. They overemphasise negative verses on Abrahamic religions while omitting positive verses. As for the negative verses on Abrahamic religions, they take them literally and apply them to the contemporary world's situation, whereas for the positive verses, they use the socio-historical context of the verses as an excuse not to value them positively. Secondly, their reading of Islam is ideological. Consequently, they reject anything which they see as non-Islamic. They interpret Western modern ideologies and Christian and Jewish traditions as nourishing each other. In other words, non-Islamic traditions' theologies and the practices of their political states are considered inseparable. As a result of the conflicts between the Western world and Muslim countries in the modern period, they reject anything related to the West, either religious or social. Thus, this type of exclusivism prevents any kind of contact point with non-Muslims, rather than focusing on conflict, dialogue and collaboration is probably a better path for Islamic theology to take.

The social rejection of non-Islamic traditions still finds proponents in the contemporary era. Muslims who live in a religiously diverse society experience the problem of how to relate themselves to other traditions. They try to find the answers to the questions of whether it is permissible to be friends with non-Muslims or if it is religiously appropriate to imitate non-Muslim customs and behaviour and so on. As noted before, the question of religious diversity is not only a theological problem but also a legal issue in some cases. So, the answers to these questions are mainly a juristic matter. Basically, there seem to be two opposing mainstream legal approaches among the contemporary exclusivist juristic schools: on the one hand, the school followed by the Egyptian Muslim Brotherhood (*wasati*) and on the other hand, the *salafi* school, whose position is quite similar to Qutb. While the first group encourages friendship with non-Muslims, the second group issues fatwas, which forbid friendship with the followers of non-Islamic traditions. Taking the Qur'anic verses 5:51–52 as starting point, Shavit evaluates the approaches of both traditions.[96] Having examined the fatwas given by both traditions,[97] he comes to the conclusion that while both groups call on Muslims to bring non-Muslims to Islam (*dawah*), the first group (*wasati*) encourages Muslims to develop good relations with non-Muslims and to judge them according to their attitudes towards Muslims, whereas the second group calls on Muslims to be loyal only to Muslims and forbid befriending non-Muslims. Both groups essentially use the same sources as references, but they interpret them with different methodologies. While the *wasati* group applies a contextual reading if necessary,[98] the *salafi* group read the Qur'an and the tradition as literally as possible because for them the Qur'anic texts and the Prophetic traditions are crucial for issuing fatwa. In light of the social implications of sociopolitical exclusivism, it can be argued that this form of exclusivism leads to marginalisation of Muslims in non-Muslim majority states and isolation of non-Muslims in Muslim majority countries. Unlike post-liberal theology's insistence on the differences of religions,[99] in this form of exclusivism, marginalisation and isolation are not only on the theological level but also on the social level. This type of exclusivism, decreeing that contacting and forming relationships with other religious groups is religiously forbidden, prevents the occurrence of social harmony and coexistence. Therefore, in recent pluralist societies, implementation of this exclusivism is rendered quite difficult.

Evaluating the second type of exclusivism (theological), this form of exclusivism seems more optimistic than the first type since it takes only theological considerations into account and does not reject sociopolitical engagement with members of non-Islamic traditions. However, it also has some problems. Firstly, as is the case in the first form of exclusivism, methodologically, their reference to the Qur'anic texts is also selective. While

102 *Islamic theology of religions*

they take seriously the verses that claim the superiority of Islam; they do not take into full account the positive verses, which indicate diversity and value non-Islamic religions.

Secondly, theologically, it seems that there is no difference on a theological level between non-Islamic religions (mainly Abrahamic religions) and unbelievers; they treat both groups in the same way. Although they do recognise the value of some non-Islamic religions' social values, their theology does not see any categorical differences between these two groups. The Qur'an itself not only accepts some social practices of some non-Islamic religions,[100] but it also values their religions. Thus their theology of religions remains incapable of doing justice to the whole Qur'anic picture of non-Muslims.

Thirdly, their use of the theory of supersessionism also seems problematic. Because of the Qur'anic refutation of some doctrines of Judaism and Christianity, they adopt a supersession theory. However, they do not explain how Islam supersedes Sabeanism, which is mentioned in the Qur'an positively. In addition, they fail to relate Islam to non-Abrahamic religions. Theologians in the contemporary period take the mediaeval theologians' supersessionism theory as a standpoint and relate Islam to the world religions from that point. However, the political, social and religious environment of the mediaeval period was very different from the contemporary period. As medievalist theologians mostly produced works on non-Islamic religions to refute their theology, without any sympathetic engagement with their beliefs or dialogue with members of non-Islamic traditions, contemporary theologians' theologies have also been influenced by these styles of polemical and apologetic refutation. Muslims in the modern world have more opportunity to discover and learn from non-Muslims than Muslims during the mediaeval period. It should also be noted that the mediaeval theologians' theology of other religions does not only present a simple intellectual or religious position towards others, but rather the relationship of these scholars with Islamic states was more complex. Lamptey identifies their attitudes towards others as '[responsive] to particular contextual issues, especially political issues related to governance and religious orthodoxy'.[101] In other words, the political situation of the Islamic states had an indirect impact on Muslim theologians' theological views on others. Some of the scholars of that time were 'political appointees or affiliates of various rulers. They were appointed to establish a basis upon which religious difference could be assessed, and they were frequently responsible for enforcing that assessment.'[102] As a result, the theological considerations of mediaeval theologians on the one hand are representing Islam as the religion of state and, on the other hand, they are still based on exegesis and doctrinal argument. Eventually, Islamic supremacy over other religions was not only based on theological premises but was also represented by Islamic states' power relations with non- Muslims and non-Islamic states.

Finally, both theological and sociopolitical exclusivism position Islam and the other religions in a clear-cut hierarchy. Within this hierarchy, Islam resides in first place, while other religions remain in second. This kind of classification prevents dynamic relations between the believers of different faiths. As Lamptey argues, hierarchy is 'insufficient in light of understanding of the religious Other as the proximate Other that blurs boundaries and compels ongoing, complex consideration'.[103] As will be seen in the next chapter, Lamptey offers a model of lateral difference instead of hierarchical difference for considering religious diversity. In the next chapter lateral and hierarchical difference will be explored in more detail.

4 Pluralism

Pluralism in the Islamic tradition is a modern concept. The Western Christian liberal theologians' appearance in the twentieth century has led some Muslim scholars, specifically those who have been educated in Western countries, to construct an Islamic pluralism. In the late nineteenth century and early twentieth century, when Muslims had started to question why the Islamic world lagged behind Europe, some Muslims found the answer in the traditionalist approaches of various aspects of Islam, such as Islamic law and Qur'anic exegesis, and in the failure to catch up with Western intellectual developments. These theologians have all departed to some extent from traditionalist approaches and offered a modernist approach to Islam. Sayyid Ahmad Khan in India and Jamaluddin Afghani and Muhammad Abduh in Egypt have been seen as the pioneers of modernist Islam.[104] Their methodology has some similarities to Islamic revivalists in terms of their approach to tradition and promoting a return to the main sources, namely, the Qur'an and the Sunnah; however, their conclusions are different. While revivalists rejected Western ideologies and values and read the main sources in a more literal way, the modernists tried to reconcile Western values and some ideologies with the main sources. Eventually, they started to promote democracy, human rights and other ideas. The first modernists' approach to non-Islamic traditions, specifically Christianity and Judaism, was not as positive as contemporary modernists. In fact, attitudes towards non-Muslims were not the first concern of these Muslim thinkers, who primarily addressed internal problems.

Subsequent scholars such as Fazlur Rahman[105] and Seyyed Hossein Nasr[106] took the early modernists' approach and led them in different directions. They developed an Islamic pluralistic approach towards non-Muslims. In the contemporary era, Farid Esack, Hasan Askari, Mahmoud Ayoub,[107] Mahmut Aydin,[108] Ali Engineer,[109] Adnan Aslan[110] and Reza Shah-Kazemi[111] all provide different pluralistic approaches written in English.

The main characteristic of Islamic pluralist theologies is that all are convinced of the universality of God and his message(s), a point they share with exclusivist theory. While exclusivism claims that the only universal message of God is Islam, however, pluralists disagree with that argument. They mainly try to reconcile the universality of God's message with the existence of other religious traditions. There is some symmetry between Christian and Islamic pluralism. Firstly, the Christian theocentric form of theology finds

104   *Islamic theology of religions*

its echo in some Muslim theologians' works. Among them, Askari, Aydin and Engineer form a theology which takes many elements from mainly Hick and other Christian theologians' theologies. Secondly, liberation theology within Christian theology has led Knitter to adopt an ethical form of pluralism. Esack also constructs a pluralist theology whose primary motivation bases on liberation theology. Apart from these two forms, some Muslim theologians (Nasr and Shah-Kazemi) adopt a Sufi-based approach, which they would call universalism. Although they are critical of certain forms of theocentric pluralism, their theology has some commonalities with the pluralistic approach. From this perspective, as I have discussed the three different forms of pluralism in Christian theology of religions in the first chapter,[112] I note that the Islamic forms of pluralism also echo the Christian forms. The philosophical-historical, ethical-practical forms of pluralism, and religious-mystical, respectively, can be related to the aforementioned Islamic forms of theologies. I am not arguing that there are distinct borders among these three types but rather that the starting point of each theologian differs. In the first type historical/philosophical engagement with the sources is more important, while the second type prioritises a search for shared moral ground and the third type takes more from the Sufi tradition. To make my argument clearer: for example, Aydin makes many references to Christian pluralists such as Smith and Hick, but he has also written on Rumi as a pluralist Sufi. From an evaluation of Aydin's writings, however,[113] it can be seen that he refers more to the historical-philosophical problems than to the Sufi tradition. Thus, from my perspective, it would be rather consistent to label Aydin's theology of religions as form of theocentric pluralism.

In the following sections I will evaluate three types of theologies, and then I will provide assessment and criticism.

4.1 Hasan Askari and the theocentric form of pluralism

Hasan Askari is one of the pluralist Muslim theologians in the contemporary period. His most well-known works on pluralism are *Spiritual Quest: An Inter-Religious Dimension*[114] and *The Experience of Religious Diversity*,[115] which he co-edited with John Hick, who supports theocentric pluralism. Askari develops the Hickian theocentric type of pluralism.

Like Hick, Askari also reads the religious differences in a metaphorical sense. He establishes four kinds of difference or diversity: literal, symbolic, static and dynamic.[116] He then makes two claims regarding the kind of conflict that religious differences might cause; firstly, literal differences are 'perceived on a static plane of reference and tend to engender destructive conflict'.[117] Secondly, symbolic differences are 'perceived on a dynamic plane of reference and tend to lead to creative conflict'.[118] It is using the second argument that Askari builds his pluralistic vision. Taking Abrahamic religions as an example, he claims that although some similarities and common ground are shared, each Abrahamic faith has an equally and differently authentic approach to the 'Absolute Truth'.[119] If we take their differences

Islamic theology of religions   105

symbolically rather than literally, he argues these differences lead to creative conflict, which on the one hand affirms other traditions while on the other hand criticises them. It is in this way that mutual awareness and a high degree of sensitivity to others might be practised.

Askari attempts to apply the idea of 'progressive revelation' in light of the Islamic perception of religious history. From this basis, he firstly explains the notion of transformation. Christianity transformed Judaism, and Islam was the extension of that transformation. To reinforce his point, Askari gives the example of Jesus. Jesus transformed Judaism through a dual movement: he provided the deeper meaning, which is the inward movement, and he also intended this meaning to apply to all humankind rather than a specific society or a chosen people, which represents the outward movement.[120] Askari believes that Christian critique of Judaism is because of Jewish exclusivism, self-righteousness and literalism. By making the Messiah's message universal and applicable to all humanity, Christianity has brought something valuable to the world. For Askari however, like Jews, Christians have also fallen into the same exclusiveness with the idea of incarnation. From that point, Islam came to light as an extension of same tradition. On the one hand it has maintained the universality of God's message as the Christians argued; on the other hand it tried to transform the idea of incarnation, which Askari sees as parallel to the idea of a 'chosen people' on the grounds that this doctrine promotes the exclusiveness of salvation only for Christian people.[121] From this perspective, Islam totally rejected the idea of the divinity of Jesus. Applying this argument to Christianity, Askari gives the Qur'anic verse of 4:171 as a reference to confirm this Islamic perception. In this verse, God warns Christians: 'do not go beyond the boundaries in your religion.' He asserts:

> The key message: 'Do not go beyond the bounds in your religion.' Going beyond the bounds in one's religion is a threat to which all religions are exposed: to equate one's own religious doctrine with the Transcendent, a tendency which seems to result from lack of distinction between the Transcendent and the immediate object of religious consciousness.[122]

Taking creative conflict among Abrahamic religions into account, Askari argues that Islam has Jesus in common with Christianity and God's oneness and transcendence with Judaism. When Islam engages in a creative conflict with Christians on Jesus, the Qur'anic denial of Jesus's divinity should be considered carefully by Christians since, for Askari, associating Jesus with God is an explicit *shirk* (Qur'anic term meaning the ascribing partners to God).[123] As for Jews, Islam's basic mission is to warn Jews of the problems inherent in their idea of 'the chosen people', which according to Askari is an implicit *shirk*.[124] This is the critical position of Islam towards the other two Abrahamic religions. However, Muslims should also criticise themselves for the sake of self-transformation. To do so, Muslims should give up the claim that Islam belongs to a particular group. Islam, to Askari, does not belong

106 *Islamic theology of religions*

to any single religious group. For this reason the historical religion of Islam has not been labelled with the Prophet's name; that is, the Muslims were not called 'the followers of Prophet Muhammad' (except by Christian critics). Askari attempts to distinguish between Islam as a universal religion and Islam as a historical foundation. He maintains that Islam should not be limited only to those who follow the Sunnah of the Prophet Muhammad.[125] Islam is the religion of those who want to submit their will to their Creator. The Qur'an mentions the other prophets such as Noah, Abraham and Moses as Muslim. If Muslims identify with these prophets, they would come to promote exclusiveness like Christians and Jews: the Qur'an blamed the Jews and the Christians for claiming Abraham as exclusively their own (3:67). On the basis of this argument, Askari warns Muslims: 'If a Muslim stops at the moment of Muhammed and begins with "*islam*" only with him, he/or she is not a "Muslim" but a "Muhammedan". He/or she is locked up in one step of the ongoing revelation of God.'[126]

However, Askari claims that if a Christian or Jew or the adherent of any religion does not associate artificial gods either implicitly or explicitly with God, he or she is a Muslim. Thus with this notion of 'Islam', the particular or historical Islam would be relativised. By distinguishing between a universal and historical Islam, Askari not only includes non-Islamic traditions within God's universal religion, he also rejects the more restrictive traditional interpretations of Islam, such as those from the classical and mediaeval period.[127] Islam has been perceived by Muslims as the final religion, but Askari rejects the rhetoric of finality in any religion. For him the claim of finality, either as a Christian phrase on the lips of Jesus ('I am the Way') or the Islamic doctrine of the idea that 'Muhammad is the seal of prophets' does not help diversity but rather causes conflict. If any religion adheres to the idea of finality, it automatically excludes other religions; however, most religions do make these kinds of claims. Askari attempts to reconcile these claims. He states that the claims of finality can be explained using four factors. Firstly, every final claim is a 'positive claim'[128] since one does not say 'I am not this' but says 'I am the Way'. Secondly, 'each claim is a summing-up, presupposing a vast set of details and essentials, or a reference to the end of a process.'[129] Thirdly, 'each is one among a number of finality-claims.'[130] Finally, those who make such a claim are either ignorant or aware that there are similar claims. If the latter, such a claim supports and defends the other.[131] For these reasons, Askari does not take finality claims literally, but rather he attempts to reconcile these claims. To summarise Askari's pluralism, firstly, he believes that there is a 'Transcendent Reality'[132] behind all religions. Secondly, religious differences should be taken symbolically, not literally. As was demonstrated, when I evaluated Hick's pluralism, Hick also develops his pluralism according to these two arguments.

4.2 Farid Esack and the ethical-practical form of pluralism

In the contemporary Islamic tradition, Farid Esack develops an ethical form of pluralism. His pluralism is based on two things: the Qur'an and his personal journey. Born in South Africa, Esack witnessed, along with his Christian and Jewish neighbours, oppression and injustice, and as a result he developed his own form of liberation pluralism. His approach is influenced by both modern Muslim intellectuals such as Fazlur Rahman and Muhammad Arkoun in terms of reading and interpreting the Qur'anic text and Latin American liberation theologians who view suffering as the most important concern for theology.

Fundamentally his theory originates from a Qur'anic vision of egalitarianism and pluralism; however, it also derives inspiration from the struggles of the prophets.[133] Esack attempted to create a convenient hermeneutical methodology, which was capable of offering solutions to the contemporary political and economic oppression in South Africa and would provide theological support to a more pluralistic approach. Esack reads the Qur'an contextually as he felt that to understand the Qur'an means 'to understand its revealed meaning in a specific past context and then to be able to contextualize [it] in terms of contemporary reality'.[134] In this respect, Esack reinterprets terms used in the Qur'an such as *tawhid*[135] (unity), *taqwā*[136] (an awareness of the presence of God), *iman* (belief),[137] *islam*[138] (submission) and *kufr*[139] (disbelief, infidelity) in a more pluralistic way. He finds exclusivist statements in the Qur'an to be contextually based and not to represent claims of a universal truth. For instance, regarding verse 5:51, which is often read as a warning for Muslims not to befriend Christians and Jews, Esack argues that the Qur'anic injunctions against affiliating with others relates to 'collaboration with the unjust and unrighteous Other, not solidarity with the exploited and marginalized Other'.[140]

His main argument depends on two realities: firstly, nobody can speak about the Quran's last decision about 'the other/s', and secondly, it is not good hermeneutics to 'apply texts of opprobrium in a universal manner to all those whom one chooses to define as "people of book" [or] "disbelievers", etc. in an ahistorical fashion'.[141] He avoids applying such verses which directly address the People of the Book, namely Christians and Jews, as if the Qur'an addressed contemporary Jews and Christians. He believes the reason for the opprobrium towards Jews and Christians in the Qur'an depends on the historical realities of Medinan society.[142] Without considering the historical environment, particularly the social and political dynamics among Muslims, Christians and Jews, we cannot interpret the Qur'an correctly.

Esack draws three conclusions from the Qur'an's position towards the 'religious other'. Firstly, the Qur'an insists on the balance between orthodoxy and orthopraxis, and it objects to the people who rejected the message of Prophet Muhammad on *tawhid* (oneness of Allah) and social justice. The Qur'an demonstrates that the rejection of *tawhid* led Meccan society to experience economic and social oppression.[143] Secondly, the Qur'an definitively condemns the People of the Book whose position towards other religions was exclusivist.[144] Esack uses the Qur'anic context to support his statements. He argues that according to the Qur'an, many Christians and Jews believed that they were special and not the same as other people. Using

108 *Islamic theology of religions*

verse 62:6, Esack states that the Qur'an's response to this kind of groundless belief is quite obvious. The Qur'an also denounces the attempt by Christian and Jews to place Abraham into their religion. 'Abraham was neither a Jew nor a Christian; rather he was one inclining toward truth, a Muslim [submitting to Allah]' (3:67). Thirdly, he claims that the Qur'an explicitly accepts religious pluralism. He uses this verse, which is related to the position of Abraham, and claims that this verse indicates the Qur'an's tendency to religious pluralism.[145] Esack maintains that the Qur'an acknowledges the de jure legitimacy of non-Islamic traditions in two ways. Firstly, the Qur'an takes the religious life of other believers into consideration: it respects and partially accepts their laws, social norms and religious practice, which were included within the Muslim-led community in Medina. He uses many examples from the Qur'an to support his argument. He argues that the People of the Book are recognised in the Qur'an as part of a single community (23:52). The Charter of Medina singles them out, especially the Jews, as being part of a single community together with the Muslims. The permission given to Muslims to consume foods which are processed in a religious way by the People of the Book and the legality of the marriages of Muslim men to chaste women of the People of Book (5:5) are explicit examples of the Quran's acceptance of other divinely ordained religions. Furthermore, to some extent the Qur'an does acknowledge the religious laws, norms and regulations of Jews and Christians (5:47).[146] Secondly, using the verses 2:62 and 5:69 as evidence, he claims that the Qur'an also accepts the salvation of faithful believers of non-Islamic religions.[147]

Even though the Qur'anic account of religious otherness is a model for Muslims, Esack believes that the reason why Muslims have restricted salvation only to Muslims, and have made the other divinely established religions 'others', can be found by examining clearly the historical development of Islamic theology and the history of relations between Muslims and other traditions as a whole. He believes that the traditional modes of exegesis circumvented the apparent inclusiveness of some Qur'anic verses. For example in verse 2:62, God says that all those who have faith will be saved, but traditional interpreters emphasise the 'supercessionism doctrine'.[148] Classic *muffasirs* (Qur'anic commentators)[149] interpreted 2:62 in two ways: either they contended that verse 3:35 abrogated this verse, or they interpreted it in other ways which avoided an inclusive meaning. In the end they left Muslims with the doctrine of supercessionism and ignored the inclusivist vision of the Qur'an.

To conclude, Esack presents two main arguments: firstly, he argues that religious plurality is the will of God, contending that the Qur'an not only accepts religious others but also accepts their spirituality and salvation.[150] Secondly, he sees a Qur'anic imperative to cooperate with others 'in common cause to serve justice and righteousness'.[151] He provides a liberation theology of religions in which 'Islam can only truly be experienced as the liberative praxis of solidarity.'[152] For him this starting point contrasts with traditional and modernist theology. He correlates good deeds with belief: in

Islamic theology of religions 109

his interpretation, the Qur'an 'places extraordinary emphasis on the binding relationship between faith (iman) and practice or what is described as
righteous deeds (a'mal al-salihat)'.[153]

4.3 Shah-Kazemi and universalism

Reza Shah-Kazemi, along with some other perennial philosophers, presents
a Sufi-based theology of religions. In this theology, he wants to move beyond
the threefold classification introduced by Race. He describes his theology of
religions as a universalist position which 'shares with pluralism the basic
premise that the major religious traditions are valid paths to salvation, but
parts company with the pluralist in asserting that this salvific efficacy stems
from the fact that these religions are divinely revealed, not humanly constructed'.[154] As for the inclusivist position, his universalism shares the assertion that 'there is a single religious essence which underlines all outward
forms.'[155] However, unlike the inclusivist position, his universalism does
not patronise and domesticate its own religious truths to other religions
but rather aims to appreciate the religious difference of others as divinely
sanctioned; in other words, 'the other in its very otherness, in all its particularities, in all its irreducible difference, is respected not simply out of a senti-
ment of religious tolerance, but on the basis of a perception that the other
is an expression of the One.'[156] As regards to exclusivism, Shah-Kazemi's
universalism shares the exclusivist position that 'one's religion is normative
and binding',[157] but it does not deny the validity of other religions.

Methodologically, Shah-Kazemi's theology of religions derives from a Sufi
hermeneutic mainly developed from Ibn al-Arabi. Sufi tradition has developed a hermeneutical approach to the Qur'an which basically focuses more
on the inward (*batn*) meaning of the Qur'anic text rather than the outward
one (*zahr*). Shah-Kazami states:

> Verses are deemed to allude to spiritual realities that may not be appar-
> ent at first sight, realities that are perceived by the Sufis in the measure
> of their contemplatively, their mystical states, their receptivity to the
> deeper meanings hidden within the text. In this connection, the fol-
> lowing saying of Prophet-designated as weak according to the crite-
> ria of hadith- is often cited in various versions: 'There is no verse of
> the Qur'ān which does not have and outward (*zahr*), and inward sense
> (*batn*), a limit (*hadd*) and a place to which one ascends (*muttala'*).[158]

Shah-Kazemi's starting point for the theological acceptance of other religions depends on his understanding of the belief of *tawhid* (the oneness of
God). He thinks that for Sufis, the belief of *tawhid* is not only a theological consideration, but also 'the whole of Sufism- its speculative metaphysics, its transformative spirituality, its soul-searching psychology, its mystical
practices and its ethical imperatives – can be seen as so much of "commen-
tary" or elaboration upon this Qur'ānic message of *tawhid*.'[159] The exoteric

110   *Islamic theology of religions*

exegesis of the Qur'anic interpretation of the belief of *tawhid* leads him to accept all sorts of diversity. According to Sufi interpretation there is only one single Real, which is God, and all other things belong to that single unity. Shah-Kazemi's theology stems from the relationship 'between oneness in diversity and diversity within oneness'.[160] Thus for him, the One, God, is present in each particular thing in the cosmos, but He is more than the sum of all particulars.[161] As the universality of God is present in every particular, including the religious others, his theology of religions accepts the religious otherness of non-Islamic religions as part of divine unity.

Shah-Kazemi offers a different interpretation of the term 'Islam', which he describes as 'quintessential' and 'universal' Islam. On the one hand he argues that there is something unique in each revealed religion, whilst on the other hand, he regards all revelations as expressions of one and the same religious essence (quintessence).[162] This notion resembles Hick's presupposition that each religion is a different response to the same divine reality. However, unlike Hick, Shah-Kazemi considers religious diversity as divinely ordained, not as different human responses to the same Reality. As presented in Askari's theology of religions, Muslim pluralists distinguish between historical and universal Islam. Shah-Kazemi also uses this distinction when he interprets the Qur'anic verses, such as 3:85, which regard Islam as the only true religion. He thinks that neither the theory of supersessionism, which claims that Islam is the only true religion accepted by God, nor the pluralist claim (mainly by Askari) that universal Islam abolishes particular and historical Islam, present a universalist vision of Islam. He claims:

> The particular and historical form of Islam is doubtless to be situated at a lower level than the universal and timeless essence, but the particular is not to be trivialized, marginalized, or invalidated by the universal. On the contrary, the particular is elevated and ennobled in the very measure that it is deemed to be an expression of the universal – the form becomes more, not less, *essential* to the extent that it is grasped as an embodiment of the essence and a vehicle leading to the essence.[163]

Thus, Shah-Kazemi utilises his exoteric hermeneutic and regards Islam as universal with historical Islam and other religions as parts of its universality. As for the question of salvation, he believes that all believers in God regardless of their religion have the same absolute spiritual equality; in other words, 'for each person is judged strictly according to his or her own state of soul, not on the basis of formal affiliation, nor on the basis of conforming outwardly to a set of formal legal rules.'[164] However, although he prioritises belief and individual piousness, he argues that salvation (entering to paradise) would only be possible by the mercy of God.[165]

4.4 Assessment and criticism

I have considered three forms of pluralism in Islamic theology of religions. The first type of pluralism sees a Transcendent Reality behind all religions, while the second type of pluralism emphasises good deeds (ethics) over doctrinal faith, and the third type underlines the universality of God with exoteric readings of the sources. Even though these types offer different forms of pluralism, all take the Qur'an as their main source for contextualising pluralism within the Islamic faith. All three theologies interpret Islam differently as to how it was traditionally regarded.

Although Shah-Kazemi does not offer his theology of religions as a form of pluralism, in this section I have categorised his theology within pluralism. This might seem a simplified overview; however, his theology objects to the supersessionist theory of Islam, as the other forms of pluralism do. Furthermore, like in the theocentric form of pluralism his theology considers God the source of diverse religions. Despite being critical of pluralism, his theology also ends up with supporting universal Islam over historical Islam. The only difference between his distinction of universal and historical Islam and Askari's is that while Askari sacrifices historical Islam for the sake of pluralism, Shah-Kazemi keeps historical Islam under the umbrella of universal Islam; in other words, in his theology, historical Islam and other religions can be incorporated with universal Islam within his Sufi exoteric methodology. Thus, the differences of religions in Shah-Kazemi's theology are not denied, but they are subordinated. Universal Islam is still regarded as normative in understanding religious others.

Looking at the Islamic form of the theocentric model (and relatively Shah-Kazemi's universalism), the main argument is that each religion has a different response to the same God. As is apparent in Askari's theology, he places more emphasis on similarities and interprets differences symbolically. He makes a distinction between universal and historical Islam to include non-Islamic traditions in the universal plan of salvation. This claim sounds more inclusivist than pluralist. Although Askari gives different nuances from Rahner, he comes to the same conclusion. In contrast to Rahner, however, he tries to use this separation to advocate pluralism, although Rahner's anonymous Christian theory suggests that even though non-Christians do not realise it, they are Christians. Moreover, Askari and other Muslims who use the idea of universal and historical Islam do not offer a model of explicit and implicit belief like Rahner. In spite of nuanced differences, they leave a door open to the claim that even though non-Muslims do not believe themselves to be Muslims, they are anonymously Muslims since, from Adam onwards, God sent a single revelation. Eventually, the advocators of a theocentric form of pluralism and universalism use this distinction to characterise the Islamic position towards non-Islamic traditions, like Rahner does,[166] but distinguishing between universal Islam and historical Islam produces more negative outcomes than positive. I will outline these problems generally and the problem of the theocentric form of pluralism in particular.

Firstly, it locates Islam in a position of superiority over non-Islamic faiths. While theocentric pluralists, by disagreeing with the traditional form of exclusivism, try to avoid a patronising attitude, they commit more or less the same mistake. Secondly, they oversimplify the differences among religions. By interpreting non-Islamic traditions as part of a universal Islamic

112 *Islamic theology of religions*

faith, the real differences of other faiths are ignored. There are distinct sects and interpretations in diverse religions. Some religions, like Christianity, have established an orthodox set of beliefs which has persisted for centuries and which differs greatly from what Muslim theocentric pluralists would interpret their beliefs to be. While Muslim theologians have shifted their beliefs for the sake of dialogue with non-Muslims, the theology they offer in fact subordinates Christians who hold Christian orthodoxy. In other words, pluralist Islamic theology aims to include non-Islamic tradition into their desired theology of religions, but they end up with affirming one specific form of theological interpretation (in Askari's case, liberal Christian theology which does not give central place to orthodox beliefs). There are many commonalities between, for example, Askari's and Hick's reading of Christian doctrines: they both believe that the doctrines of incarnation and Trinity lead to the exclusivist claims of Christian tradition. However, for mainstream orthodox Christianity any reductive interpretation of Christ's divinity is not acceptable. Thus, this form of theology of religions limits itself to the truths of one form of a specific religion. Muslim or Christian pluralists, or a believer of any religious background, may agree that there is an ultimate Reality behind all world religions' traditions, they may agree on certain things, but their theology fails to relate their belief to an orthodox believer of any particular religion.

Thirdly, in Hick's theocentric model religions are human responses to the ultimate Reality, whereas in the theocentric Muslim pluralists' theology, religions are part of the same divine plan of God. If this is the case, relating Islam with Buddhism or other non-theistic religions seems problematic. Buddha is the founder of Buddhism – his teachings have become the main sources of Buddhism – but Buddha never claimed to be either a prophet or to have been revealed by any ultimate power. From this perspective, Muslim theologians' theory that all religions belong to the Islamic faith collapses. The final point, which also relates to the third point, is that Muslim theologians of the theocentric form of pluralism relate Islam more with Judaism and Christianity, and they show us how the three Abrahamic religions should be perceived in terms of theology, but they do not show how Islam is related to non-Abrahamic faiths. They give such an abstract definition; that is, 'there is an Ultimate Reality behind all religions.' They are somehow successful in showing that that same ultimate Reality is behind Christianity and Judaism, but they are not interested in how other world religions are related to this. For example, Ayoub claims that in verse 2:62 and 5:69, Sabians addresses those who do not have a divine scripture. He maintains that

> Muslims have written much about the identity of the Sabeans. I would say that they represent all people who have no Book- that is, people who are not Jews and Christians but who have an idea of, and in some way worship, a transcendent Supreme Being, or God.[167]

However, he does not go into further detail on how the category of the Sabians might be related to other world religions. There should be a clear explanation of how the God of Islam as the source of every religion relates to such religions as Buddhism, where there is no concept of God or Hinduism in which there are multiple Gods. To make such an argument there should be a clear examination of each religion. From this perspective, rather than abstract claims about the unity of religions, there is a need for more solid claims which are firmly supported by study and engagement with particular religions. From this point of view, for Islamic theology of religions the tools of comparative theology would be useful as it requires a deep engagement with other tradition/s other than their own. For Muslims, rather than theorising non-Islamic religions in the light of statements of their own religious text, the real engagement with non-Islamic religions through their texts and teachings would increase Muslims' awareness of the real differences.

Examining Esack's form of ethical-practical pluralism, his theology offers something new to the Islamic theology of religions. Like Knitter, he is not so interested in the theological similarity or differences of religions, rather he believes that liberation is the main issue. He offers a dynamic meaning for such words as *kufr*, *iman*, *islam*, and others. He sees an important correlation between faith and good deeds. His special emphasis on liberative action is a result of his struggle against the Apartheid regime in South Africa. His contribution to the field of theology of religions is considerable and effective. He changes the direction of the discussion. While theocentric pluralists focus more on the ultimate Reality, his main focus is cooperation with non-Muslims for a good cause.

Esack's reading of negative verses about the People of the Book is contextual. As has been shown before, Rahman had already offered a contextual reading of the Qur'an, according to which the Qur'anic verses are historically conditioned. There is always a reason behind the revelation of any verse, and to understand that reason we should go back to the Qur'anic times and then deduct an ethical conclusion for the contemporary context. Applying this hermeneutical approach, Esack interprets the negative verses in the People of the Book as existing not because of their ontology but rather because their actions were negative. It is not that Christians or Jews are cursed by God but their negative actions which were cursed. This interpretation contrasts with that of Qutb. As has been mentioned, for Qutb, the bad action of the People of the Book is an ontological problem. Esack's and Rahman's interpretations of this issue are more suitable to the Qur'anic vision in general than Qutb's.

Although Esack's theology places less emphasis on the salvation problem and more on liberation praxis, he still believes that God accepts non-Islamic religions' salvific efficacy. He does not answer the question of whether non-Islamic traditions have the same efficacy as Islam, but he does assert that faithful believers would be saved. The faithful believers are not restricted to any social-religious community. Those who are both outside of 'Islamic' tradition and within 'Islamic' tradition and have faith, which is directly related to good deeds, will be saved. The presupposition here is again that every person is somehow related to the universality of God's message, which has been described in Islamic sources. Like theocentric theologians, Esack also

114 *Islamic theology of religions*

falls into inclusivism. To combine the universality of God with the particularity of other religions is not easy task. As it has been argued, like theocentric pluralists, Esack's theology presupposes the idea that there is a single unity behind every religion. As I have argued, for such a big claim to be substantiated, there should be a clear examination of non-Abrahamic faiths, which demonstrates how they are related to that single unity.

Esack's form of pluralism is a response to the first type of exclusivism (sociopolitical) I have discussed. As I have shown, the extreme form of exclusivism, represented by Qutb and the *Salafi* school, rejects any relations with non-Muslims. However, Esack calls on Muslims to cooperate with non-Muslims against oppression. His arguments are important and valuable, but it should be noted that cooperation with non-Muslims against oppression is different from believing that they belong to the same unity. Both theocentric and ethical pluralism pay more attention to commonalities and ignore differences.

Pluralist Muslim theologians do not go as far in their beliefs as Christian theologians since each religion's dynamic is different. While Christianity's main doctrines are incarnation and Trinity as a result of Jesus's specific relation with God, in Islamic theology the main authority is the Qur'an. Pluralist Christian theologians construct their theology of religions by rejecting these doctrines, or they reinterpret them in a way that is fundamentally different from Christian orthodoxy. For any Muslim, however, either exclusivist or pluralist, replacing the Qur'an with such other concepts is unacceptable. The main and fundamental starting point for Muslim pluralists is the Qur'an, whereas for Christian pluralists, there is no such an authority. This difference explains why pluralist Muslim theologians' theology of religions sometimes falls into inclusivism in certain respects. The Qur'anic position towards other religions can be read as an inclusivist position. From an overall perspective, the Qur'an simultaneously accepts and rejects non-Islamic traditions (categorical 'yes' and 'no'). However, unlike the standard inclusivist theologies, Islamic inclusivism should not project its own beliefs onto other religions. In other words, the differences and commonalities of non-Islamic religions should be treated in the same manner. While accepting the similarity of other faiths with Islam, their differences should not be subordinated. This position will be explored more deeply in the final chapter. Another difference between the nature of Islamic and Christian theology of religions is that for Christians, the problem of salvation was an institutional matter. The creed of 'no salvation outside of the Church' was constructed through the early institutionalisation of Christianity. On the other hand, in Islamic theology salvation has never been a matter of institutionalisation. Despite the doctrine of supersessionism, Muslim theologians have not constructed any doctrine similar to that of no salvation outside of the Church. In fact, in Islamic theology the problem of salvation is not as apparent as in Christian theology. As a result, whether we consider the classical period or the contemporary period, Muslims pay less attention to this issue than Christians.

Conclusion

I have evaluated different voices from the Muslim world on the issue of theology of religions. Each position is valuable; each theologian represents his or her own particular perspective. Exclusivists and pluralist Muslims agree on the universality of God and his single religion. There is only one single way for the whole humanity. While exclusivist Muslims do not include non-Muslims in that single religion, pluralist Muslims put the believers of non-Islamic religions into God's single religion. From this perspective, pluralist Muslims reinterpret the meaning of Islam and offer a universal vision of Islam as submission to God regardless of religious boundaries.

I have used Race's threefold classification to describe Christian theology of religions in the previous chapters. In spite of some problems, I have argued that Race's classification offers a good overview of Christian theology of religions. Despite some efforts by Muslim and non-Muslim theologians, applying Race's classification in Islamic theology to provide analysis of the different positions is not as easy as in Christian theology. As has been indicated, Muslim pluralists' theology of religions claims to be pluralist but falls into inclusivism in certain perspectives. Furthermore, I have also shown that an effort to put exclusivist theology into the inclusivist category fails because of its different responses to two main questions: whether non-Islamic faiths lead to salvation and whether non-Islamic faiths have been touched by God's message. For exclusivists, the answer to both questions is no, while for pluralists it is yes. From this perspective, Race's classification does not fully help us to contextualise the Islamic theology of religions.

Exclusivist Muslim theologians offer an interpretation of non-Islamic faiths based on hierarchical relations. Their theology does not help in engaging in a truthful dialogue with the believers of other faiths. On the other hand, pluralist Muslim theologians' emphasis on the similarities between religions also fails to realise the otherness of non-Islamic religions. The ethical form of pluralism attempts to solve this problem by offering liberative praxis as the most important part of religions, but it also fails since the theology behind that form of pluralism is the same theology as the theocentric form. Thus, Muslim theologians should try to seek a new way to integrate Islamic religions with non-Islamic faiths. The next chapter will focus on Jerusha Lamptey's theology of religions that attempts to address these problems.

Notes

1 Jacques Waardenburg (ed.), *Muslim Perceptions of Other Religions* (New York, Oxford: Oxford University Press, 1999). The author only presents the historical progress of Muslim study of non-Islamic religions. He neither evaluates different theological approaches nor touches on the legal issues. He gives a good overview of how Muslims have studied non-Islamic religions throughout history: the Early Period: 610–650 CE, pp. 3–17; the Medieval Period: 650–1500 CE, pp. 18–69; the Modern Period: 1500–1950 CE, pp. 70–84; the Contemporary Period: 1950–1995 CE.

116 Islamic theology of religions

2 Paul Knitter, *Introducing Theologies of Religions* (Maryknoll, NY: Orbis Books, 2009), part 1, see especially 19–56.

3 Alan Race, *Christians and Religious Pluralism* (London: SCM Press, 1983/1993), 38.

4 Gavin, D'Costa, *Christians and the World Religions: Disputed Questions in the Theology of Religions* (Chichester: Wiley-Blackwell, 2009), 7.

5 Muhammad Hassan Khalil, *Islam and the Fate of Others: The Salvation Question* (New York: Oxford University Press, 2012).

6 Ibid., 7.

7 Ibid.

8 Ibid.

9 Gavin D'Costa, *Theology and Religious Pluralism: The Challenge of Other Religions* (Oxford: Basil Blackwell, 1986), 4.

10 Rifat Atay, "Religious Pluralism and Islam: A Critical Examination of John Hick's Pluralistic Hypothesis" (PhD diss., University of St. Andrews, 1999).

11 Ibid., 14–18.

12 Ibid., 27.

13 Imam Maturidi is a founder of one of the Sunni Islamic schools. He is a Hanafi theologian, jurist and Qur'anic commentator. See W. Madelung, "al-Māturīdī," in *Encyclopaedia of Islam*, Second Edition, eds. P. Bearman, T. Bianquis, C. E. Bosworth, E. van Donzel and W. P. Heinrichs. Brill Online, 2015. Reference. University of Bristol (15 October 2014), available at: http://referenceworks.brillonline.com/entries/encyclopaedia-of-islam-2/al-maturidi-SIM_5045.

14 Atay, "Religious Pluralism and Islam," 28–29.

15 Ibid., 36.

16 Ibid., 37.

17 Ibid., 43.

18 Lewis Winkler, *Contemporary Muslim and Christian Responses to Religious Pluralism: Wolfhart Pannenberg in Dialogue with Abdulaziz Sachedina* (Eugene: Pickwick Publications, 2011), 41.

19 Ibid., 44.

20 Ibid., 47.

21 For the inclusivist position he uses Aydin's "Religious Pluralism: A Challenge for Muslims- a Theological Evaluation," *Journal of Ecumenical Studies* 38/3 (Summer 2001): 330–352. For pluralism he uses "Religious Pluralism," in *Muslim and Christian Reflection of Peace: Divine and Human Dimension*, eds. J. Dudley Woodberry, Osman Zumrut and Mustafa Koylu (Lanham: University of Press of Amerika, 2005), 89–99.

22 Adnan Aslan, "Islam and Religious Pluralism," *The Islamic Quarterly* 40/3 (1996): 172–186.

23 Aslan defines himself neither as pluralist nor inclusivist. However, Aydin in several occasions promotes pluralistic views. See the previously mentioned bibliographies.

24 D'Costa, *World Religions*, 24. D'Costa describes universal-access exclusivism using four main principles. Firstly, there will be an opportunity for those who have not heard the message of the Gospel to hear it either at the point of death or after death. Secondly, since by his middle knowledge, God knows who would or would not accept the Gospel, God will apply the Gospel even if the person never hears Gospel in his or her lifetime. Thirdly, we cannot exclude the possibility of salvation for the un-evangelised since we do not and cannot know how God will reach them. Finally, 'explicit faith and baptism are the normal means to salvation; there can be other means that act as a preparation (*preparatio*) to salvation, which will eventuate in final salvation.' These preparations might take place either through following natural revelation in nature, or following the good through conscience and reason, or through an element within their religion

Islamic theology of religions 117

but not through the religion per se. The final remark conforms to the restrictive inclusivist position (Ibid., 29).

25 Khalil, *Salvation Question*, 11.
26 Qamar-ul Huda, "Knowledge of Allah and Islamic View of Other Religions," *Theological Studies* 64 (2003): 278–305.
27 The Qur'an, 5:48.
28 The Qur'an, 49:13.
29 The Qur'an, 2:256.
30 The Qur'an, 5:2.
31 The Qur'an, 5:8.
32 The Qur'an, 3:64.
33 The Qur'an, 2:62/5:69.
34 The, Qur'an, 3:19.
35 The Qur'an, 3:85.
36 The Qur'an, 9:29.
37 The Qur'an, 3:67–68.
38 The Qur'an, 2:111–112.
39 The Qur'an, 5: 51.
40 The Qur'an, 2:120.
41 The Qur'an, 9:30.
42 The Qur'an, 3:70–71.
43 The Qur'an, 5:82.
44 As in the case of John 14:6 and Acts 4:12, Christian exclusivist theology takes its root from mainly these two verses. However, in Islamic discourse, not only are there such exclusivist verses like these two Biblical passages, but also, there are such verses that directly criticise the practice and belief systems of Christianity and Judaism.
45 The Qur'an, 2:106.
46 For a critical overview of this verse, see John Burton, "The Exegesis of Q.2:106 and the Islamic Theories of *Naskh: mā nansakh min āya aw nansaha na'ti bi khairin minhā aw mithlihā*," *Bulletin of the School of Oriental and African Studies* 48/3 (1985): 452–469. For further discussion of the theory of *naskh*, see "The Interpretation of Q.87, 6–7 and the Theories of *Naskh*," *Der Islam* 62 (1985): 5–19.
47 Yohanan Freidman, *Tolerance and Coercion in Islam: Interfaith Relations in the Muslim Tradition* (New York: Cambridge University Press, 2003), 21. For further discussion on two different views on abrogation see especially, 21–27.
48 For some classical and modern interpreters' interpretation of these two verses, see Mahmoud Ayoub, *The Qur'an and Its Interpreters, Volume II: The House of 'Imran* (Albany: State University of New York Press, 1992). For the verse 3:19, see 66–68 and the verse 3:85, and see also 241–243.
49 Abdulaziz Sachedina, "Political Implications of the Islamic Notions of "Supersession' as Reflected in Islamic Jurisprudence," *Islam and Christian-Muslim Relations* 7.2 (1996)" 159–168.
50 Fazlur Rahman, *Islam and Modernity: Transformation of an Intellectual Tradition* (Chicago: University of Chicago Press, 1982), 5.
51 Waardenburg, *Muslim Perceptions*, in the Medieval Period, 20.
52 In fact in Muslim societies there were two distinct classes: Muslims and non-Muslims. The non-Muslims were also divided into two main sections: those who have divine revelation – Christians, Jews, Zoroastrians and Sabians – and those who are the polytheists (*mushrikun*). The members of the first groups were allowed to live within Islamic communities as long as they paid the tax to the authorities. However, the second group was not recognised and asked to come to belief to live in the Islamic states. In fact, when Prophet Muhammad conquered Mecca, he did not force the polytheists of Mecca to convert to Islam. In fact,

118 *Islamic theology of religions*

during later phase of the Prophet's ministry, to make it easier for non-believers to convert to Islam, the Qur'an itself in 9:60 declares that alms should be given to those whose hearts are reconciled to Islam. However, after the death of the Prophet, it was not permitted for unbelievers who publicly denounce Islam to live in Islamic communities.

53 Waardenburg, *Muslim Perceptions*, 20.
54 If we compare with Knitter's classification of theology of religions positions in *Introducing Theology of Religions* (part 1, 19–56), the classical Islamic view tended towards a model of *Replacement* rather than *Fulfilment*.
55 William L. Cleveland, *A History of the Modern Middle East*, Third Edition (Oxford: Westview Press, 2004), 163.
56 See for further exploration of the Western imperialism's influence of Islamic world, for example, David K. Fieldhouse, *Western Imperialism in the Middle East 1914–1958* (New York: Oxford University Press, 2006).
57 See, Irfan A. Omar (ed.), *Muslim View of Christianity: Essays on Dialogue by Mahmoud Ayoub* (Maryknoll, NY: Orbis Books, 2007), specifically 50–57.
58 Adullah Saeed, *Interpreting the Qur'ān: Towards a Contemporary Approach* (Abingdon, New York: Routledge, 2006), 17.
59 Hasan al-Banna is a co-founder of Muslim Brotherhood organisation of Egypt. For a good overview of his thoughts on social implication of Islam, see, for example, http://m.www.islamicbulletin.org/free_downloads/resources/between_ yesterday_and_today.pdf (accessed in 20 October 2014).
60 Ana Soage, "Islamism and Modernity: The Political Thought of Sayyid Qutb," *Totalitarian Movements and Political Religions* 10/2 (June 2009): 189–203.
61 Such as Abu Ala al-Mawdudi and Izzat Darwaza.
62 Adullah Saeed, *Interpreting the Qur'ān*, 18.
63 Qutb's assumption on the Islamic system resides with the Prophet Muhammad and rightly guided Four Caliphs. According to Qutb, the perfect Islamic system was established by Prophet Muhammad and his Companions, and the first Four Caliphs maintained this system. Thanks to this system, for a thousand years Muslims basked in the blessing of the first period. However, Muslims later imported foreign elements from Greek philosophy, Persian mythology, Jewish tales, and Christian theology (Soage, "Islamism and Modernity").
64 Sayyid Qutb, *In the Shade of the Qur'an*, vol. 16, 1951–1965, 98, available at: http://ia700803.us.archive.org/27/items/InTheShadeOfTheQuranSayyidQutb/ volume_16_surahs_48–61.pdf (accessed in 10 September 2015).
65 Ibid., 98.
66 Sayyid Qutb, *In the Shade of the Qur'an*, vol. 7, 1951–1965, 10, available at: http://ia700803.us.archive.org/27/items/InTheShadeOfTheQuranSayyidQutb/ Volume_7_surah_8.pdf (accessed in 10 September 2015).
67 Sayyid Qutb, *In the Shade of the Qur'an*, vol .2, 1951–1965, 349, available at: http://ia700803.us.archive.org/27/items/InTheShadeOfTheQuranSayyidQutb/ Volume_2_surah_3.pdf (accessed in 10 September 2015).
68 Ibid.
69 Qutb argues that '(t)he principle of *"no compulsion in religion'* should be read in conjunction with another one that states: '*Make ready against them whatever force and war mounts you can muster, so that you may strike terror into the enemies of God who are also your own enemies, and others besides them of whom you may be unaware, but of whom God is well aware'*" (8: 60). Qutb, *In the Shade of the Qur'an*, vol. 2, 353, emphasis in originial.
70 Sayyid Qutb, *In the Shade of the Qur'an*, vol. 8, 1951–1965, 19, available at: http://ia700803.us.archive.org/27/items/InTheShadeOfTheQuranSayyidQutb/ Volume_7_surah_8.pdf (accessed in 10 September 2015).
71 Ibid.

Islamic theology of religions 119

72 Since, for Qutb, all 'divine message had the common goal of establishing the principle of God's oneness, calling on mankind to believe in it, and reject all pagan beliefs' (Qutb, *In the Shade of the Qur'an, vol. 4*, 168.), Prophet Muhammad is the last prophet and messenger of God to all humanity. As a result, all people 'regardless of their religion, creed, belief, race, and nationality, are called upon to believe in his message as he preached it in essence and detail' (Ibid., 165).
73 Qutb, Ibid., 166.
74 Sayyid Qutb, *In the Shade of the Qur'an, vol. 1*, 1951–1965, 78, available at: http://ia700803.us.archive.org/27/items/InTheShadeOfTheQuranSayyidQutb/Volume_1_surah_1–2.pdf (accessed in 10 September 2015).
75 Sayyid Qutb, *In the Shade of the Qur'an, vol. 3*, 1951–1965, 342, available at: http://ia700803.us.archive.org/27/items/InTheShadeOfTheQuranSayyidQutb/Volume_3_surah_4.pdf (accessed in 10 September 2015).
76 Ibid., 343.
77 Yasir Qadhi, "The Path of Allah or the Paths of Allah? Revisiting Classical and Medieval Sunni Approaches to Salvation of Others," in *Between Heaven and Hell: Islam, Salvation and the Fate of Others*, ed. Mohammad Khalil (New York: University of Oxford Press, 2013), 110–122, 112.
78 He uses the Qur'anic verses 3:85 and 3:19 as examples.
79 Ibid., 113.
80 Ibid., 114.
81 Ibid.
82 Qadhi here uses mediaeval Muslim scholar al-Nasafi's argument, 115.
83 Ibid., 119.
84 Tim Winter, "Realism and the Real," in *Between Heaven and Hell: Islam, Salvation and the Fate of Others*, ed. Mohammad Khalil (New York: University of Oxford Press, 2013), 128.
85 Ibid.
86 Ibid., 136.
87 'Abd al-Salām ibn Ibrāhīm, *Irshād al-murīd sharḥ Jawharat al-tawḥīd*, published in the margin of *Ḥāshiyat al-amīr 'alā sharḥ 'Abd al-Salām 'alā al-jawhara fī 'ilm al-kalām* (Cairo: Muḥammad 'Alī Ṣubayḥ, 1953), 146 cited in Winter, "Realism and the Real," 137.
88 Ibid., 140.
89 Khalil, *Salvation Question*.
90 Ibid., 17–24.
91 Khalil lists four categories of Ghazali's theory of excuse. The first category includes those who never hear of the Prophet; they will be excused. The second group is those who rejected the message of Prophet after they encountered it in its true form; they will be damned. Those who heard only a negative message about Islam belong to third category; they will also be excused. Finally, the fourth category is those who actively investigated the Islamic message after encountering it in its true form; they will be damned if they do not accept it. (Khalil, *Salvation Question*, 36.)
92 Ibid., 141–142.
93 Gavin D'Costa, *Vatican II: Catholic Doctrines on Jews and Muslims* (Oxford: Oxford University Press, 2014), 63. He uses Luke 12: 47–48 and Timothy 1:13 as justification.
94 Ibid., 64. According to Aquinas's theory, if a child was raised by wolves and never has heard the Gospel, God would either reveal himself through inspiration (interior revelation or angelic communication) or send someone to preach the faith to him. Although Aquinas did not think that a wolf-child would be saved by virtue of invincible ignorance, later some other Christian theologians developed this theory and argued that the non-reached might be saved (see D'Costa, *Vatican II*, 64–80).

120 *Islamic theology of religions*

95 Ibid., 80.
96 Uriya Shavit, "Can Muslims Befriend Non-Muslims? Debating al-walā' wa-al-barā' (Loyalty and Disavowal) in Theory and Practice," *Islam and Christian-Muslim Relations* 25/1 (2014): 67–88.
97 For the first group he examines Yusuf al-Qaradawi's fatwas on the issue, who is the most well-known Islamic jurist of the Muslim Brotherhood in the contemporary era.
98 For example, al-Qaradawi does not ignore the Qur'anic verses 5:51–52, which prohibit extending friendship to non-Muslims. However, he believes these verses cannot be applied for all Jews and Christians and others for the reason that this kind of interpretation would contradict other Qur'anic verses, such as 60:8, 30:21. Thus, as a *wasati* principle, 'these verses must be contextualised, the command to disavow infidels should be interpreted as applying exclusively to those who are hostile to Islam and who fight against Muslims; those enemies, as opposed to infidels in general, are not to be assisted or taken as confidants' (Shavit, "Can Muslims Befriend Non-Muslims?", 79).
99 While post-liberal theology of religions promotes good neighbourhood (in Knitter's words), the sociopolitical exclusivism does not allow any kind of relation. From this perspective, the isolation and marginalisation in this form is much deeper.
100 For example, see the Qur'anic verse 5:5, which declares that the food prepared by the People of the Book is acceptable to Muslims and that Muslim men can marry non-Muslim brides.
101 Jerusha Lamptey, *Never Wholly Other: A Muslima Theology of Religions* (New York: Oxford University Press, 2014), 48.
102 Ibid., 48.
103 Ibid., 77.
104 See for example, Albert Haurani, *Arabic Thought in a Liberal Age, 1798–1939* (Cambridge: Cambridge University Press, 1983); Muhammad Zaki Badawi, *The Reformers of Egypt: A Critique of al-Afgani, 'Abduh, and Ridha* (Slough: Open Press, 1976); and Christian W. Troll, *Sayyid Ahmad Khan: Reinterpretation of Muslim Theology* (New Delhi: Vikas Publishing House, 1978).
105 Rahman's particular contribution to Islamic science is his methodology, both in the interpretation of the Qur'an and Islamic law. He has offered a modernist approach for both Islamic subjects. He has not particularly focused on theology of religions, but in his *Major Themes of the Qur'an* he offers a contextual reading of the Qur'an which indirectly relates to the Islamic perception of the other two Abrahamic faiths. In this book he adds a particular appendix with the title 'The People of the Book and Diversity of Religions'. See *Major Themes of the Qur'an* (Chicago, London: University of Chicago Press, 2009).
106 Seyyed H. Nasr, "Islam and Encounter of Religions and Islam's Attitude towards Other Religion History," in *The Religious Other: Towards a Muslim Theology of Religions in a Post-Prophetic Age*, ed. Muhammad Suheyl Umar (Lahore: Iqbal Pakistan Academy, 2008), 59–81 and 121–134. See also "The Islamic View of Christianity," in *Christianity through Non-Christian Eyes*, ed. Paul Griffiths (Maryknoll: Orbis Books, 1990), 126–134.
107 Omar, *Muslim View of Christianity* and Mahmoud Ayoub, "Islam and the Challenge of Religious Pluralism," *Global Dialogue* 2/1 (Winter 2004): 53–64.
108 Mahmut Aydin, "Is There Only One Way to God," *Studies in Interreligious Dialogue* 10 (2000): 148–158; "Religious Pluralism: A Challenge for Muslims-Theological Evaluation," *Journal of Ecumenical Studies* 38/2–3 (2001): 330–352; "Islam and Diverse Faiths: A Muslim View," in *Islam and Interfaith Relations*, eds. Perry Schmith-Leukel and Lloyd Ridgeon (London: SCM Press, 2007), 33–54; and "A Muslim Pluralist: Jalaluddin Rumi," in *The Myth of Religious Superiority: A Multifaith Exploration*, ed. Paul Knitter (Maryknoll: Orbis Books, 2005), 220–236.

Islamic theology of religions 121

109 Ali Engineer, "Islam and Pluralism," in *The Myth of Religious Superiority: A Multifaith Exploration*, ed. Paul Knitter (Maryknoll: Orbis Books, 2005), 211–219.

110 Adnan Aslan, "Islam and Religious Pluralism," *The Islamic Quarterly* 40/3 (1996): 172–186.

111 Reza Shah-Kazemi, *The Other in the Light of One: The Universality of the Qur'ān and Interfaith Dialogue* (Cambridge: Islamic Text Society, 2006) and "Beyond Polemics and Pluralism: The Universal Message of the Qur'an," in *Between Heaven and Hell: Islam, Salvation and the Fate of Others*, ed. Mohammad Khalil (New York: University of Oxford Press, 2013), 88–104.

112 Three-bridges, religious-mystical, philosophical-historical and ethical-practical, originally introduced in John Hick and Knitter (eds.), *The Myth of Christian Uniqueness: Toward a Pluralistic Theology of Religions* (London: SCM Publisher, 1987) but later utilised by Knitter in *Theologies of Religions*.

113 For Aydin, Islamic religious pluralism is the idea that 'Paradise is not restricted only to those who follow the teaching of the Prophet Muhammad' (Aydin, "Religious Pluralism"). Quoting Hick's most famous idea that religions are different human responses to the same ultimate Reality, Aydin argues that since God is present in all religion, God gives equal opportunity to the followers of major world religions for ultimate fulfilment. From this basis, the theocentric form of pluralism defines the term 'Islam' differently from the past. Aydin also relativises historical Islam for the sake of pluralism. He claims, like Hick, that Muslim theology should also undergo an Islamic-based 'Copernican Revolution', which is 'to put at the centre the meaning of the term *Islam* namely, submission and obedience to Allah, rather than the institutionalised religion of the Prophet Muhammad, in order to rescue themselves from absolutizing their own religion by excluding the other' (Aydin, Ibid.). Within this argument, he includes non-Islamic traditions in God's universal religion. Despite differences, the believers of non-Islamic faiths are also part of universal Islam, thus they are Muslim. Aydin states 'those who submit and surrender themselves to Allah without associating anything or anyone with Allah should be considered by Muslims as persons whose rewards are assured by Allah in the Hereafter' (Aydin, Ibid.). As we see from the arguments Aydin uses to justify a pluralistic approach, it seems that his pluralism is more based on the theocentric form of pluralism rather than a Sufi-based approach.

114 Hasan Askari, *Spiritual Quest: An Inter-Religious Dimension* (Pudsey, West Yorkshire: Seven Mirrors Publishing, 1991).

115 Hasan Askari, "Within and Beyond Experience of Religious Diversity," in *The Experience of Religious Diversity*, eds. John Hick and Hasan Askari (Gower, Aldershot: Gower Publishing, 1985), 191–218.

116 Ibid., 191.

117 Ibid.

118 Ibid., 192.

119 Ibid., 194.

120 Ibid., 195.

121 Ibid.

122 Ibid., 196.

123 Ibid., 197–198.

124 Ibid., 198.

125 Ibid., 199.

126 Ibid.

127 Ibid.

128 Ibid., 208.

129 Ibid.

130 Ibid.

131 Ibid.

122 *Islamic theology of religions*

132 Ibid., 216.
133 Farid Esack, *Qur'an, Liberation and Religious Pluralism: An Islamic Perspective of Interreligious Solidarity against Oppression* (Oxford: One World Publication, 1996), 83.
134 Ibid., 61.
135 Ibid., 90–94.
136 Ibid., 87–90.
137 Ibid., 117–125.
138 Ibid., 126–134.
139 Ibid., 134–144.
140 Ibid., 184.
141 Ibid., 147.
142 Ibid., 152.
143 Ibid., 155.
144 Ibid., 158.
145 Ibid., 159.
146 Ibid., 159–160.
147 Ibid., 159.
148 Ibid., 162.
149 Such as al-Zamakhshari and al-Tabari, who are ones of the most influential *mufassirs* of classical period. See Esack, *Qur'an, Liberation and Religious Pluralism*, 162–163 and especially footnote 15.
150 Ibid., 155–161.
151 Ibid., 180.
152 Ibid., 110.
153 Farid Esack, *The Qur'an: A User's Guide* (Oxford: One World Publication, 2005), 146.
154 Reza Shah-Kazemi, *The Other in the Light of the One: The Universality of the Qur'ān and Interfaith Dialogue* (Cambridge: The Islamic Text Society, 2006), xxiv.
155 Ibid., xxv.
156 Ibid.
157 Ibid., xxvi.
158 Ibid., 63–64.
159 Ibid., 74.
160 Ibid., 75.
161 Ibid., 97.
162 Ibid., 140–141.
163 Reza Shah-Kazemi, "Beyond Polemics and Pluralism," in *Between Heaven and Hell: Islam, Salvation and the Fate of Others*, ed. Mohammad Khalil (New York: University of Oxford Press, 2013), 97.
164 Shah-Kazemi, *The Other*, 186.
165 Shah-Kazemi, "Beyond Polemics," 90.
166 When Rahner came across a Buddhist thinker who asked Rahner what he would think if he had been called an 'anonymous' Zen Buddhist, his answer was: 'I feel myself honoured by such an interpretation, even if I am obliged to regard you as being in error or if I assume that, correctly understood, to be a genuine Zen Buddhist is identical with being a genuine Christian.' Rahner, "The One Christ and the Universality of Salvation," in *Theological Investigations*, vol. 16, 219.
167 Omar, *Muslim View of Christianity*, 14.

Bibliography

Askari, Hasan. *Spritual Quest: An Inter-Religious Dimension.* Pudsey, West Yorkshire: Seven Mirrors Publishing, 1991.

———. "Within and beyond Experience of Religious Diversity." In *The Experience of Religious Diversity*, edited by John Hick and Hasan Askari, 191–218. Gower, Aldershot: Gower Publishing, 1985.

Aslan, Adnan. "Islam and Religious Pluralism." *The Islamic Quarterly* 40/3 (1996): 172–186.

Atay, Rifat. "Religious Pluralism and Islam: A Critical Examination of John Hick's Pluralistic Hypothesis." PhD diss., University of St Andrews, 1999.

Aydin, Mahmut. "Is There Only One Way to God." *Interreligious Dialogue Studies* 10 (2000): 148–158.

———. "Islam in a World Diverse Faiths: A Muslim View." In *Islam and Interfaith Relations*, edited by Perry Schmith-Leukel and Lloyd Ridgeon, 33–54. London: SCM Press, 2007.

———. "A Muslim Pluralist: Jalaluddin Rumi." In *The Myth of Religious Superiority: A Multifaith Exploration*, edited by Paul Knitter, 220–236. Maryknoll, NY: Orbis Books, 2005.

———. "Religious Pluralism." In *Muslim and Christian Reflection of Peace: Divine and Human Dimension*, edited by J. Dudley Woodberry, Osman Zumrut and Mustafa Koylu, 88–99. Lanham: University of Press of Amerika, 2005.

———. "Religious Pluralism: A Challenge for Muslims—a Theological Evaluation." *Journal of Ecumenical Studies* (Summer 2001): 330–352.

Ayoub, Mahmoud. "Islam and the Challenge of Religious Pluralism." *Global Dialogue* 2/1 (Winter 2000): 53–64.

———. *The Qur'an and Its Interpreters, Volume II: The House of 'Imran*. Albany: State University of New York Press, 1992.

Badawi, Muhammad Zaki. *The Reformers of Egypt: A Critique of al-Afgani, 'Abduh, and Ridha*. Slough: Open Press, 1976.

Burton, John. "The Exegesis of Q.2: 106 and the Islamic Theories of Naskh: mā nansakh min āya aw nansaha na'ti bi khairin minhā aw mithlihā." *Bulletin of the School of Oriental and African Studies* 48/3 (1985): 452–469.

———. "The Interpretation of Q.87, 6–7 and the Theories of *Naskh*." *Der Islam* 62 (1985): 5–19.

Cleveland, William L. *A History of the Modern Middle East*. Third Edition. Oxford: Westview Press, 2004.

D'Costa, Gavin. *Christianity and World Religions: Disputed Questions in The Theology of Religions*. Oxford: Wiley-Blackwell, 2009.

———. *Theology and Religious Pluralism: The Challenge of Other Religions*. Oxford, New York: Basil, Blackwell, 1986.

———. *Vatican II: Catholic Doctrines on Jews and Muslims*. Oxford: Oxford University Press, 2014.

Engineer, Ali. "Islam and Pluralism." In *The Myth of Religious Superiority: A Multifaith Exploration*, edited by Paul Knitter, 211–219. Maryknoll, NY: Orbis Books, 2005.

Esack, Farid. *Qur'an, Liberation and Religious Pluralism: An Islamic Perspective of Interreligious Solidarity against Oppression*. Oxford: One World Publication, 1996.

———. *The Qur'an: A User's Guide*. Oxford: Oneworld Publication, 2005.

Fieldhouse, David K. *Western Imperialism in the Middle East 1914–1958*. New York: Oxford University Press, 2006.

Freidman, Yohanan. *Tolerance and Coercion in Islam: Interfaith Relations in the Muslim Tradition*. New York: Cambridge University Press, 2003.

124 *Islamic theology of religions*

Haurani, Albert. *Arabic Thought in a Liberal Age, 1798–1939.* Cambridge: Cambridge University Press, 1983.

Huda, Qamar-ul. "Knowledge of Allah and Islamic View of Other Religions." *Theological Studies* 64 (2003): 278–305.

Khalil, Muhammad Hassan. *Islam and the Fate of Others: The Salvation Question.* New York: Oxford University Press, 2012.

Knitter, Paul. *Introducing Theologies of Religions.* Maryknoll, NY: Orbis Books, 2009.

Lamptey, Jerusha. *Never Wholly Other: A Muslima Theology of Religions.* New York: Oxford University Press, 2014.

Madelung, W. "al-Māturīdī." In *Encyclopaedia of Islam.* Second Edition, edited by P. Bearman, T. Bianquis, C.E. Bosworth, E. van Donzel and W.P. Heinrichs. Brill Online, 2015. Reference. University of Bristol. 15 October 2014. http://reference works.brillonline.com/entries/encyclopaedia-of-islam-2/al-maturidi-SIM_5045.

Nasr, Seyyed Hossein. "Islam and Encounter of Religions and Islam's Attitude towards Other Religion in History." In *The Religious Other: Towards a Muslim Theology of Religions in a Post-Prophetic Age*, edited by Muhammad Suheyl Umar, 83–120. Lahore: Iqbal Pakistan Academy, 2008.

———. "The Islamic View of Christianity." In *Christianity through Non-Christian Eyes*, edited by Paul Griffiths, 126–134. Maryknoll, NY: Orbis Books, 1990.

Omar, Irfan A., ed. *Muslim View of Christianity: Essays on Dialogue by Mahmoud Ayoub.* Maryknoll, NY: Orbis Books, 2007.

Qadhi, Yasir. "The Path of Allah or the Paths of Allah? Revisiting Classical and Medieval Sunni Approaches to Salvation of Others." In *Between Heaven and Hell: Islam, Salvation and the Fate of Others*, edited by Mohammad Khalil, 110–122. New York: University of Oxford Press, 2013.

Qutb, Sayyid. *In the Shade of the Qur'an, vol. 1*, 1951–1965. http://ia700803.us.archive.org/27/items/InTheShadeOfTheQuranSayyidQutb/Volume_1_surah_1–2.pdf (accessed September 10, 2015).

———. *In the Shade of the Qur'an, vol. 2*, 1951–1965. http://ia700803.us.archive.org/27/items/InTheShadeOfTheQuranSayyidQutb/Volume_2_surah_3.pdf (accessed September 10, 2015).

———. *In the Shade of the Qur'an, vol. 3*, 1951–1965. http://ia700803.us.archive.org/27/items/InTheShadeOfTheQuranSayyidQutb/Volume_3_surah_4.pdf (accessed September 10, 2015).

———. *In the Shade of the Qur'an, vol. 7*, 1951–1965. http://ia700803.us.archive.org/27/items/InTheShadeOfTheQuranSayyidQutb/Volume_7_surah_8.pdf (accessed September 10, 2015).

———. *In the Shade of the Qur'an, vol. 8*, 1951–1965. http://ia700803.us.archive.org/27/items/InTheShadeOfTheQuranSayyidQutb/Volume_7_surah_8.pdf (accessed September 10, 2015).

———. *In the Shade of the Qur'an, vol. 16*, 1951–1965. http://ia700803.us.archive.org/27/items/InTheShadeOfTheQuranSayyidQutb/volume_16_surahs_48–61.pdf (accessed September 10, 2015).

Race, Alan. *Christians and Religious Pluralism.* London: SCM Press, 1983/1993.

Rahman, Fazlur. *Islam and Modernity: Transformation of an Intellectual Tradition.* Chicago: University of Chicago Press, 1982.

———. *Major Themes of the Qur'an.* Second Edition. Chicago, London: University of Chicago Press, 2009.

Rahner, Karl. *Theological Investigations, Vol.16: Experience of the Spirit: Source of Theology.* London: Darton, Longman & Todd, 1979.

Sachedina, Abdulaziz. "Political Implications of the Islamic Notions of 'Supersession' as Reflected in Islamic Jurisprudence." *Islam and Christian-Muslim Relations* 7/2 (1996): 159–168.

Saeed, Adullah. *Interpreting the Qur'ān: Towards a Contemporary Approach.* Abingdon, New York: Routledge, 2006.

Shah-Kazemi, Reza. "Beyond Polemics and Pluralism: The Universal Message of the Qur'an." In *Between Heaven and Hell: Islam, Salvation and the Fate of Others,* edited by Mohammad Khalil, 88–104. New York: University of Oxford Press, 2013.

———. *The Other in the Light of One: The Universality of the Qur'an and Interfaith Dialogue.* Cambridge: Islamic Text Society, 2006.

Shavit, Uriya. "Can Muslims Befriend Non-Muslims? Debating al-walā' wa-al-barā' (Loyalty and Disavowal) in Theory and Practice." *Islam and Christian-Muslim Relations* 25/1 (2014): 67–88.

Soage, Ana. "Islamism and Modernity: The Political Thought of Sayyid Qutb." *Totaliritarian Movements and Political Religions* 10/2 (June 2009): 189–203.

Troll, Christian W. *Sayyid Ahmad Khan: Reinterpretation of Muslim Tehology.* New Delhi: Vikas Publishing House, 1978.

Waardenburg, Jacques, ed. *Muslim Perceptions of Other Religions.* New York, Oxford: Oxford University Press, 1999.

———. *Muslim and Others: Relations in Context.* Berlin: Walter Gruyter, 2003.

Winkler, Lewis. *Contemporary Muslim and Christian Responses to Religious Pluralism: Wolfhart Pannenberg in Dialogue with Abdulaziz Sachedina.* Eugene: Pickwick Publications, 2011.

Winter, Tim. "Realism and the Real." In *Between Heaven and Hell: Islam, Salvation and the Fate of Others,* edited by Mohammad Khalil, 123–155. New York: University of Oxford Press, 2013.

4 Jerusha Lamptey's theology of religions

Introduction

In the previous chapter, I have outlined Islamic theology of religions and argued that none of the theologies I have examined offer a sufficient framework to address the Islamic understanding of other religions. In this chapter, however, I will offer Jerusha Lamptey's theology as an alternative theology, which might be considered as departing from both traditional and contemporary liberal Muslim theologians' theologies. What makes Lamptey a unique theologian is the type of methodology she uses. She combines several different approaches and offers her owns. In this chapter, I will focus on Lamptey's theology of religions. Before discussing her intellectual ideas, it is important to provide some biographical information.

She earned her BA in Anthropology and Religion in 1997 at the American University, Washington D.C. After completing her BA she received a Fulbright Scholarship and carried out research in Ghana between 2000 and 2002. Her experiences there led her to her conversion to Islam.[1] She received her master in Islamic sciences at the Graduate School of Islamic and Social Sciences in Leesburg, Virginia, in 2004, and her PhD in theological and religious studies with a focus on religious pluralism at Georgetown University in 2011. She is currently working at Union Theological Seminary Faculty as an assistant professor of Islam and ministry.

Her recent book *Never Wholly Other: A Muslima Theology of Religious Pluralism*[2] will be the main source which I will look at in this chapter, although relevant articles[3] and book chapters[4] will also be examined. In addition, the works that she has mainly used to construct her theology of religions will be examined throughout this chapter.

Two reasons make Lamptey unique and worthy of study: firstly, her contribution to the field of theology of religions and, secondly, the methodology she uses. She offers something new in the Islamic theology of religions. As I have outlined in the previous chapter, Muslim scholars have followed two different ways in articulating the Islamic view of other religions: they either ignore any goodness or truths in non-Islamic religions, or they equate non-Islamic religions with Islam. Both positions fail to adequately value the real otherness of non-Islamic religions. From that perspective, appreciating the

Jerusha Lamptey's theology of religions   127

insights and problems of these two positions, Lamptey's theology of religion can be seen as an alternative.

I have presented Williams's theology of religions in the second chapter of this work. There I have argued that his theology of religions shows a radical openness towards other, when put into practice, although he outlines a more exclusivist theology at theoretical level. On the other hand, Lamptey's theoretical framework provides her own form of theology of religions with a great openness towards the difference of the religious other. There seems to be some contradictory elements within these two theologians' theologies that derive from their specific contexts. For example, the difference between a young Muslim woman who seeks to address religious pluralism from a more feminist-oriented point of view versus a senior Christian male theologian who takes Christian orthodoxy as starting point to respond to religious pluralism and the search for building a new theology of religions within the Islamic theology of religions versus being critical of theorising an alternative model within the Christian theology of religions. Even though, these elements seem to contradict each other; in fact they can be complementary. Whilst Williams does not seek to develop his theology of religions, but in practice he addresses many questions raised within Christian theology of religions, Lamptey proposes her theology of religions with specific attention to what has been produced in Islamic theology of religions. So, it is safe to assume that the former engages with theology of religions mostly in practice, whereas the latter builds a theology which might require a practical application. Moreover, Lamptey's Muslima theology[5] (with her own words) approach does not necessarily contradict Williams's theology as both take into consideration religious differences. Her approach to theology of religions derives from the idea that differences are a matter which needs to be addressed. Consequently, she uses Christian feminist theologians who request to address the difference of religions in her methodology. Additionally, both Lamptey and Williams are critical of the theocentric form of pluralism, which prioritises the sameness/similarities of religions. Hence, it appears that both theologians have some common concerns in their response to religious pluralism in spite of the differences in their theological approaches.

This chapter will focus on Lamptey's theology of religions. Firstly, it will consider the typology she has outlined for contemporary theology of religions in Islamic discourse. Secondly, each stage of Lamptey's threefold methodological development will be given. Thirdly, it will move onto Lamptey's theology of religions, and finally, some analytical remarks will be offered in conclusion.

1 A map of contemporary Islamic theology of religions

Lamptey analyses contemporary Islamic theology of religions in the light of how theologians appreciate similarities and differences. As outlined in the previous chapter, scholars who examine Islamic responses to religious

128 *Jerusha Lamptey's theology of religions*

diversity mainly borrow Race's typology and apply it to Islamic theology of religions. However, Lamptey does not use Race's classification as her primary way of organising contemporary Islamic theology of religions. She examines contemporary Islamic responses to religious diversity using three different categories: prioritisation of sameness, simultaneous affirmation of sameness and difference, and prioritisation of difference.

The first group overemphasises the commonality among religions while ignoring differences. I have categorised them as advocates of a theocentric form of pluralism in the previous chapter. Lamptey examines some contemporary Muslim theologians' theology of religions, including Ali Engineer,[6] Abdulaziz Sachedina[7] and Mahmut Aydin,[8] and she shows how they fail to see the differences of non-Islamic religions. As I have pointed out in the previous chapter, the theocentric form of pluralism in the Islamic tradition does not go as far as Hick does in Christianity, although there is considerable overlap with the Hickian theocentric model. The common point between these theologians is that each highlights the Qur'anic verses on the single unity of all religions while disregarding other Qur'anic verses related to differences. As a result of their overdependence on the sameness of religions and the use of the Qur'anic verses in that direction, when Lamptey analyses Engineer's pluralism, she claims that Engineer uses the Qur'anic verses in the same manner as the exclusivist theologians. She contends:

> While sameness, unity, and respect in the face of diversity are core aspects of the Qur'an, they do not exist in isolation. Engineer does not probe their relationship to more "pluralism-ambivalent" aspects of the Qur'an, such as *shirk* (ascribing partners to God). Rather, he employs a selective textual methodology that prioritizes sameness and fails to substantially engage difference. Notably, the selective textual methodology (proof texting) that Engineer employs to affirm religious pluralism and stress sameness is the same methodological approach used by other historical and contemporary scholars to arrive at an exclusivist reading of the text that prioritizes difference. In both cases, only aspects of the Qur'an that bolster the respective positions- that is, pluralism or exclusivism- are acknowledged, and all other aspects of the text that run counter to or complexify these conclusions are ignored or summarily dismissed.[9]

She raises similar critiques against both Sachedina and Aydin, contending that Sachedina 'reduces the importance of the external differences introduced by revelation'.[10] Similarly, she contends that Aydin oversimplifies religious differences and overemphasises the sameness of religions. She thinks that all three theologians regard differences as boundaries that create conflict. Thus, they devalue and downplay differences and emphasise sameness.[11]

The second group confirms religious differences and sameness simultaneously. In the second group she evaluates perennial philosophers such as Seyyed Hossein Nasr,[12] Reza Shah-Kazemi[13] and a more particularist

Jerusha Lamptey's theology of religions 129

theologian Muhammad Legenhausen.[14] Again, as has been pointed out in the previous chapter, the first two theologians offer a mystical form of pluralism. Unlike the theocentric form of pluralism, this form of pluralism attaches importance to religious differences as well. In that form, divine unity is affirmed, and divine unity has been regarded as the source of diversity. All three of these theologians offer a vision of pluralism which explicitly contrasts with Hick's pluralism and implicitly with the theocentric form of Islamic pluralism. Rather than considering world religions as historically and culturally conditioned responses to the same Reality (as in Hick's case), they regard diverse religions as divinely intended.[15]

Shah-Kazemi and Legenhausen label their theology of religions universalism and nonreductive pluralism, respectively. They both accept the salvific efficacy of non-Islamic religions in certain aspects, though accepting the supersessionism theory. Shah-Kazemi promotes a Sufi approach in which non-Islamic religions were considered both salvifically effective and divinely ordained.[16] However, on the one hand, Legenhausen displays similarities with Christian post-liberal theologians in placing too much emphasis on differences and the incommensurability of religions.[17] On the other hand, unlike most post-liberals, he accepts the salvific efficacy of non-Islamic traditions. Although both theologians value non-Islamic religions, they classify Islam as the only true religion among others. As a result, Lamptey criticises them for providing a hierarchical classification of religions.[18] She contends that

> separation and hierarchical evaluation maintain boundaries and difference, and although sameness is acknowledged it is not permitted to eradicate or blur such boundaries . . . [for] Legenhausen, divine revelation is acknowledged in respect to other religions, but divine revelation also creates bounded communities that are deontologically commanded in successive and linear order without any overlap.[19]

The third group of theologians Lamptey examines rejects sameness and places much more emphasis on differences to affirm the superiority of the Islamic faith. Her third group resonates one the one hand with exclusivist theology and on the other hand with post-liberal theology of religions. In this section, Lamptey primarily evaluates Winter,[20] and interestingly she also places Legenhausen in this group as she thinks Winter's and Legenhausen's theologies overlap in certain aspects. I have categorised Winter as representative of exclusivist theology in the Islamic tradition in the previous chapter. Briefly, I explained that Winter's theological view regarding non-Islamic faiths is that Islam supersedes all other religions, which are corrupted and no longer valid. Thus Islam is the only true religion and the one which leads its believers to salvation. Lamptey believes that although Winter and Legenhausen construct different forms of theology of religions, they use generally similar notions such as supersession, salvation, divine mercy and tolerance to construct their approaches.[21] Winter, however, is a classical

130 Jerusha Lamptey's theology of religions

exclusivist who reiterates the mediaeval form of exclusivism, while Legenhausen attempts to develop a theology that accepts goodness and truths in other religions but also ranks Islam in the highest position among others. Although both theologians underline the need for tolerance and dialogue with other faiths, Lamptey thinks that the way they approach tolerance is 'provocative'. She claims:

> Winter advocates for a tolerance that is humble, worldly, and paternalistic, a tolerance that recognizes valid origins but makes no pretense about legitimacy. Legenhausen advocates for a tolerance that rests upon some degree of recognition of the truth and guidance in other traditions, and recognition that salvation is connected to divine mercy alone. The need to explicitly make this caveat about tolerance while promoting an exclusive theology is provocative.[22]

Lamptey's critique of both theologians' creation of a hierarchical classification of religions is important, but her claim that exclusivist theology leads to intolerance seems an overreaching claim. Firstly, it is necessary for her to define 'tolerance' and 'intolerance' and then consider whether theological exclusivism is connected to social and political intolerance. In the previous chapter, I offered two forms of exclusivism: sociopolitical and theological. While the sociopolitical form of exclusivism leads to intolerance, theological exclusivism does not necessarily lead to social and political exclusivism. Although Winter's theology fails to establish a fruitful engagement with non-Muslims, to label his theology as intolerant is unfair. Secondly, Legenhausen's theology of religions can be used as an example of post-liberal particularism in the Islamic tradition. Borrowing from Knitter, I have labelled post-liberal theology the 'Acceptance Model', which accepts other religions the way they are in reality. Thus, Lamptey's criticism of Legenhausen also seems to fail. However, both Winter's and Legenhausen's theologies of religions, with their emphasis on supersessionism, have some problems, which I have demonstrated in the previous chapter.

There seems to be a considerable overlap between Lamptey's and Race's respective classifications in certain areas. Her three distinct categories correspond to pluralism, inclusivism and exclusivism, respectively, though her nuancing differs from Race. However, it should be also noted that although Lamptey's first and third categories correspond to Race' pluralism and exclusivism, respectively, her second category does not correspond directly to inclusivism. In the second category, she includes a Sufi approach, which is considered to be closer to pluralist theology than inclusivist. Furthermore, for Race's classification, the key criterion is whether a particular theology of religions accepts non-Christian religions as valid religions that lead to salvation. Lamptey, however, categorises each response according to whether non-Islamic traditions resemble or differ from Islam. In other words, Lamptey's classification neither takes religious epistemology or soteriology as a starting point, but rather she constructs her classification with regards to attitudes to similarity and difference of diverse religions. Despite some similarities, it should be noted that Race's classification is much broader than Lamptey as there have been more theological responses to religious pluralism in the Christian tradition. Moreover, scholars like Lamptey, including myself, mainly use English or translated works, while in the Islamic tradition theologians produce such works in their local language. Apart from these three categories, Lamptey also presents Esack and al-Faruqi[23] as alternatives to those as she thinks both these authors present different and more acceptable approaches.

As I have demonstrated in the previous chapter, Esack presents a liberation theology of religions that prioritises the struggle against oppression as the most important common ground among religions. When Esack outlines his theology, he offers dynamic interpretations of such terms used in the Qur'an as *iman*, *islam*, disbelief, People of Book and more. His interpretation of these terms appeals to Lamptey since she believes that Esack successfully offers a complex and dynamic negotiation between the Qur'anic categories of the religious other.[24] Like Esack, Lamptey also interprets the Qur'anic categories in a dynamic way. Lamptey also admires al-Faruqi's theology of religions. There are two notions of al-Faruqi's theology that Lamptey utilises. Firstly, al-Faruqi believes that 'divine transcendence implies that all men are equally creaturely, and hence, nothing differentiates them from one another except personal achievement.'[25] Lamptey also develops her theology in accordance with the universality of divine transcendence and its confrontation with each human being. Secondly, al-Faruqi's notion of *din al-fitra* (natural religion) presumes that each human being possesses *din al-fitra*. Traditionally, *din al-fitra* has been interpreted as the religion of Islam, but for al-Faruqi all religions, including Islam, are assessed and reformed by it. Lamptey in her theology of religions does not use this notion; instead she uses the notion of *taqwā* (piety, God-consciousness), which is not identified strictly with Islamic belief but rather can be possessed and manifested by all humanity.

Lamptey wants to move beyond all three categories and offer something new to the current discussion. Though appreciating each response of theologians to religious pluralism, and seeing them as valid and valuable, she thinks that the theologians she has analysed assume that the conception of religious difference must be interpreted as something dividing humanity 'through the erection of clear, static, and impermeable boundaries'.[26] Thus, they either ignore and isolate difference or rank it hierarchically. Furthermore, she contends that all three responses fail to 'integrate – rather than prioritize – a number of diverse topics including religious sameness, religious difference, interaction, dynamic relationality, and the teleological value of religious difference'.[27] These failures of contemporary discourse on religious pluralism lead her to develop her own theology of religions, which will be discussed in the next section.

132 *Jerusha Lamptey's theology of religions*

2 Lamptey's theology of religions

As discussed previously, Lamptey starts her theology of religions by questioning how to relate the diverse religions to Islam. Her primary concern is how to understand the believers of other faiths and how to relate their otherness to the Islamic faith. For Lamptey, contemporary trends in Islamic theology of religions see religious communities 'as being wholly discrete, clearly defined, and unchanging entities',[28] thus it is necessary and urgent 'to search for an alternative conception of difference, a conception that is not premised upon discrete and fixed boundaries.[29] As a result, she offers a Muslima theology of religions in Islamic tradition. She deliberately chooses to use the term 'Muslima theology' rather than Islamic feminism due to controversy surrounding the usage of the latter term. Muslima is an Arabic term which refers to a female Muslim. She describes her approach as follows:

> [M]y approach arises out of my positioning as a believing and practicing Muslim. More importantly, it indicates that I endeavor to articulate a theology of religions through a critical reappraisal and revisiting of the central Islamic sources, primarily the Qur'ān. This theology of religions is rooted in the Islamic tradition while simultaneously probing and testing the bounds of that tradition.[30]

The reasons why she has termed her theology of religions as Muslima theology depend on her experience and theoretical choice. Experientially, she wants to show her experience as a woman. Theoretically, she benefits from Muslim women scholars' methodology of interpretations of the Qur'an and non-Muslim feminist theologians' theological positions towards the believers of other religions.

2.1 Methodology

Like many other contemporary theologians, Lamptey also uses the Qur'an as the main source to construct her theology of religions. Apart from theological exclusivists who take Islamic tradition and traditional theologians seriously, the advocators of all other forms make use of the Qur'an as the primary source, and they use Sunnah and other sources if necessary, though using different interpretation methods. Although Lamptey does not reject the authority of other sources, she believes the hermeneutical method she utilises to interpret the Qur'an also helps her make use of other sources.[31] Thus, her theology of religions does not promote a Qur'an-only approach but promotes a new method of interpretation of the Qur'an.

Lamptey follows three stages in her methodology of Muslima theology of religions, which I will summarise here briefly before explaining them in detail. In the first stage, she examines Muslim women's interpretation of the Qur'an. Her aim is to take seriously the conceptual and hermeneutical contributions of Muslim women interpreters of the Qur'an, specifically their insights on the conception of sexual differences, and then to apply these to other faiths. Since Muslim women's approaches to the religious other does not satisfy Lamptey, she moves onto the next stage, where she examines feminist non-Muslim theologians' approaches to religious pluralism. In the final stage, she engages with Izutsu's intra-Qur'anic and synchronic semantic methodology as she believes Izutsu's hermeneutical approach can help her develop her Muslima theology of religions.

In addition to these three stages, she also utilises Jonathan Smith's concept of the proximate other. Smith, in *Differential Equations*,[32] claims that the most basic sense of other is generated by the binary opposition of *IN/OUT*,[33] or *WE (HUMAN)/THEY (NOT HUMAN)*.[34] For Smith, in these two binary oppositions, the concept of other is a remote other, which is not perceived as problematic and dangerous.[35] In other words, in that notion of otherness, the other is perceived either as *LIKE-US* or *NOT-LIKE-US*; either they are in or out. He adds a third form of otherness, the proximate other/the near neighbour, which is the most complex and troublesome. In this conception, the other is perceived as *TOO-MUCH-LIKE US*, or it claims *TO-BE-US*. Smith's concept of the proximate other is the starting point for Lamptey to develop her theology of religions. When she relates non-Islamic religions to Islam, she uses proximate otherness. For Lamptey the religious other as proximate other 'blurs boundaries and compels ongoing, complex theological and practical consideration'.[36]

The following sections will discuss the three stages of Lamptey's methodology in turn.

2.1.1 Contribution of Muslim women interpreters of the Qur'an

Lamptey's Muslima theological approach takes its roots from contemporary Muslim women's interpretations of the methodology of Qur'anic study. Since she urges reinterpretation of the Qur'an, it is necessary for her to consider different methodological approaches in a contemporary context. For her, contemporary women's approach to the Qur'an is vital to contextualise her theology of religions for two reasons. Firstly, in Islamic history, women were either silent, silenced or generally unheard. They suffered from interpretative voicelessness; that is to say, their voice was excluded in Islamic tradition. Secondly, the main contribution of women interpreters is to highlight the Qur'anic conception of human difference, specifically biological and sexual difference.[37] Thus, drawing on their methodologies, Lamptey attempts to generalise and utilise their methodologies for treating the conception of religious differences. In other words, she takes the methodological frameworks based on sexual differences and then applies it to religious difference.

From this perspective, she analyses contemporary Muslim women such as Amina Wadud,[38] Asma Barlas[39] and Riffat Hassan.[40] Lamptey draws three methodological conclusions from each of these Muslim women's interpretations.

134 *Jerusha Lamptey's theology of religions*

Firstly, the main characteristic of these women's interpretations is that they promote reinterpretation of the Qur'an. In other words, they offer an alternative rereading of the Qur'an, relative to both the traditional and modern exegetical methodologies.[41] Their rereading of the Qur'an takes the Qur'an itself as the primary source to understand its own context and meaning: this requires a 'close intratextual reading; cross referencing of grammar, syntax, terminology, and structure; contextualization and recontextualization; and elucidation of larger Qur'ānic themes, [so that] the Qur'ān becomes the principal source of its own intratextual explication'.[42] Their promotion of the Qur'an as the primary source emanates from the fact that traditionally Muslims have used sources other than the Qur'an, especially *aḥādīth* (narratives about the life, sayings and praxis of Prophet) to justify a patriarchal reading of the Qur'an.[43] Thus, they take the Qur'an as an interpretative tool of the Qur'an itself. These intratextual and cross-referencing outcomes help Lamptey to move her theology onto the next stage, where she utilises Izutsu's semantic methodology.

Secondly, these three women believe that every attempt to interpret the Qur'an is an act of human interpretation.[44] Wadud believes that there is no method of interpreting the Qur'an that is fully objective. Every interpreter makes some kind of subjective choice. Some details of exegetes' interpretations reflect their subjective choices, not necessarily the intent of the text.[45] As a result, the Qur'anic text is polysemic, which means that it is open to multiple interpretations. For these scholars, the content of interpretation is directly connected with the methodological approach of interpreters. This second methodological outcome directs Lamptey to appreciate all the attempts of contemporary Muslims in addressing the question of religious pluralism since each theologian reflects his or her own methodological reading of the Qur'an. Of course that is not to say that all offer the exact meaning of the words of God, which would lead to relativism, but rather they offer them as possible interpretations.

Finally and most importantly, contemporary Muslim women offer a novel understanding of the Qur'anic discourse on men and women. Traditionally, Muslim scholars have created a static hierarchical ranking between men and women, which subordinated women and placed them in a position as if they had an indirect relationship with God. Using their methodological insights however, Muslim women attempt to show that men and women are the same with respect to creation. Wadud, for instance, takes the Qur'anic rhetoric of 'believing men' and 'believing women' and argues that there is no essential difference between men and women with regard to creation in the purpose of the Book and in the reward it promises.[46] Barlas similarly indicates that God does not privilege men as men or subordinate women as women.[47] Hassan also makes a similar argument when she states,

> Not only does the Qur'ān make it clear that man and woman stand absolutely equal in the sight of God, but also that they are "members"

and "protectors" of each other. In other words, the Qur'ān does not create a hierarchy in which men are placed above women, nor does it pit men against women in an adversary relationship.[48]

Despite the underlying sameness of men and women, these scholars are also aware of difference, although they believe that sexual difference should never lead to hierarchical differentiation and that sexual difference is irrelevant with regard to moral agency.[49] From this perspective, using such Qur'anic verses as 33:35, 116:17 and 48:5–6, Wadud and Barlas offer *taqwā* (piety, God-consciousness) as a test of hierarchical differences between sexual groups.[50] *Taqwā*, for Muslim feminist scholars, should be assessed at the individual level rather than based on affiliation with a particular sex. These scholars use the concept of *taqwā* to respond to sexual differences by deconstructing gender hierarchies. What matters before God is not biological sex but level of piety, and both men and women have the same potential for *taqwā*. Lamptey wishes to go a step further and to utilise the concept of *taqwā* for another level of difference, religious difference. It becomes the focal point of Lamptey's theology of religions.

In spite of using the methodological frameworks of these Muslim women, Lamptey does not follow their approaches to religious differences. Wadud does not discuss religious diversity separately, although both Hassan and Barlas address the Islamic response to religious pluralism.[51] Their approach does not satisfy Lamptey, however, as she thinks that Hassan's engagement with the religious other is an example of the first model she has offered, prioritising similarity over difference (theocentric pluralism in my classification).[52] In addition for Lamptey, Barlas's approach does not promote a dynamic relationship with the other; rather, in her theology, religious otherness is defined as an opposition.[53]

Lamptey's treatment of Muslim women is very clever and impressive. Although these women successfully give a voice to women who have been subordinated in terms of their engagement with religious pluralism they repeat the early model of pluralism, which is the theocentric model. Like Rahman, whose methodology also has been adapted by these women, or others who were the first individuals in the modern era to respond to religious pluralism, they have developed a theocentric model of pluralism. Since every theory is a product of a certain time and culture, their treatment of religious difference at that time can be considered authentic and appropriate. In recent decades, there has been a shift from pluralism to particularism, from sameness to difference within Christian theology of religions. The appearance of particularism caused even pluralist theologians to revise their version of pluralism. Knitter can be used as an excellent example in this respect. We are left in a position to either confirm sameness or difference. However, Lamptey attempts to treat sameness and difference equally since an either/or position does not help us to fully contextualise the religious other. In the next chapter, I will also attempt to respond to this problem

136 *Jerusha Lamptey's theology of religions*

by utilising the methodologies of theologians I have given throughout the preceding chapters.

As a consequence of Lamptey's dissatisfaction with contemporary Muslim approaches to religious others, she turns her focus to non-Muslim feminist theologians' theology of religions and aims to find the methodological and conceptual conclusions within these approaches to apply them to her theology of religions. The next section will focus on Lamptey's use and treatment of feminist theologians' perceptions of the religious other.

2.1.2 *Contributions of non-Muslim feminist theologians*

Feminist theologians' theological perceptions of religious diversity have a very significant place in Lamptey's theology of religions. They provide something which Muslim theologians have not offered, an applicable methodology and sources which address religious diversity, sameness and difference and criticise the theology of religions, in particular the positions on Race's typology: exclusivism, inclusivism and pluralism. Lamptey analyses some contemporary feminist theologians[54] but does not necessarily support all she has engaged with. She seeks to integrate feminist theologians' theology into her Muslima theology approach. Even though she aims to transform women's otherness into religious otherness, she is aware that that kind of transformation amounts to oversimplification.[55]

Lamptey takes two major conclusions from contemporary feminist theologians. Firstly, taking the core point of Ursula King's, Jeannie Hill Fletcher's, MacGarvey's[56] and Kwok's theologies, she attempts to implement in Islamic discourse the idea that religious difference does not divide humanity 'through the erection of clear, static, and impermeable boundaries'.[57] From this perspective she takes Hill Fletcher's contribution of identity,[58] Kwok's critique of the category of reified religion[59] and McGarvey's explanation of the focus on either sameness or difference.[60] In her Muslima theology she aims to follow these scholars in attempting to move beyond the standard models and to construct a new model.[61]

Secondly, she combines these feminist approaches with Muslim women interpreters for her Muslima theology. In her theology she aims to diverge from standard models of theology of religions (including exclusivism, inclusivism and pluralism) that are based on difference or sameness alone and instead to articulate an integrated, multifaceted alternative. She wants to treat both religious sameness and difference equally as well as showing the relationship between the two. She contends:

> In reference to religious difference, *Muslima* theology will challenge the fixation with viewing difference as dividing humanity through the erection of clear, static, and impermeable boundaries. In contrast, it will utilize the insights of identity theory to explore the complex and dynamic web of relationality that exists within the Qur'ānic discourse on the religious Other.[62]

2.1.3 Contribution of Izutsu's semantic analysis

The third methodological approach Lamptey considers is Toshihiko Izutsu's semantic[63] analysis of the Qur'an. There are two conclusions of Izutsu's methodology from which Lamptey benefits. Firstly, like Muslim women interpreters, Izutsu's Qur'anic interpretation methodology also prioritises intratextuality. Lamptey extends the boundaries of the ideas she has taken from Muslim women interpreters and combines it with Izutsu's semantic field approach.[64] Secondly, Izutsu's semantic analysis distinguishes between the basic and relational meanings of the words that are used in the Qur'an. According to Izutsu, in addition to their basic meaning, every word has a relational meaning, 'a connotative meaning defined by its complex and particular relations to other Qur'ānic words and concepts'.[65]

Lamptey is attracted to Izutsu's semantic analysis because it helps her examine the usage of the terms in the Qur'an and place them in a dynamic relationship. Izutsu's semantic analysis offers 'multiple relationships to many other words that properly belong to other fields'.[66] Taking this into account, Lamptey's Muslima theology seeks to address the problem of religious relationality. Although she uses Izutsu's methodology, she disagrees with Izutsu's examination of Qur'anic religious classification. Izutsu essentially classifies religious diversity into two groups: *mu'min* (believer) and *kāfir* (disbeliever). According to Izutsu, these groups are opposites.[67] For Lamptey however, belief and disbelief should not necessarily be understood as opposites. The main object of her theology is to offer a 'holistic mapping of the Qur'an's dynamic religious relations and categories'.[68]

Having established the three tenets of Lamptey's methodology, the next section will focus on Lamptey's theology of religions.

2.2 Lamptey's theology of religions

As has been outlined, Lamptey's theology of religions combines different methodologies and offers an authentic and alternative theology. I will outline her theology of religions using four claims. Firstly, Lamptey claims that religious difference should be understood as lateral, not hierarchical. Secondly, the concept of *taqwā* should be a means of hierarchical difference among people rather than the religions themselves. Thirdly, the attainment of salvation should be seen as something that is individually achieved, not something that requires membership of a specific group. Finally, every religious community is subject to corruption, or change, including the Islamic community.

Starting with the first claim, Lamptey borrows the Muslim interpreter Barlas's distinction of biological differences.[69] Barlas offers two forms of sexual differences: lateral and hierarchical. While lateral difference is divinely intended, hierarchical difference is not sex specific and is instead on the basis of *taqwā*. Expanding these two forms of difference, Lamptey claims that difference among religions should be understood as lateral.[70] In this

138 *Jerusha Lamptey's theology of religions*

respect she rejects the exclusivist claim of the superiority of Islam. She provides three characteristics of lateral difference. Firstly, lateral difference is a group phenomenon. 'It primarily refers not to individual particularities but rather to patterns and trends of difference at the group level.'[71] She believes that as groups, the Sabians, Magians, Jews, Children of Israel, Nazarenes and the People of the Scripture, who are mentioned in the Qur'an, plainly fulfill the first characteristic of lateral difference: they denote difference that exists on a collective level rather than on the individual level.[72] Secondly, lateral difference is divinely intended; in other words, it is not a consequence of the human error of corruption. Thirdly, this form of difference never serves 'as the basis of evaluation'.[73] This argument does not mean that Lamptey rejects any kind of evaluation, rather she thinks that any singular evaluation would not be ascribed to an entire group. Thus, by placing religions laterally Lamptey believes that although each religion's laws and practices might be different, this does not mean that one is superior to the other. What makes people, not religions, superior is *taqwā*. She contends that 'the hierarchical exhortation to *taqwā* is something common in all revelations whereas the lateral laws, rites, and ways are particular to each revelation.'[74]

Her second claim occupies an extremely significant place in Lamptey's theology of religions. By distinguishing between lateral and hierarchical difference, she places *taqwā* above such terms as *iman* and *islam*. While exclusivist theologians believe that these terms cannot be applied to non-Muslims, pluralist theologians interpret these terms differently and expand their usage. For instance, the theocentric form of pluralism promotes the idea of universality of *islam* and *iman*.

Lamptey's prioritising of *taqwā* helps her accept the religious other as both the same and different simultaneously. She defines *taqwā* as follows, 'Taqwā is piety, but piety is devotion to God, awe of God, mindfulness or consciousness of God, worship of God, and even fear of God.'[75] Further, she shows different usages of *taqwā* in the Qur'an to be related not only to belief but also to action,[76] an orientation toward God and a constant awareness of God[77] as a framework for social and familial relations.[78] She believes that *taqwā* is not something that can be achieved once and completely, rather it is something that is active and constantly striven for and sustained.[79]

Lamptey does not reject the concept of *iman* and *islam*, but rather she prioritises *taqwā*. She is aware of different categories used in the Qur'an to address religious diversity. In this respect she analyses categories such as *iman* (belief), *islam*[80] (submission), *hanif*[81] (nondenominational monotheism), *kufr*[82] (disbelief), *shirk*[83] (ascribing partners to God) and *nifaq*[84] (hypocrisy), like Esack does. Unlike Esack, however, Lamptey also looks at these words in connection with the concept of *taqwā* and in their intratextual relations to each other.

From this perspective, Lamptey presents the different manifestations of each category to show their relations with *taqwā* and each other. She differentiates three different facets of *taqwā*. The first tenet of *taqwā* is 'recognition of and attitude towards God', in other words, a recognising of God's

Jerusha Lamptey's theology of religions 139

existence and understanding of God's power'.[85] While the concepts of *iman*, *islam* and *hanif* are used in positive relations with the concept of *taqwā*, other concepts are used in a negative way in the Qur'an. For example, the Qur'anic verse 8:2[86] describes those who are faithful (*mu'minun*) as the ones who put their trust (*tawakkul*) in their Lord. Lamptey interprets 'to put trust in the Lord' as a recognizing of God and his power. In contrast to *iman*, those who commit *kufr* or *shirk* show a negative attitude toward the recognition of God. Thus those who perform *kufr* display a lack of appreciation for God's abundant favours.[87] In terms of the recognition of God, *iman* and *kufr* seem to be opposite to each other (belief and disbelief). From this perspective, the question can be asked whether those who do not have the concept of God can be categorised as disbelievers. Lamptey does not classify people who do not recognise God's existence as disbelievers, and for her *kufr* cannot be used as an absence of belief.[88] She contends:

> One of most striking aspects of the Qur'ānic discourse is that it does not discuss people who do not recognize the existence of God. In other words, there is no discourse aimed at atheism or a group of people that could be considered atheists. This is an especially important point in reference to common English translations of some of the hierarchical concepts. For example, *kāfir* (disbeliever) is commonly translated as "unbeliever," thereby implying the utter absence of belief. The Qur'ān, however, depicts all of humanity as acknowledging the existence of God.[89]

The second tenet of *taqwā* is 'humankind's response to God's guidance'.[90] Taking the example of *iman*, there are several characteristics of *iman* as a response to God's guidance. Those who manifest *iman* in God's guidance do so insofar as they 'hear and obey revelation',[91] 'revelation increases their iman',[92] and '[they] do not draw distinctions among God's revelations or messengers'.[93] Similar to *iman*'s relationship with *taqwā*, other categories also have different characteristics. Generally, categories of *iman*, *islam* and *hanif* manifest an active and positive response to God's guidance, whereas *kufr*, *shirk* and *nifaq* are deliberate denials of God's guidance.

The third tenet of *taqwā* is relates to the 'type and nature of actions'.[94] In this sense, *taqwā* is not only related to belief but also to action. *Taqwā* is associated with 'praying, giving charity, performing good deeds, and demonstrating kindness in social and familial relations'.[95] As with recognition of God and response to God, some categories manifest with the concept of *taqwā* positively, while others do not respond positively. Here, Lamptey quotes several verses regarding each category to demonstrate that belief and action are two dimensions of *taqwā*.[96]

From her description of each category, it would be useful to establish some implementations for better understanding. Firstly, Lamptey believes each category is not defined by a single trait. The characteristics of each term are complex and interconnected. She states that 'each concept is complex and multifaceted; each is defined by an intricate array of central characteristics in

140 *Jerusha Lamptey's theology of religions*

terms of the belief, responses, actions, and interactions.'[97] Secondly, according to her understanding of all the concepts, they are dynamic and defined by an active and deliberate nature: 'They do not denote fixed or static positions but rather dynamic manifestations that can increase and decrease.'[98] Thirdly, because of their complexity of dynamism, it is not possible to prioritise one above the others.[99] Taking the concept of *taqwā* together with its interaction with other categories, hierarchical difference would be among people, not religions. The Qur'anic categories are not bounded to a particular religion, but rather there is a dynamism between the act of faith and action and their relationship. From this viewpoint, her third claim is related to her understanding of *taqwā*.

Lamptey's third claim is that salvation is reached individually; it is not bound to a particular group (religion) since she identifies a lateral difference among religions and hierarchical difference among people who seek *taqwā*. She asserts:

> The key is that neither reward nor punishment will be determined solely by membership in a particular religion. It will be determined by certain beliefs, actions, and relationships, wherever they may be found – and, perhaps more precisely, wherever they may be found in a persistent pattern, whether positive or negative.[100]

By stating her belief that salvation is achieved individually, she disagrees with both pluralists and exclusivists. For exclusivist theologians, salvation is only possible by following Islamic beliefs and practices, but they do not directly claim all non-Muslims will not be saved. Pluralists accept other religions as possible ways of salvation, thus they equate Islam with other religions. In contrast, Lamptey neither equates other religions with Islam nor seems to reject the salvific means of non-Islamic beliefs. She believes that recognition of Muhammad as Prophet is part of *iman* and *islam*, but it is not a prerequisite of salvation. There are some other concepts of salvific values such as good works, praying, giving alms, believing in God and believing in judgement, which the Qur'an affirms. Thus for her, it is not possible to prioritise one over the others; even if this was possible, it would be the recognition of God which would take first place. As a result of the Qur'an's depiction of every person as conscious of God, however, it is difficult for Lamptey to use this argument of the recognition of God as being the singular threshold criterion. She contends that 'since the Qur'ānic discourse depicts dynamic levels and degrees of *taqwā*, it is hard to determine what would count as the lowest level or the cutoff point.'[101] Even though Lamptey makes distinction between unbeliever and disbeliever (while belief in God is absent in the first, there is a deliberate rejection of belief in the second), she does not say more about how we should place non-theistic religions like Buddhism into this discussion. Like pluralist theologians who make with certitude such claims as that 'there is a Transcendent reality behind all religions', Lamptey also uses the assumption of the Qur'anic depiction of *din al-fitra* (natural religion), assuming the probability that believers of non-theistic religions have (unconsciously) the belief of God. From this perspective, Lamptey's theology of religions requires more attention to relate non-theistic religions in her theology of religions. It is necessary to make one final point regarding Lamptey's perception of salvation. Like pluralist theologians she uses the Qur'anic verse 5:18 to oppose the idea of chosenness or salvation's dependence on a single religion.[102] Unlike pluralists, however, again she reiterates the individual nature of achieving salvation.

Lamptey's final claim is that every religious community is subject to change. According to the Qur'anic account, the books of the Jews and Christians have been changed or corrupted. Consequently, traditionally Muslims have regarded other religions as corrupted. Furthermore, the Qur'an also states that the words of God (the Qur'an) are protected by God.[103] However, Lamptey distinguishes between the divine protection of the Qur'an and its interpretation or implementation. She claims that '[e]ven if the Qur'ān has divine protection for its textual integrity, this does not prevent its message from being interpreted and enacted in ways inconsistent with *taqwā*.'[104]

Nevertheless, Lamptey thinks that corruption and change do not have the same meaning. While corruption (*tahrif*) has a negative meaning, change does not necessarily amount to corruption. She believes that 'corruption should be understood as that which impedes the manifestation of *taqwā*, not as any and all change within religious communities. Based on these brief observations, the purpose of lateral religious difference must transcend contextual responsiveness alone.'[105] It is not clear whether she is arguing that non-Islamic religions are corrupted or changed or whether changes in Islamic faith are negative (*tahrif*/corruption) changes or not.

Like Williams, Lamptey also starts her theology with taking religious differences into account. Unlike Williams, she ends up with affirming the similarities. The reason for that might be because of the nature of the subject of theology of religions. Williams is sceptical about the usefulness of any model within theology of religions, but Lamptey offers her own form of theology of religions. Besides as has been pointed out before, while Williams responds to religious pluralism he sometimes employs comparative theology to underline how similar themes in diverse religions can be understood differently, that is, the concepts of revelation and prophethood in Islam and Christianity. However, although Lamptey takes religious differences as starting point, she does not discusses how a specific religion, in her case Islam, would respond to the differences of other faiths which might disagree with fundamental Islamic beliefs. For example, the question can be asked whether Islamic and Christian understandings or whether their perceptions of revelation are similar or not. Even though Lamptey is aware of the differences of religions, she does not specify these differences for the sake of a constructed theology of religions. Moreover, she takes such concepts in the Qur'an as something that can be found in diverse world religions. The dilemma here lays the fact that theology of religions takes a single religion as starting point and tries to make sense of other religions from this specific

142 *Jerusha Lamptey's theology of religions*

religion's point of view. The main object there is how someone's own religion is related to other religions. Thus, like many other theologians who offer their own form of theology of religions, Lamptey does not involve the religious truths of other religions. This not only prevents acceptance of others as the way they express them, but it also prevents learning from the other. What is missing in Lamptey's theology is a comparative perspective. But as has been pointed out at the beginning of this chapter, her theology has not settled enough that needs to be tested and developed. In spite of this, the starting point of her theology is quite important and valuable.

Lamptey's theology of religions tends to give less attention to the controversial verses of the Qur'an regarding the People of the Book. Although she offers lateral difference as a way of conceptualising differences among religions, it is not fully clear whether she values non-Islamic religions or believers of non-Islamic faiths. For example, when she discusses the People of the Book, she claims that they cannot be viewed automatically as disbelievers based on their affiliation as People of the Book. If they are defined as disbelievers, it is because of their manifestation of disbelief. On the contrary, if they are described as believers, it is not because they follow the path of Prophet Muhammad but rather because they manifest the act of belief. She further contends that the followers of Prophet are also described as believers owing to their manifestation of belief.[106] From this viewpoint, it is not clear whether it is religion itself or the acts of people that legitimate their being called either believers or disbelievers. Furthermore, her notion of lateral difference allows each religion to be considered the same in the eyes of the universal message of God. This idea is important, but what about Qur'anic criticisms of some fundamental beliefs of Christianity? Can we label these different types of worldviews as simply lateral? The pluralist reading of both Muslim and Christian theocentric pluralists share essentially the same concept, that is, the concept of God, although the orthodox reading of both religions conflicts in certain aspects. Considering both accounts, the next chapter raises some questions, for instance, if we believe in the same God and attempts to discover some possible responses.

Conclusion

Lamptey's theology of religions can be regarded as a new contribution to Islamic discourse. It challenges contemporary theologies of religions. In the contemporary discussion of religious diversity, theologians either offer a view of non-Islamic religions as invalid or corrupted, or they simply reject the differences of other religions. Lamptey's theology of religions, however, treats religious difference seriously, while at the same time it aims to affirm similarities or sameness. For Lamptey, the other is a proximate other that is near to the Islamic faith with all kinds of complexity, relationality and boundaries.

In Christian theology of religions, there have been diverse responses to religious pluralism. In the Islamic tradition, however, the responses to religious diversity remain limited. Thus far I have offered both diverse responses from both traditions and a consideration of Williams's and Lamptey's theology of religions in more detail. Both Lamptey and Williams take religious difference seriously; they both start their theology with difference, although Williams ends by confirming difference, while Lamptey reaffirms sameness in certain respects. In other words, the first remains particularist, the second pluralist. Both positions have their own deficiencies and strengths. The next chapter will present some arguments for an alternative theology of religions.

Notes

1 For more biographical information, see this interview with US NPR News: http://www.npr.org/templates/story/story.php?storyId=19235263 (accessed in 20 August 15).
2 Jerusha Lamptey, *Never Wholly Other: A Muslima Theology of Religious Pluralism* (New York: Oxford University Press, 2014).
3 Jerusha Lamptey, "Mapping' the Religious Other: The Second Vatican Council's Approach to Protestantism," *Journal of Ecumenical Studies* 45/4 (Fall 2010): 604–615.
4 Jerusha Lamptey, "From Sexual Difference to Religious Difference: Towards a Muslima Theology of Religious Pluralism," in *Muslima Theology: The Voices of Muslim Women Theologians*, eds. Ednan Aslan, Elif Medeni and Marcia Hermansen (Berlin: Peter Lang GmbH, 2013), 231–245, "Lateral and Hierarchical Religious Difference in the Quran: Muslima Theology of Religious Pluralism," in *Understanding Religious Pluralism: Perspective from Religious Studies and Theology*, Kindle Edition, eds. Peter Phan and Jonathan Ray (Eugene: Pickwick Publication, 2014), 5637–5963, "Embracing Relationality and Theological Tensions: Muslima Theology, Religious Diversity," in *Between Heaven and Hell: Islam Salvation and the Fate of Others*, ed. Mohammad Khalil (New York: Oxford University Press, 2013), 235–254.
5 The concept of Muslima theology is very recent in Islamic studies. Recently, some Muslim women, including Jerusha Lamptey, have started to use the label 'Muslima theology' instead of feminist Islamic theology. See Ednan Aslan, Marcia Harmensen and Elif Medeni (eds.), *Muslima Theology: The Voice of Muslim Women Theologians* (Frankfurt: Peter Lang Edition, 2013). This book collects many Muslim women's articles on different topics, including Islamic law, interpretation of the Qur'an, Hadith methodology, theology of religions and so on.
6 Ali Engineer, "Islam and Pluralism," in *The Myth of Religious Superiority: A Multifaith Exploration*, ed. Paul Knitter (Maryknoll: Orbis Books, 2005), 211–219.
7 Abdulaziz Sachedina, "The Qur'an and Other Religions," in *The Cambridge Companion to the Qur'an*, ed. Jane Dammen McAuliffe (Cambridge: Cambridge University Press, 2006), 291–309.
8 Mahmut Aydin, "Religious Pluralism: A Challenge for Muslims – a Theological Evaluation," *Journal of Ecumenical Studies* 38/2–3 (Spring Summer 2001): 330–352, "A Muslim Pluralist: Jalaluddin Rumi," in *Myth of Religious Superiority*, ed. Paul Knitter (Maryknoll, NY: Orbis Books, 2005), 220–236.
9 Lamptey, *Never Wholly Other*, 54.
10 Ibid., 56.
11 Ibid., 71.
12 Seyyed Hossein Nasr, "Islam and the Encounters of Religions," in *The Religious Other: Towards a Muslim Theology of Religious Other in a Post-Prophetic Age*, ed. Mahammad Suheyl Umar (Lahore: Iqbal Academy Pakistan, 2008), 83–120.

144 *Jerusha Lamptey's theology of religions*

13 Reza Shah-Kazemi, *The Other in the Light of One: The Universality of the Qur'ān and Interfaith Dialogue* (Cambridge: Islamic Text Society, 2006).

14 Muhammad Legenhausen, "NonReductive Pluralism and Religious Dialogue," in *Between Heaven and Hell: Islam Salvation and the Fate of Others*, ed. Mohammad Khalil (New York: Oxford University Press, 2013), 154–175.

15 For a good comparison between Hick's and Nasr's theology of religions, see Adnan Aslan, *Religious Pluralism in Christian and Islamic Philosophy: The Thought of John Hick and Seyyed Hossein Nasr* (Abingdon, Oxon: Routledge, 1994).

16 Reza Shah-Kazemi, "Beyond Polemics and Pluralism: The Universal Message of the Qur'an," in *Between Heaven and Hell: Islam Salvation and the Fate of Others*, ed. Mohammad Khalil (New York: Oxford University Press, 2013), 88–102.

17 Legenhausen, "NonReductive Pluralism," 156.

18 Lamptey, *Never Wholly Other*, 66.

19 Ibid., 72.

20 Tim Winter, "The Last Trump Card: Islam and Supersession of Other Faiths," *Studies in Interreligious Dialogue* 9/2 (1999): 133–155.

21 Lamptey, *Never Wholly Other*, 69.

22 Ibid., 70.

23 Ismail Raji al-Faruqi, *al Tawḥīd: Its Implications for Thought and Life* (Herndon: International Institute of Islamic Thought, 1992), *Islam and Other Faiths* (Leicester: Islamic Foundation and International Institute of Islamic Thought, 1998), "The Essence of Religious Experience in Islam," *Numen* 20/3 (1973): 186–201.

24 Lamptey, *Never Wholly Other*, 75–76.

25 Al-Faruqi, *Islam and Other Faiths*, 42.

26 Lamptey, *Never Wholly Other*, 77.

27 Ibid., 77.

28 Ibid., 4.

29 Lamptey, "From Sexual Differences," 231.

30 Lamptey, *Never Wholly Other*, 7.

31 Ibid., 10.

32 The full text is available in Jonathan Z. Smith, *Relating Religions: Essays in the Study of Religion* (Chicago: University of Chicago Press, 2004).

33 Lamptey, *Never Wholly Other*, 230.

34 Ibid., 231.

35 Ibid., 245.

36 Lamptey, "From Sexual Difference," 235.

37 Lamptey, *Never Wholly Other*, 81, "Embracing Rationality," 239.

38 Amina Wadud, *Qur'an and Woman: Rereading the Sacred Texts from a Woman's Perspective* (New York: Oxford University, 1999), "Towards a Qur'anic Hermeneutics of Social Justice: Race, Class and Gender," *Journal of Law and Religion* 12/1 (1995–1996): 37–50.

39 Asma Barlas, *Islam: Unreading Patriarchal Interpretations of the Qur'an* (Austin: University of Texas Press, 2002) and "Women Reading of the Qur'ān," in *Cambridge Companion to the Qur'ān*, ed. Jane Dammen McAuliffe (Cambridge: Cambridge University Press, 2006), 255–273.

40 Riffat Hassan, "Feminism in Islam," in *Feminism and World Religions*, eds. Arvind Sharma and Katherine K. Young (Albany: State University of New York Press, 1999), 248–278, and *Religious Conservatism: Feminist Theology as a Means of Combating Injustice toward Women in Muslim Communities Cultures* (undated), available at: http://www.irfi.org/articles/articles_101_150/religious_conservatism.htm (accessed in 30 March 2015).

41 For example, Wadud underlines three categories of women interpretation of the Qur'an: traditional, reactive and holistic. It is the final one where she develops her own methodology. See Wadud, *Qur'an and Women*, 1–3.

Jerusha Lamptey's theology of religions 145

42 Lamptey, *Never Wholly Other*, 84.
43 Hassan, *Religious Conservatism*, Barlas, "Women Reading of the Qur'an," 259–260.
44 Barlas, *Islam: Unreading Patriarchal*, 17, Wadud, *Qur'an and Women*, 1.
45 Wadud, *Qur'an and Women*, 1. Barlas also supports similar ideas. See *Unreading Patriarchal*, 5.
46 Wadud, *Qur'an and Women*, 15.
47 Barlas, *Unreading Patriarchal*, 11.
48 Hassan, "Feminism in Islam," 255.
49 Barlas, *Unreading Patriarchal*, 10–11.
50 Wadud, *Qur'an and Women*, 37, Barlas, *Unreading Patriarchal*, 144.
51 See for Riffat Hassan, "The Qur'anic Perspective on Religious Pluralism," in *Peace-Building by, between, and beyond Muslims and Evangelical Christians*, eds. Mohammed Abu-Nimer and David Augsburger (Lanham: Lexington Books, 2009), 91–101, and for Fatma Barlas, "Hearing the Word, as a Muslim: Thirteen Passages of the Qur'ān and Religious Difference," (paper presented at Cornell University Vespers, November 2007).
52 Lamptey, *Never Wholly Other*, 93. Although, Wadud does not provide a settled approach of religious pluralism, she touches on that subject. But her engagement also is an example of first model of Lamptey's classification.
53 Lamptey, *Never Wholly Other*, 95.
54 Including Jeannine Hill Fletcher, "Shifting Identity: The Contribution of Feminist Thought to Theologies of Religious Pluralism," *Journal of Feminist Studies in Religion*, 19/2 (Fall 2003): 5–24, and *Monopoly on Salvation? A Feminist Approach to Religious Pluralism* (New York: Continuum, 2005), Rosemary Ruether, *Sexism and God-Talk: Toward a Feminist Theology* (Boston: Beacon, 1993) and "The Future of Feminist Theology in the Academy," *Journal of the American Academy of Religion* 53/4, 75th Anniversary Meeting of the American Academy of Religion (December 1985): 703–713; Marjorie Hewitt Suchocki, "In Search of Justice: Religious Pluralism from a Feminist Perspective," in *The Myth of Christian Uniqueness: Toward a Pluralistic Theology of Religions*, eds. John Hick and Paul Knitter (Maryknoll, NY: Orbis Books, 1987), 149–161; Kate McCarthy, "Women's Experience as a Hermeneutical Key to a Christian Theology of Religions," *Studies in Interreligious Dialogue* 6/2 (1996): 163–173; Ursula King, "Feminism: The Missing Dimension in the Dialogue of Religions," in *Pluralism and the Religions: The Theological and Political Dimensions*, ed. John D'Arcy May (Herndon: Cassell/Wellington House, 1998), 40–58; Rita Gross, "Feminist Theology as Theology of Religions," in *Cambridge Companion to Feminist Theology*, ed. Susan Frank Parsons (Cambridge: Cambridge University Press, 2006), 60–78; Kwok Pui Lan, *Postcolonial Imagination and Feminist Theology* (Louisville: Westminster John Knox, 2005), and some more other.
55 Lamptey, *Never Wholly Other*, 115.
56 Kathleen McGarvey, *Muslim and Christian Women in Dialogue: The Case of Northern Nigeria* (Oxford: Peter Lang, 2009).
57 Lamptey, *Never Wholly Other*, 115.
58 Hill Fletcher offers an identity which is hybrid and always embedded in a complex web of dynamic, intersecting relations, not something static and homogenous. Lamptey, "Embracing Rationality," 242.
59 Kwok's critique of pluralism as a Western imposition forces Lamptey to go beyond pluralism, which she has more sympathy with than the other two models.
60 'McGarvey notes the inability of pluralism to deal simultaneously with sameness and difference, which results in either a singular focus on sameness (as if there is no Other) or a singular focus on difference (as if the Other is too Other).' Lamptey, *Never Wholly Other*, 116.

146 *Jerusha Lamptey's theology of religions*

61 Ibid., 121.
62 Ibid.
63 Izutsu explains semantics as 'an analytic study of the key-terms of a language with a view to arriving eventually at a conceptual grasp of the weltanschauung or world-view of the people who use that language as a tool not only of speaking and thinking, but, more important still, of conceptualizing and interpreting the world that surrounds them'. *God and Man in the Qur'an: Semantics of the Qur'anic Weltanschauung* (Kuala Lumpur: Islamic Books Trust, 2008), 3.
64 Izutsu defines semantic fields in this way: '[n]o key-word stands alone and develops in isolation from other key-words of varying degrees of importance. Each key-word is accompanied by others, and together they form a complex network of keywords which we call in semantics a "semantic field".' *The Concept of Belief in Islam: A Semantic Analysis of Īmān and Islām* (Kuala Lumpur: Islamic Book Trust, 1993), 282.
65 Lamptey, *Never Wholly Other*, 124.
66 Izutsu, *Semantic Analysis*, 23–24.
67 Ibid., 96.
68 Lamptey, "Embracing Relationally," 243.
69 Barlas, *Islam: Unreading Patriarchal*, 145.
70 Lamptey, *Never Wholly Other*, 140.
71 Ibid.
72 Ibid., 156.
73 Ibid., 40.
74 Ibid., 248.
75 Ibid., 145.
76 She uses the Qur'anic verses 23:57–62 as examples. Ibid., 146.
77 The Qur'an 2:18.
78 The Qur'an 4:21, 46:15, 31:14–15, 29:8.
79 Lamptey, *Never Wholly Other* 148.
80 Ibid., 202–205 and 221–223.
81 Ibid., 194–197 and 215–217.
82 Ibid., 197–202 and 217–221.
83 Ibid., 190–197 and 212–215.
84 Ibid., 205–207 and 223–224.
85 Ibid., 184.
86 'True believers (*mu'minūn*) are those whose hearts tremble with awe when God is mentioned, whose faith increases when God's revelations are recited to them, who put their trust in their Lord' (8:2).
87 Ibid., 197.
88 Ibid., 197.
89 Ibid., 184–185.
90 Ibid., 208.
91 See verses 2:285, 24:51.
92 See verses 8:2, 9:24.
93 See verses 2:285, 3:119.
94 Lamptey, *Never Wholly Other*, 225.
95 Ibid.
96 From this perspective, like Esack, Lamptey also uses belief and right action as two inseparable parts. However, unlike Esack, she does not intend to offer a liberative, praxis-based theology of religions.
97 Lamptey, *Never Wholly Other*, 237.
98 Ibid., 237.
99 Ibid., 238.
100 Lamptey, "Embracing Relationally," 246.
101 Lamptey, *Never Wholly Other*, 239.

Jerusha Lamptey's theology of religions 147

102 Lamptey, "Embracing Relationality," 246.
103 Qur'an 15:9: 'We, indeed We, it is We who have sent down the Reminder, and indeed it is We who will preserve it.'
104 Lamptey, *Never Wholly Other*, 252.
105 Ibid.
106 Lamptey, "Lateral and Hierarchical Difference" (Kindle Edition).

Bibliography

al-Faruqi, Ismail Raji. *Al Tawḥīd: Its Implications for Thought and Life*. Herndon: International Institute of Islamic Thought, 1992.
———. "The Essence of Religious Experience in Islam." *Numen* 20/3 (1973): 186–201.
———. *Islam and Other Faiths*. Leicester: Islamic Foundation and International Institute of Islamic Thought, 1998.
Aslan, Adnan. *Religious Pluralism in Christian and Islamic Philosophy: The Thought of John Hick and Seyyed Hossein Nasr*. Abingdon, Oxon: Routledge, 1994.
Aydin, Mahmut. "A Muslim Pluralist: Jalaluddin Rumi." In *The Myth of Religious Superiority: A Multifaith Exploration*, edited by Paul Knitter, 220–236. Maryknoll, NY: Orbis Books, 2005.
———. "Religious Pluralism: A Challenge for Muslims – a Theological Evaluation." *Journal of Ecumenical Studies* (Summer 2001): 330–352.
Barlas, Asma. "Hearing the Word, as a Muslim: Thirteen Passages of the Qur'ān and Religious Difference." Paper presented at Cornell University Vespers. November 2007.
———. *Islam: Unreading Patriarchal Interpretations of the Qur'an*. Austin: University of Texas Press, 2002.
———. "Women Reading of the Qur'ān." In *Cambridge Companion to the Qur'ān*, edited by Jane Dammen McAuliffe, 255–273. Cambridge: Cambridge University Press, 2006.
Engineer, Ali. "Islam and Pluralism." In *The Myth of Religious Superiority: A Multifaith Exploration*, edited by Paul Knitter, 211–219. Maryknoll, NY: Orbis Books, 2005.
Fletcher, Jeannine Hill. *Monopoly on Salvation? A Feminist Approach to Religious Pluralism*. New York: Continuum, 2005.
———. "Shifting Identity: The Contribution of Feminist Thought to Theologies of Religious Pluralism." *Journal of Feminist Studies in Religion* 19/2 (2003): 5–24.
Gross, Rita. "Feminist Theology as Theology of Religions." In *Cambridge Companion to Feminist Theology*, edited by Susan Frank Parsons, 60–78. Cambridge: Cambridge University Press, 2006.
Hassan, Riffat. "Feminism in Islam." In *Feminism and World Religions*, edited by Arvind Sharma and Katherine K. Young, 248–278. Albany: State University of New York Press, 1999.
———. "The Qur'anic Perspective on Religious Pluralism." In *Peace-Building by, between, and beyond Muslims and Evangelical Christians*, edited by Mohammed Abu-Nimer and David Augsburger, 91–101. Lanham: Lexington Books, 2009.
———. *Religious Conservatism: Feminist Theology as a Means of Combating Injustice toward Women in Muslim Communities Cultures*. undated. www.irfi.org/articles/articles_101_150/religious_conservatism.htm (accessed March 30, 2015).
Izutsu, Toshihiko. *The Concept of Belief In Islam: A Semantic Analysis of Īmān and Islām*. Kuala Lumpur: Islamic Book Trust, 1993.

148 *Jerusha Lamptey's theology of religions*

———. *God and Man in the Qur'an: Semantics of the Qur'anic Weltanschauung*. Kuala Lumpur: Islamic Books Trust, 2008.

King, Ursula. "Feminism: The Missing Dimension in the Dialogue of Religions." In *Pluralism and the Religions: The Theological and Political Dimensions*, edited by John D'Arcy May, 40–58. Herndon: Cassell/Wellington House, 1998.

Lamptey, Jerusha. "Embracing Relationality and Theological Tensions: Muslima Theology, Religious Diversity." In *Between Heaven and Hell: Islam Salvation and the Fate of Others*, edited by Mohammad Khalil, 235–354. New York: Oxford University Press, 2013.

———. "From Sexual Difference to Religious Difference: Towards a Muslima Theology of Religious Pluralism." In *Muslima Theology: The Voices of Muslim Women Theologians*, edited by Ednan Aslan, Elif Medeni and Marcia Hermansen, 231–245. Berlin: Peter Lang GmbH, 2013.

———. "Lateral and Hierarchical Religious Difference in the Quran: Muslima Theology of Religious Pluralism." In *Understanding Religious Pluralism: Perspective from Religious Studies and Theology*. Kindle Edition, edited by Peter Phan and Jonathan Ray. Eugene: Pickwick Publication, 2014.

———. "Mapping the Religious Other: The Second Vatican Council's Approach to Protestantism." *Journal of Ecumenical Studies* 45/4 (Fall 2010): 604–615.

———. *Never Wholly Other: A Muslima Theology of Religions*. New York: Oxford University Press, 2014.

Lan, Kwok Pui. *Postcolonial Imagination and Feminist Theology*. Louisville: Westminster John Knox, 2005.

Legenhausen, Muhammad. "NonReductive Pluralism and Religious Dialogue." In *Between Heaven and Hell: Islam Salvation and the Fate of Others*, edited by Mohammad Khalil, 154–175. New York: Oxford University Press, 2013.

McCarthy, Kate. "Women's Experience as a Hermeneutical Key to a Christian Theology of Religions." *Studies in Interreligious Dialogue* 6/2 (1996): 163–173.

McGarvey, Kathleen. *Muslim and Christian Women in Dialogue: The Case of Northern Nigeria*. Oxford: Peter Lang, 2009.

Nasr, Seyyed Hossein. "Islam and Encounter of Religions and Islam's Attitude towards Other Religion in History." In *The Religious Other: Towards a Muslim Theology of Religions in a Post-Prophetic Age*, edited by Muhammad Suheyl Umar, 83–120. Lahore: Iqbal Pakistan Academy, 2008.

Ruether, Rosemary. "The Future of Feminist Theology in the Academy." *Journal of the American Academy of Religion* (75th Anniversary Meeting of the American Academy of Religion) 53/4 (December 1985): 703–713.

———. *Sexism and God-Talk: Toward a Feminist Theology*. Boston: Beacon, 1993.

Sachedina, Abdulaziz. "The Qur'an and Other Religions." In *The Cambridge Companion to the Qur'an*, edited by Jane Dammen McAuliffe, 291–309. Cambridge: Cambridge University Press, 2006.

Shah-Kazemi, Reza. "Beyond Polemics and Pluralism: The Universal Message of the Qur'an." In *Between Heaven and Hell: Islam, Salvation and the Fate of Others*, edited by Mohammad Khalil, 88–104. New York: University of Oxford Press, 2013.

———. *The Other in the Light of One: The Universality of the Qur'an and Interfaith Dialogue*. Cambridge: Islamic Text Society, 2006.

Smith, Jonathan Z. *Relating Religions: Essays in the Study of Religion*. Chicago: University of Chicago Press, 2004.

Suchocki, Marjorie Hewitt. "In Search of Justice: Religious Pluralism from a Feminist Perspective." In *The Myth of Christian Uniqueness: Toward a Pluralistic Theology of Religions*, edited by John Hick and Paul Knitter, 149–161. London: SCM Press, 1987.

Wadud, Amina. *Qur'an and Woman: Rereading the Sacred Texts from a Woman's Perspective*. New York: Oxford University, 1999.

———. "Towards a Qur'anic Hermeneutics of Social Justice: Race, Class and Gender." *Journal of Law and Religion* 12/1 (1995–1996): 37–50.

Winter, Tim. "The Last Trump Card: Islam and Supersession of Other Faiths." *Studies in Interreligious Dialogue* 9/2 (1999): 133–155.

5 Theology of religions reassessed

Introduction

In the previous chapters, I analysed a range of different approaches in both Islamic and Christian theology of religions and gave special attention to Williams's and Lamptey's theology of religions as examples of nuanced approaches which attempt to hold together both similarity and difference. I argued that both Williams's and Lamptey's theology of religions challenge the settled classifications in their particular traditions. In other words, one part of their theology seems to belong to a particular type, whilst other aspects suggest different types, thus they seem to belong multiple types. This challenges the notion that any adequate theological response to religious diversity will fit easily into a single category or typology.

In this chapter, I will first discuss some arguments relating to theology of religions and its connection with comparative theology. Then I will move on to review some of the important issues, which I have highlighted throughout the whole study, relating to a possible alternative Islamic theology of religions. I will argue that Islamic theology of religions needs to engage at a deeper level with non-Islamic religions' teachings and texts to offer a comprehensible theology which will do justice to the similarities and differences of diverse religions. In connection with this topic, by utilising comparative theology, I will look at the nature of God and revelation in Islam and Christianity to explore the similarities and differences between the two traditions in these areas.

1 Theology of religions: outcomes and problems

Throughout the previous chapters, I have outlined the contemporary discussion among Christian and Muslim theologians in their approaches to religious pluralism. I have also shown that there has been much more diversity in the responses from Christian theologians than among Islamic approaches. There are a few reasons why Muslims have not produced as many diverse approaches. Firstly, the origin of the subject is based mainly on Western Christianity. Secondly, throughout history, Muslims have not only understood the subject theologically but also as a legal matter: the status of non-Muslims in Islamic societies is regarded as a legal issue. Thirdly, the dynamics of Islamic studies have primarily led Muslims to repeat the interpretations of scholars considered as authorities from the mediaeval period of Islamic history. This form of methodology which followed traditional Islamic scholarship and Qur'anic exegesis was broken off in the late nineteenth century by a number of innovative Islamic thinkers.[1] As I have presented, the extreme form of exclusivism (social exclusivism) and pluralism departed from traditional scholarship and exegesis in terms of using a different methodology for approaching the Qur'an and Sunnah. It is these two approaches that have offered something new in the Islamic responses to religious diversity. Consequently, there are a few comments that should be highlighted in the overall discussion of Islamic theology of religions.

Firstly, I previously claimed that the discussion among pluralists and particularists has been an important contribution in Christian theology of religions. The criticisms from both sides have paved the way for mutual benefit. On the one hand, theologians have shown the inadequacy of their opponents' positions. On the other hand, they have taken others' criticisms into account so that they can strengthen their positions. For instance, developments in Hick's and Knitter's theologies can be seen as the product of these discussions (although their modified theologies still have certain problems). In the long term, both theologians have revised their theology of religions and offered something different from their original theology.[2]

It is reasonable to argue that, unlike Christian theologians, Muslim theologians have not engaged deeply with each other's theology of religions. Recently, young scholars such as Khalil and Lamptey have provided an overview of Islamic theology of religions and raised critiques against what has been produced in recent decades. What is interesting is that while in the modern development of Christian theology of religions, exclusivism, inclusivism and pluralism emerged chronologically,[3] in contemporary Islamic theology of religions, pluralism and sociopolitical exclusivism emerged in response to modernity and traditional approaches. In other words, when, in the modern and contemporary eras, Muslims started to question the place of Islam among world religions, the pluralistic opinion alongside with socio-historical exclusivism have become the only alternative views to the traditional Islamic view. Recently, theologians such as Winter and Qadhi have revised the traditional form of exclusivism in the light of discussion provided within Islamic theology of religions.

Moreover, the particularist position, with a few exceptions, is almost omitted in Islamic theology of religions. For example, Legenhausen, as has been previously mentioned, offers a particularist theology in which Islam and other religions' particularity are confirmed. Even though his theology offers something different within Islamic theology, this has still not led to sufficient discussion among Muslim theologians. Thus, due to lack of engagement, Muslim theologians have not developed yet their positions in light of criticism from alternative positions as Islamic theology of religions is less mature than Christian theology of religions.

152 *Theology of religions reassessed*

Secondly, even though Muslim theologians (mainly liberal) have not sufficiently discussed the term 'religion' in the modern context, they have produced a theology in the light of the theologies of their Christian counterparts. Recently, there has been discussion over the term 'religion', which has been thought to be a Eurocentric concept. In general, particularist Christian theologians use that critique to indicate that the modern concept of pluralism is not innocent. They make a connection between European imperialism and pluralism. Thus, they focus on the root of the studies of 'religions' and argue that Eurocentrism shapes these studies of religion. For instance, Jenny Daggers claims that the motivation behind modern and contemporary liberal pluralist theology is Eurocentric imperialism. She starts by looking deeply at the root of the term 'religion'. She claims that the category of religion is 'a tripartite, emergent from Christian theology during modernity, as Christianity increased, transcended, and diminished, and persisted in contemporary religious studies and Christian theology'.[4] She examines the concept of religion as Christianity increased, was transcended and finally diminished in light of three historical developments. Firstly, the increase of Christianity covers the era of expansionist colonialism, in which Christianity was regarded as the one true religion.[5] In this period, she examines philosophers and theologians such as Kant, Schleiermacher and Clarke who contextualise Christianity as an absolute and universal religion 'either displacing the religions, or in softer rhetoric as their fulfillment, given that they are destined to wither away under the impact of European modernity'.[6] Secondly, Daggers shows how a concept of religion was developed which transcended Christianity, 'the notion of an absolute religion transcending Christianity, and incorporating all the religions'.[7] So there was a shift from Christianity as an absolute religion, which absorbed other religions to 'an absolute religion' that transcends Christianity. For Daggers, later twentieth-century liberal pluralist theologians have continued to use this category. Finally, the concept of religion underwent a third shift as Christianity diminished under the impact of secularisation. With this shift, religion is portrayed as 'a diminishing, archaic, and redundant separate sphere, irrelevant to the brave new secular world of modernity and destined to wither away'.[8]

Similar to Daggers, Hugh Nicholson and Tomoko Masuzawa also show the continuity between European imperialism and universalist presuppositions. Masuzawa, in her *The Invention of World Religions* offers an historical account of the idea of 'world religions'. She claims that the emergence of the world religions discourse is Eurocentric and Eurohegemonic.[9] Nicholson also proposes a similar view of the concept of religion. He argues that 'there is an intrinsic connection between, on the one hand, the universalistic presuppositions of the comparative enterprise as conventionally understood, and, on the other, the perpetuation of imperialistic attitudes.'[10] I do not intend to judge the concept of religion and its historical developments. Nevertheless, these scholars' judgements seem to be consistent to some extent and worthy of consideration. Firstly, as I have previously indicated, pluralism owes its appearance in Islamic theology of religions to liberal Christian

Theology of religions reassessed 153

theologians. What has been produced by liberal Christians has to some extent been revised in Islamic terms by Muslims. It is also more than a coincidence that Muslim liberal pluralist theologians were mainly educated in Western countries and most probably adopted European values in their revisions of Islamic thought. Secondly, as a result of the hegemony of European universalism, the twentieth century has witnessed many works by Muslim scholars who have tried to reconcile European Enlightenment values and Islamic beliefs. In other words, the Enlightenment values have provided a test for Muslims to prove that their religion is not archaic and is consistent with liberal values.

It should also be noted that although these scholars have shown continuity between European colonialism and studies of 'religion', as Hedges points out, relating religions to each other is not only limited to a Western academic perspective.[11] For example, when Muslims started to study non-Islamic religions, they also created distinctions and judged other religions in the light of their own beliefs. Wardenburg discusses some considerations regarding early Muslims' study of non-Muslims. Firstly, non-Islamic traditions were judged by the Qur'an, which is a chronologically later revelation. Secondly, that revelation was believed to provide the formal standards and categories for non-Muslims as well as substantial knowledge about non-Muslims and their religious beliefs and doctrines. Thirdly, early prophetic revelations, before Prophet Muhammad, were regarded as valid since they were seen as the origin of monotheistic religion. Fourthly, there was recognition of a kind of primordial religion that was 'a primal and fundamental consciousness of God (*fitra*), which has been implanted in each human being at birth'.[12] Islam, however, was seen as the true expression of the eternal and primordial religion.

Thirdly, it should also be noted that in spite of the imperialist context of the world religions discourse, the spirit of Islamic and Christian pluralist theology of religions had been useful in terms of interfaith engagement. The early pluralists had also become the advocators of interfaith dialogue among Muslims. Pluralism was the only alternative model to two groups: on the one hand, the sociopolitical exclusivists who did not want to have any kind of positive interaction with non-Muslims and, on the other hand, traditionalist Muslims who were silent on many issues. As an alternative to these two groups, Muslim pluralists have opened up a fresh pathway with the help of their engagement with Western intellectuals. It should be noted, however, that although all proponents of dialogue activities were not necessarily pluralists,[13] the role of pluralist theologians cannot be denied. Thus, it could be claimed that the emergence of pluralist theory in Islamic theology of religions was necessary to foster good relations with non-Islamic communities. In spite of its usefulness, Islamic pluralism has its problems, which have been discussed in previous chapters. Yet, the concern I have raised throughout this entire study may lead Islamic theology of religions to another direction. As I have previously claimed, Islamic pluralism needs more attention by deeply engaging with non-Islamic religions' texts and

154 *Theology of religions reassessed*

teachings, which might direct Islamic responses to religious diversity from a more theoretical engagement towards a more practical one.

Fourthly, there has been some discussion of the utility of the theology of religions. In the first chapter, I provided an overview of the discussion over Race's threefold typology, and I claimed that his classification would be useful in combination with other typologies. Furthermore, I have not placed comparative theology as an alternative to theology of religions but rather argued that these should operate together. Recently, some comparative theologians argue that the area of theology of religions is no longer useful. For instance, Schebera argues that 'a theology of religions has reached an impasse, which limits its ability to foster religious dialogue among religious practitioners of the religions of the world.'[14] He further contends that discussions of typologies in theology of religions repeated 'the same arguments or tweaked the underlying theology to try to show the superiority of one model over the other'.[15]

Christian comparative theologians have offered comparative theology as an alternative to theology of religions since they believe that comparative theology will lead to more effective dialogue than a theology of religions. Schebera claims that as a theology of religions begins its dialogues with certain a priori conditions, the outcome of dialogue is already predetermined by its methodology. Thus, the other partner in the dialogue would not be convinced that there was a real encounter. He argues:

> Instead of broad, generalized comparisons between religions, it seems to make more sense to compare particular points between religions. This includes a comparative analysis between particular texts, symbols, personalities, teachings, classics, in an attempt to see if the understanding of that particular point might illuminate the understanding of its parallel in the other religion engaged in the dialogue.[16]

Although I do not wholly agree with him in terms of locating comparative theology as an alternative to theology of religions, his point seems to also be a crucial one for Muslims. Both theology of religions and comparative theology seek to address religious diversity. However, while theology of religions is an internal negotiation between a specific religion's claims for universal truth, comparative theology is an external engagement with a focus on learning from the other. In other words, the former focuses on the theoretical framework for making sense of religious diversity whilst the latter involves a deep learning from the other religions through their perceptions. They both address religious diversity but from different perspectives. If we regard them as two alternative approaches to diversity, our conclusion will support one over the other. Conversely, if we consider them as complementary to each other, then we could utilise one's tools to make the other more comprehensible. Considering the fact that Islam within its sources addresses the religious other, one cannot simply bypass theology of religions and promote comparative theology only. However, similar to Christian theologians who write about the theology of religions, Muslim theologians also start with general ideas which aim to cover all religions. For Muslims, rather than offering only abstract arguments related to world religions, to offer a theology based on comparison of similar natures of faiths would be more challenging. From this aspect, Islamic theology of religions need to operate with in conjunction with comparative theology to offer more nuanced theology of religions which would do justice to difference of other religions.

Fifthly, from the overall approach of theology of religions, it might seem necessary to feel obligated to follow one specific position on a typology. In practice, however, the positions on a typology should not be seen as complete alternatives to one another. One can build a theology which combines aspects from different theology of religions positions. For instance, Feldmeier considers himself one-third inclusivist, one-third perennial-pluralist and one-third postmodern mutualist.[17] The reason why he does not confine himself to a single type is that he does not want to sacrifice the truths in other positions while depending on one position. He claims that

> a theology of religions needs to live in a creative tension between paradigms of truth claims and what they point to (*veritas semper major est*). The key point here is that objective truth itself is known paradigmatically and no paradigm can subsume all other paradigms or include all legitimate or important truths.[18]

He then contends that according to circumstances (dialogue environment), one can perhaps seek a common spirit while sitting and singing together with Hindu, Sufi and Christian mystics, while in another forum it might be more useful to operate with Knitter's acceptance model to express religious differences.[19] While evaluating Williams's theology of religions, I have shown that his theology of religions does not wholly fit into any single type. I also have presented how Lamptey's theology of religions challenges with other settled theology of religions in Islamic discourse. Furthermore, as has been consistently reinforced in previous chapters, no theology of religions is exempt from critiques and flaws, including the ones I have shown a favourable tendency towards. There are great insights in each type as well as deficiencies. Rather than being confined to one specific theology of religions, allowing creative cooperation among the models would be much more helpful. Based on the discussion provided in the previous chapter, I will now raise some concerns for a potential Islamic theology of religions.

2 Important issues for an Islamic approach to theology of religions

First and foremost, like most Muslim theologians, either exclusivists or pluralists, the starting point for an Islamic theology of religions should be the Qur'anic revelation. But we should be aware that, overall, the Qur'an itself offers a complicated theology of religions. While some texts focus on the

156 *Theology of religions reassessed*

particularity of the Islamic belief, at times it sounds inclusivist or even pluralistic. The ambiguity of the Qur'anic texts concerning non-Islamic traditions illustrates that the issue is complicated, and there will be no clear and immediate answer to the issue.

The Qur'an on the one hand values non-Islamic religions, mainly Judaism and Christianity; on the other hand, it criticises their belief systems and practices. Despite its critiques, the Qur'an does not categorise them as invalid religions. Muslim theologians later developed a supersessionist theory, however, in which non-Islamic religions are regarded as theologically invalid. Although, in the Islamic states non-Muslims, mainly Jews, Christians and Zoroastrians, are allowed to stay with the condition of paying tax,[20] their religions were theologically categorised as false religions. Atay argues that

> Islam has been sociologically inclusivist, eschatologically exclusivist and politically pluralist in its relations towards other religions. . . . Jews, Christians and Zoroastrians have been treated differently from other traditions in legal terms, but eschatologically, like the followers of other religions, they were deemed not to be saved either.[21]

Thus, treating non-Islamic religions as theologically invalid but allowing their practices seems to contradict with how Islamic states treated the disbelievers (*kāfir*: the term does not include Jews and Christians but originally referred to Meccan polytheists, apostates from Islam and followers of rival prophets after Prophet Muhammad's death). The legitimacy of non-Islamic religions comes from their reception of a divine, prophetic message. Furthermore, the Qur'anic verses do not use the terms of replacement or supersessionism when criticising the belief systems of Christians and Jews.[22] As has been shown before, the theory of supersessionism is not the Qur'anic account, but it is a matter of interpretation by Muslim theologians. As a result, the supersessionist theory cannot be used for categorising non-Islamic traditions. As Lamptey points out, the historical development of Islamic theology was not only theologically motivated, but politics and governance also had an influence on the theologians who developed what became orthodox theology.[23]

Overall, the Qur'anic argument seems to offer a complex picture of Christian and Jewish traditions. While the Qur'an sets out its own distinctive belief system, it is the very nature of the text to claim its particular and unique status. The Qur'anic language of exclusivism should be understood as its particularism, not as the deliberate exclusion of other religions. According to the Qur'an, there are true elements in non-Islamic religions in spite of the false elements. Muslims' positions towards religious others should not depend on falsification of other religions, however, but on a confidence in the particular truth of their own religion. Furthermore, the Qur'an itself declares: 'And assuredly We have raised in every community an apostle saying: worship Allah and avoid the devil (16:36).' This statement does not necessarily suggest that Muslims should regard other religions' religious figures as prophets, but rather the verse verifies the universality and validity of the divine message outside of Islam.

Some theologians in Christian traditions utilise Trinitarian belief while articulating a theological response to other religions. Among them, for instance, D'Costa, Panikkar, Williams and Daggers seem to offer a theology of religions in which their faith's distinctiveness is protected but also open to other religions. Williams's and Panikkar's positions have already been discussed, thus it is not necessary to repeat them here.

D'Costa does not seek to undermine the truths of other religions since, according to his Trinitarian theology, goodness and truth are not only limited to Christianity but can also be found within other religions – justified on the grounds that the Holy Spirit is working outside of Christianity. Yet, it would be wrong to exaggerate the level of acceptance D'Costa invokes as, even though he recognises that the Holy Spirit works in other religions, he still maintains that their beliefs, as a whole, are not compatible with the revelation received from Christ. D'Costa believes that Jesus is the only revelation to be provided by God; hence, there is no possibility for new revelations after the coming of Christ. Although D'Costa clearly disagrees with inclusivist theologians who display a higher degree of certainty about where exactly the Holy Spirit is working in other religions and as a result accept the salvific means of other religions,[24] he states that the Holy Spirit may operate in non-Christian religions 'in so much as some of their teachings relate to Christ, either explicitly or implicitly'.[25] The Qur'anic account of Jesus as one of the greatest prophets can be provided as one example of explicit affirmation from a non-Christian tradition; while Muhammad's teaching about the care of widows when no one is looking after them can also be seen as an implicit recognition of the Holy Spirit's action.[26] He considers both cases as a type of *preparatio evangelica* (preparation for the Gospel).[27] D'Costa does not agree that following non-Christian religions may lead to salvation due to the Holy Spirit's actions. Yet, despite this apparent 'exclusivist' orientation, he continues to argue that his Trinitarian orientation is dialectically more sustainable and has realistic limits because it accepts the 'real otherness' of other religions; it promotes 'openness (taking history seriously), tolerance (or negative civic religious rights) and equality (in terms of human dignity)'.[28] D'Costa's language seems offensive. Rather than prioritising the particularity of his own belief, he chooses to claim the superiority of Christianity.

Similar to D'Costa, Daggers also takes Trinitarian belief seriously. As an alternative to the tripartite concept of religion constructed as part of the development of modern European intellectual hegemony, she offers a recentred vision Christianity, which returns to orthodox claims of Christianity combined with post-liberal ideas. She utilises Lindbeck's cultural-linguistic approach,[29] Fletcher's feminist hybridised identities[30] and the transformed cultural practices of Kathryn Tanner[31] together with Asian and European Trinitarian theology of religions. As an alternative to the modern conception

158 *Theology of religions reassessed*

of religion, she offers her theology of religions hoping to '[release] the Trinitarian universalism that inheres within Christian theology from its Eurocentric moorings, and [relocate] this Christian universalism within one incommensurable religious tradition among others'.[32] Although she does not develop her own Trinitarian argument, she shows as favourable towards the Asian theologians' Trinitarian perspective, particularly the work of Amos Yong. As previously demonstrated, D'Costa's Trinitarian theology admits that the work of the Holy Spirit in non-Christian religions is *praeparatio evangelica*. Some Asian theologians challenge this view, however, and offer a more mutual and complementary perspective on Trinitarian theology.[33] For instance, Yong, a Penetecostalist theologian, argues that non-Christian religions should not be regarded as merely *praeparatio evangelica*. He

> distinguishes the economy of the Spirit from that of the Word, then proposes non-Christological criteria for discerning the work of the Spirit among adherents of other religions. He attempts to mobilize the universality of the Holy Spirit to overcome problems arising from the historical particularity of Jesus.[34]

Daggers believes that Asian theologians' critiques of *praeparatio evangelica* as a theological understanding of religious pluralism seem to offer alternatives to European theologians.[35]

These proposals, offered by Christian theologians, are within the framework of Trinitarian belief and cohere to some extent with Christian faith. However I would argue that some aspects or features of their proposals are useful even outside the framework of Trinitarian faith and do not depend solely upon it. Therefore, such positions inspire me to imagine new ways of locating Islam among world religions. That is to say, their theology of religions is both faithful to their own beliefs and doctrines and manages to keep together Christianity's particular claims with a universal scope for God's activity. Explaining this in Islamic terms, God's divine message is universal as it is not restricted only to Islam; however, what we know from the Qur'an is that God has perfected his religion in that particular message, the Qur'an.[36] However, this does not necessarily mean that there is no divine message in other religions. The verse which suggests that every community is given a prophet can be used as justification for accepting that there are multiple divine messages. However, that cannot justify the pluralist position that each is equally true or false. From the Islamic position, Muslims believe that what is given them is true, but that does not necessarily lead to a dismissal of the true elements in other religions.

Secondly, the Qur'an does not cover everything. The Qur'anic texts are limited to certain verses in which many issues such as belief, religious practices and social life are discussed. In spite of the limits of the text, throughout history Muslims have developed considerable works regarding the beliefs of non-Islamic religions. The presuppositions given by the Qur'an shaped the minds of Muslims to contextualise the belief systems of non-Islamic traditions. Given the limited amount and the complexity of Qur'anic verses on non-Muslims, it is better not to think that the Qur'an is supposed to teach everything about religious others but rather that it is the duty of Muslims to engage with non-Islamic traditions themselves to achieve a better understanding. It is a fact that in the contemporary environment, there is a movement towards dialogue. The main aim of the works produced by contemporary pluralist Muslims is to offer a theological basis for dialogue, and in this they have some success, even if some aspects of their work are problematic.

As pointed out before, Muslims in the contemporary period either have not taken into account the differences of other faiths by emphasising similarities or have simply dismissed other religions as a whole. Previously I have shown the failure of both positions. I want to return to the pluralist argument, which I find most problematic, which uses the concept of a universal *islam* to justify a pluralistic vision of Islam. While doing this, they equate Islamic belief with non-Islamic religions without deeply engaging with the beliefs and practices of non-Islamic religions. They make generalisations about non-Islamic religions as if they had been constructed in the same way as historical Islam. However, considering the beliefs and practices of diverse religions, the picture they draw seems not to be entirely right. It seems that to make such big general claims, certain forms of comparison between different faiths is required. For example, when Muslims say that God sent the same divine message to every community, which legitimises the pluralistic interpretation, it may seem that this claim contains within it the idea that the concept of revelation in every single religion is the same. Such claims can only be proved or disproved through attention to the specific religions and through sensitive and accurate comparisons.

From this perspective, there is a need to compare some of the apparently similar features or aspects of different religions. I will particularly compare two central notions, God and revelation, in Islam and Christianity. However, although I am aware of the fact that Islam and Christianity are not static religions and that interpretation and application can vary from person to person or culture to culture,[37] it seems useful to compare some of the central notions of both religions, which are held by many members of that religion and have remained relatively stable over time.

Thirdly, as the issue of salvation has been placed at the centre of theology of religions, theologians who have offered a theological position have theorised on how salvation is possible outside of a single faith. Previously, I claimed that the issue of salvation has not been at the centre of Islamic belief, whilst Muslims have paid more attention to whether non-Islamic religions are true or false. However, traditionally, Muslims regard Islamic beliefs as the only way that leads to heaven. While they have placed too much emphasis on the role of belief, the Qur'an balances belief with practice (good deeds).[38] Traditionally, Muslims thought that for Muslims, the requirement to earn God's mercy for the next world is both orthodoxy and orthopraxy.[39] Esack's and Lamptey's emphasis on good deeds seems to be consistent with the

160   *Theology of religions reassessed*

whole of Qur'anic arguments in terms of rewards and punishment. Besides, Lamptey's focus on an individual level of salvation, rather than institutional, and Williams's 'don't know-ism' seems to fit best. As Lamptey clarifies that the Qur'anic treatment of punishment and rewards is not affiliated with any religion. However, as Muslims we know that by following Islamic beliefs (orthodoxy and orthopraxy) in the next world, there will be consequences (either reward or punishment) of our acts, but we do not know how much of non-Islamic religions' true elements would lead their believers to be punished or rewarded. On a general note, Muslim and Christian theologians can probably agree on the single point that it is God who will decide who will be saved or not.

In view of these proposals, it should also be noted that to expect every participant of interfaith dialogue to have the same form of theology of religions and the same motivation is unrealistic. Every attempt to formulate a theology of religions is valuable, but any alternative theology of religions might appear to solve the problems of others and simultaneously create new problems. Thus, rather than judging theologies of religions as a whole, I use Keith Ward's definition of 'open' and 'closed' theology. He offers an 'open' and a 'closed' theology as alternatives to each other. He establishes six main features for open theology, which are as follows:

> It will seek a convergence of common core beliefs, clarifying the deep agreements which may underline diverse cultural traditions. It will seek to learn from complementary beliefs in other traditions, expecting that there are forms of revelation one's own tradition does not express. It will be prepared to reinterpret its beliefs in the light of new, well-established factual and moral beliefs. It will accept the full right of diverse belief-systems to exist, as long as they do not cause avoidable injury or harm to innocent sentient beings. It will encourage a dialogue with conflicting and dissenting views, being prepared to confront its own tradition with critical questions arising out of such views. And it will try to develop a sensitivity to the historical and cultural context of the formulation of its own beliefs, with preparedness to continue developing new insights in new cultural situations.[40]

In contrast to an open theology, Ward defines a 'closed' theology using four characteristics:

> [It will insist] on the total distinctiveness of its own beliefs, excluding others from any share in important truths. It rejects all contact with other systems of belief. It rejects any development of knowledge which would force a reinterpretation of its own tradition. It will, if possible, restrict or prevent the expression of criticism or dissent. It will seek to suppress other religions. It will insist that it possesses a complete or sufficient understanding of truth, which change could only impair or destroy.[41]

Theology of religions reassessed 161

Ward further adds that no theology is wholly open or wholly closed.[42] Having an open theology as much as is possible would lead to more fruitful interfaith engagements. As has been previously argued, such theologies of religions, as Barth's in Christian theology or Qutb's in Islamic theology, would not be helpful pragmatically, not because they do not take Christian or Islamic beliefs seriously but because they do not allow any cross-religious interaction. From the way I presented both Lamptey and Williams, it seems that both of their theology of religions seem to be examples of 'open' or partially open theologies. As Ward points out no theology is wholly open and closed, their theology in certain aspects seeks to be manifested by other religions. While Williams, as a senior theologian, has had more opportunity to practice interfaith engagement and to develop his position more deeply, Lamptey's theology also seems to be promising for future engagement. Thus, unlike pluralists' insistence that only pluralist views offer more openness towards other religions, it seems that the most important thing is not whether or not one's theology accepts all religious tradition as equal but whether or not one's theology is open to the differences of other religions and the possibility of changing or revising its positions about the religious other on the basis of such engagement.

For the purpose outlined here, the next section will focus on the nature of God and revelation in Islam and Christianity to get a better sense of difference understanding of these two themes in Christianity and Islam. Although I do not aim to construct any comparative theology methodology, I believe that to present different understandings of these two themes will supply a preliminary basis for comparative theology. From this respect, a comparative perspective of these two themes gives us a reason why theology of religions should be in conjunction with comparative theology. As has been presented before, while so-called Muslim pluralist theologians construct their theology of religions, they have such presuppositions that think non-Islamic religions have similar understandings of phenomena such as God, revelation and so on. By presenting different ideas on the same God and revelation, I aim to show that to reach a conclusion of what Muslim or Christian pluralist theologians offer is not as easy as they present.

3 Do Muslims and Christians believe in the same God?

The nature of the question of whether Muslims and Christians believe in the same God is complicated. I will argue that the answer to this question is not a simple yes or no. As both faiths share a belief in monotheism, when theologians argue that these faiths do not believe in the same God, they produce such reasons that to some extent recognise commonalities but ultimately confirm different perceptions of God. Furthermore, since there have been different theologies among both Muslim and Christian theologians, the counter question could be asked, do different Muslim and Christian communities always believe in the same God? Apparently, it seems that the answer to this question varies according to the theological position of the theologians.

162 *Theology of religions reassessed*

For instance, Christian and Muslim pluralist theologians seem to have a shared concept of God. If we look at Hick's and Askari's descriptions of 'God' or 'ultimate Reality', we see that from their perspective, the idea of the same God is quite apparent. From Hick's experience of other religions, Hick not only claims that Muslims and Christians believe in the same God but that other world religions that have the concept of God share the same God with Christians. He claims that just as in a Christian church, in a Jewish synagogue, a Muslims mosque, a Sikh gurdwara and a Hindu temple, 'God is worshiped as the maker of heaven and earth.'[43] Because of their phenomenological similarities, Hick argues that God worshipped in different religious temples is the same. Although Askari does not follow the same phenomenological comparisons among diverse religions, his theology of religions consequently confirms that there is a Transcendent Reality underlying all world religions.[44] As a result of their perception of God, pluralist theologians have been criticised within and outside their faith. For instance, Reçber claims that the picture of God which has been offered by Hick is not the equivalent of the Islamic or Qur'anic God.[45] He looks at Hick's reflection on *al-Haqq*,[46] compares it with the Qur'anic usage and consequently argues that Hick's ideas on al-Haqq are not compatible with an Islamic account (most probably orthodox Islam). In response to Reçber, Hick uses Muslim Sufis such as Ibn al-Arabi and Rumi to defend his initial claims.[47] What is interesting here is that the so-called pluralists, either Christian or Muslim, challenge the orthodox understanding. For example, Turner claims that

> Pluralists' [Hick] imagination of God does not fit either an Islamic or Christian God. First, Christians and Muslims believe that there is one and only one God; polytheism is rejected, and there is no multiplicity of gods. Secondly, they are agreed that there is no multiplicity of God; God is utterly simple, without compassion and without distinction.[48]

Moreover, as a result of their removal of such doctrines as incarnation and Trinity, Christian theologians also distinguish between the orthodox and the pluralist understandings of God. The compatibility of Christian and Muslim pluralists' assumptions about God, together with the criticisms of their views, is only one part of the discussion; whether the orthodox reading of both traditions' God is compatible or not has been the main debate between Christians and Muslims.

Historically, Muslims and Christians have developed different theologies of God. Consequently, each group has had difficulties accepting the other's perceptions of God. In spite of some commonalities, the Christian doctrines of incarnation and Trinity for Muslims, and the Islamic denial of these doctrines for Christians, have led them to refute the other's God. Considering orthodox responses to the debate surrounding the issue of the same God, I will consider two remarkable public statements, one from a Christian perspective and one from a Muslim perspective: the statements of the Second Vatican Council and the initiative *A Common Word*. I will then consider a

Theology of religions reassessed 163

helpful book exploring the issue of whether or not Christians and Muslims worship the same God: Miroslav Volf's book on Allah.

Firstly, the documents produced at the Second Vatican Council discussed Muslims and their beliefs, including belief in God. This was the first time in Christian history that a Christian institution had spoken positively about Muslims.[49] The Second Vatican Council has prioritised commonalities between Christianity and other faiths. As for Islamic beliefs, despite omitting the term 'Islam' for the religion of Muslims, Muhammad as the Prophet of Islam, and the Qur'an as the holy book of Muslims, the council has focused on what is common between Islam and Christianity. *Nostra Aetate* 3 declares:

> The Church regards with esteem also the Moslems. They adore the one God, living and subsisting in Himself; merciful and all- powerful, the Creator of heaven and earth, (5) who has spoken to men; they take pains to submit wholeheartedly to even His inscrutable decrees, just as Abraham, with whom the faith of Islam takes pleasure in linking itself, submitted to God. Though they do not acknowledge Jesus as God, they revere Him as a prophet. They also honor Mary, His virgin Mother; at times they even call on her with devotion. In addition, they await the day of judgment when God will render their deserts to all those who have been raised up from the dead. Finally, they value the moral life and worship God especially through prayer, almsgiving and fasting.[50]

Furthermore, *Lumen Gentium* 16 also describes Muslims as those 'who, professing to hold the faith of Abraham, along with us adore the one and merciful God, who on the last day will judge mankind'.[51] From both texts alone, even though it is difficult to argue whether the council confirms that Muslims and Christians believe in the same God, to use the text as evidence for this claim is much easier than for the opposite claim. On the other hand, it is clear that the Second Vatican Council has led many Christian theologians to comment positively about Islamic beliefs.[52] Moreover, Pope John Paul II on several occasions confirmed that Muslims and Christians believe in the same God. In one of his famous speeches, addressing young people in Morocco in August 1985, he stated:

> For us, Abraham is a very model of faith in God, of submission to his will and of confidence in his goodness. We believe in the sane God, the one God, the living God, the God who created the world and brings his creatures to their perfection. . . . I believe that we, Christians and Muslims, must recognize with joy the religious values that we have in common, and give thanks to God for them. Both of us believe in one God the only God, who is all Justice and all Mercy; we believe in the importance of prayer, of fasting, of almsgiving, of repentance and of pardon; we believe that God will be a merciful judge to us at the end of time, and we hope that after the resurrection he will be satisfied with us and we know that we will be satisfied with him.[53]

164 *Theology of religions reassessed*

As can be seen from both the council documents and the comments by Pope John Paul II, rather than focusing exclusive attention on what divides the two faiths, they emphasise the commonality between the Islamic and Christian God but leave the differences open to interpretation. In fact elsewhere in the council documents, the Christian Trinitarian understanding of God has been confirmed several times. Furthermore, in spite of his positive comments on the Islamic understanding of God, Pope John Paul in his *Crossing the Threshold of Hope*[54] harshly criticises Islamic doctrines of God. He states:

> In Islam, all the richness of God's self-revelation, which constitutes the heritage of the Old and New Testament, has definitively been set aside. He is ultimately a God outside of the world, God is only Majesty, never Emmanuel. Islam is not religion of redemption. There is no room for the Cross and the Resurrection. Jesus is mentioned, but only as a prophet. The tragedy of redemption is completely absent. For this reason not only theology but also anthropology of Islam is very different from Christianity.[55]

These comments from Pope John Paul show that his response to Islam was not entirely positive and is different in tone from the Vatican Council's teaching, which perhaps spoke more positively and emphasised what was held in common for pragmatic reasons. However, even in the Vatican II documents, there are suggestions that non-Christian religions do not have the fullness of truth and are defective or lacking in some way, so the pope's critique of Islam could not be totally read as his statements contradict with Vatican II's teachings.

Secondly, A Common Word (ACW)[56] letter has led to a fruitful engagement between Christians and Muslims. Ironically, this has its origins in a controversy following from critical comments about Islam from another pope, Benedict XVI, in his Regensburg Lecture. A total of 138 prominent Muslim scholars, politicians and leaders who follow the two biggest Islamic denominations, Sunni and Shia, and other Islamic sects such as Ismalian and Jaafari, have signed an open letter to Christian leaders calling for peace and understanding between the two faiths. In essence, the letter addressed two themes: belief in one God and cooperation for world peace. The letter quoted several Biblical texts together with the Qur'anic verses and hadiths. On the issue of world peace, the letter used the rhetoric of love of God and love of neighbour, deliberately echoing Jesus's summary of the Jewish Law in the Gospels. The letter consisted of three parts: 'Love of God', 'Love of Neighbour' and 'A Common Word Between Us and You'. Regarding the first two parts, the parallel Qur'anic and Biblical verses are used to indicate that love of God and love of neighbour are common grounds between Islam and Christianity. As for the final part, the letter essentially describes the Islamic understanding of God as a common core of the two faiths.

Theology of religions reassessed 165

There are a few theological considerations that are worth noting. Firstly, the unity of divine revelations is confirmed. It states that in spite of our differences, 'it is clear that the two Greatest Commandments are an area of common ground and a link between the Qur'an, the Torah and the New Testament.'[57] ACW cites the Qur'anic verses 16:39 and 57:25 to approve the single unity of revelations. Secondly, the unity of God is also regarded as a commonality between Islam and Christianity. Quoting the Qur'anic verse 3:64,[58] Christians are asked to come together with Muslims on the common essentials of both faiths. Ultimately, the common essence of both faiths is seen as 'we shall worship none but God, and that we shall ascribe no partner unto Him, and that none of us shall take others for lords beside God.' From this common ground, it is quite clear that ACW implicitly rejects the Christian doctrine of God. Thirdly, the Islamic understanding of Jesus Christ is also confirmed. ACW demonstrates that Muslims are not against Christians since they recognise Jesus as a prophet.

Since it has been announced, an incredible number of Christian religious leaders, theologians and even politicians have responded to the letter.[59] Generally, the letter is welcomed by Christians as it is the first letter produced by Muslims for expanding peace and understanding between Christians and Muslims. However, some responses were not necessarily theologically grounded. There are some serious responses from Christian theologians, which should be taken into account. For instance, Troll argues that as a common element, the unity of God should be approached carefully because there are fundamental disagreements between Muslims and Christians on how God is worshipped and understood. For Christians, God is known and worshipped as the 'Father, Son and Spirit'.[60] He further states that 'it is important for Muslims approaching dialogue with Christians to understand that this Trinitarian monotheism is central to Christian belief and worship and is not an aspect of Christianity that can be negotiated away.'[61]

Williams, in a similar way to Troll, emphasises the difference between the two faiths. As for the unity of revelation, he indicates that the role of the Qur'an in Islam is not the same as the Bible in Christianity. He states that

> Christians understand the primary location of God's revealing Word to be the history of God's people and above all the history of Jesus Christ, whom we acknowledge as the Word made flesh, to which the Bible is the authoritative and irreplaceable witness.[62]

On the other hand, Muslims understand that 'the word is supremely communicated in what Mohammed is commanded to recite.'[63] His concern for the unity of God is also related to the previous response. Williams, in his response, from a Trinitarian perspective, explains how the unity of God is perceived by Christians. In short, Williams tries to show that even though that Muslims and Christians agree on the unity of God, they approach that unity differently.

166 *Theology of religions reassessed*

Both theologians' concerns seem consistent. Despite the good intention of the ACW, the letter dismisses different perceptions of God. Although it aimed to enrich dialogue between Muslims and Christians, as Hoover states the letter 'retains the inclusive supremacy of Islam, that is, the mainstream and traditionally orthodox doctrine that Islam recapitulates what is essential in preceding religions such as Judaism and Christianity'.[64] On the question of the same God, it does not concern itself with what the different faiths actually believe. There is a provocative statement in the ACW that claims that though Christians perceive Jesus differently, 'Christians themselves have never all agreed with each other on Jesus Christ's nature.'[65] In fact, the methodology that has been used in the Second Vatican Council and the Common Word are more or less similar. There are many parallelisms between these documents. Madigan argues that

> one might read their letter [ACW] as a first collective Muslim response to *Nostra Aetate*, a response that agrees to adopt the same approach as the Council: the bracketing of differences in order to affirm common beliefs, and an appeal to work together for justice and peace in the world.[66]

Both documents confirm the commonality of a monotheistic belief. Different from Vatican II, it implicitly rejects the Christian doctrine of God, whereas Vatican documents are silent on the Islamic doctrine of God. Moreover, they approach the other from their own religious viewpoint. They selectively chose either the Biblical or the Qur'anic verses to affirm that similar teaching is found in both traditions.[67] They both agree that there is one God who is worshipped by two traditions. They are intentionally silent, however, about whether the one God worshipped by Christians and Muslims is the same or not. It is difficult to reconcile both faiths' doctrines on God because of the Qur'anic rejection of a Trinitarian God.

Recently, the Protestant theologian Miroslav Volf has authored a book, *Allah: A Christian Response*,[68] in which he argues that Christians and Muslims worship the same God. Volf offers an intellectual assessment of the notion of the 'same God'. His book is a continuation of Yale Divinity School scholars' response to ACW. Like the ACW letter, he hopes to achieve two goals: theological and practical. He claims that world peace will only be achieved if believers of the two faiths understand that they worship a 'common God'.[69] He starts by looking at the problem from an historical perspective in the first part of the book. He uses Nicholas of Cusa and Luther as examples that historically illustrate the idea that Muslims and Christians believe in the same God. His use of these two figures as examples is important, as they have challenged Islamic beliefs intellectually without promoting war with Muslims. He argues that Nicholas chiefly affirms that the Islamic God does not contradict with the Trinity. The Trinity denied by Muslims is also not affirmed by Christians.[70] Furthermore, in terms of the Islamic understanding of divine unity, Nicholas thinks that 'what Muslims

Theology of religions reassessed 167

say about the one God presupposes the kinds of beliefs Christians affirm about the Trinity.'[71] Although Luther's position towards an Islamic God is not as positive as Nicholas's position, Volf still finds Luther's approach helpful. For Volf, what Luther offers shows that there is commonality between the Muslim and Christian views of God.[72] Volf takes this discussion a step further. He establishes his methodological framework to confirm that Muslims and Christians believe in the same God.

Methodologically Volf establishes two rules as his starting point; 'concentrate on what is common' between two faiths and 'keep an eye out for what is decisively different'.[73] Taking John 14:7–9 and several other Biblical passages as examples, Volf creates an analogy of a common God between Christianity and Judaism and applies it to an Islamic understanding of God. In spite of the different understanding of God between Jews and Christians, Christians commonly agreed that Jews and Christians believe in the same God. For that reason, Volf utilises that common view and takes it a step further. For the first rule, Volf turns to the Biblical and the Qur'anic passages to indicate that there is *similarity in description of God*[74] and *similarity in God's commands*, (emphasis in origianl).[75] Volf states that Muslims and Christians agree on four points in terms of similarity in God's description. Firstly, 'there is one God, the one and only divine being' (Mark 12:29, Qur'an 47:19). Secondly, 'God created everything that is not God' (Gen.1:1, Qur'an, 42:11). Thirdly, 'God is different from everything that is not God' (1 Tim. 6:16, Quran, 6:13). Fourthly, 'God is good' (1 John 4:16, Qur'an, 85:14). Regarding the similarity in God's commandments, Volf thinks that Muslim and Christian worship and practice both involve love of God and love of neighbour, which are two great, shared commandments between two faiths.[76] To Volf, worship of God is related to love of God and love of neighbour. He claims that when we love God, we directly worship God, while when we love our neighbour, we indirectly worship God.[77] From the similarity in God's description and his commandments, Volf affirms that the object of worship in both Christianity and Islam is the same.[78]

In terms of the different approaches of Islam and Christianity on the Trinity, Volf takes the mainstream orthodox reading of the doctrine of Trinity and attempts to show that there is no contradiction between Islamic and Christian beliefs on monotheism. He interprets the numerical understanding of Trinity as something that Islam and Christianity deny. He raises some Islamic objections to Trinity and then carefully responds to each of them.[79] He presents Islamic objections as if Muslims reject the Trinity because they think Christians divide divine essence. In fact, he finds mediaeval Muslim commentator al-Razi as the scholar who validates his statement. Al-Razi simply believed that Christians were 'affirming the existence of several 'self-subsisting essence[s]'.[80] Volf argues that this kind of doctrine is 'pure unbelief', not only from an Islamic perspective but also from a Christian perspective. Volf identifies the Islamic rejection of the Trinity in the same manner as the Jewish rejection of the Trinity. He states that '[n]either Jewish rejection of the Trinity nor the accusation that Christians are idolaters

168 *Theology of religions reassessed*

has led Christians to assert that Jews believe in a different God.'[81] In short, Volf claims two things: 'Christians deny what Muslims deny' (there is no God but God) and 'Christians affirm what Muslim affirm' (God is one and only).[82]

All of Volf's theological comments on the issue of the same God are related to sociopolitical reconciliation between Muslims and Christians. In other words, in this particular work, doctrinal and soteriological issues are secondary for Volf. His concern is to offer a theological solution which promotes religious harmony and world peace. His efforts and consideration about world peace are undeniably important. He offers a theological base for Christian readers to accept that Christianity and Islam worship the same God.

Sidney Griffith harshly criticises Volf's theological arguments. He contends that the reference point of difference between Islam and Christianity is Jesus's identity, which Volf has not taken into consideration. He states 'the Qur'an does not reject only unorthodox Christian doctrines of the Trinity, as some have thought; by denying the divinity of Jesus, the Qur'an rejects the entire doctrine of the Trinity, root and branch.'[83] For Griffith, rather that glossing over this basic difference, to admit the incommensurability of Muslim and Christian views on this issue is a more effective way to deal with the different understandings between Islam and Christianity. Griffith, however, does not directly argue that Muslims and Christians do not believe in the same God. For him, the answer is both yes and no. In terms of identity, Muslims and Christians believe in one, single Creator. In terms of how they refer to God's identity, however, Griffith argues that Muslims deny what Christians believe.

D'Costa also criticises Volf's methodology and theological arguments. In terms of methodology, D'Costa provides two critiques. Firstly, D'Costa finds Volf's application of Jewish-Christian relations to Muslim-Christian relations problematic. He maintains that the nature of the first relation is *sui generis* and methodologically cannot be applied to Islam. Secondly, D'Costa rightly criticises Volf's moral argument, which he believes 'fails to secure any conclusion on the question of truth'.[84] For D'Costa, Volf's emphasis on commonality is 'a possible category mistake'. He claims that Jewish-Christian history demonstrates that believing in the same God has not necessarily led to social peace or cooperation. He further argues that peace and harmony should not be reduced to the commonplace. From his experience, he believes that while he is opposed to nuclear weapons along with Hindus and Buddhists, they do not have to have a common monotheistic belief to cooperate on this issue. One can argue, however, that disagreement between two Abrahamic religions on God's nature is different from disagreement between monotheistic and polytheistic or nontheistic religions. Ideally, disagreements or commonality in religious arguments should not be a determinant for peaceful coexistence. Practically however, some disagreements have had a considerable negative impact. For instance, Volf uses the Malaysian case[85] several times in the book to indicate the necessity of a common God. In 2007, the Malaysian government addressed the 1986 law banning the word 'Allah' in non-Muslims' publications, a law they decided to apply to the Catholic weekly newspaper, *Herald*. The *Herald* appealed against the initial ban, and in 2009 a court ruled in its favour. Some Muslim groups were outraged and took a defiant stand against the decision. As a result, a series of firebomb attacks were carried out on places of Christian worship by Muslim groups. Of course, this situation cannot be used as the only justification for a common God, but overemphasis on the belief in a different God may cause conflict within multicultural societies.

Volf's common God argument is partially approved by Shah-Kazemi; however, he does not explicitly argue that Muslims and Christians believe in the same God, as Volf does. He argues that the question of whether Muslims and Christians believe in the same God comprises positive and negative elements: the answer needs to be 'yes' objectively and metaphysically and 'no' subjectively and theologically.[86] Methodologically, Shah-Kazemi uses two steps. Firstly, he compares the Islamic conception of God's essence and the attributes of God and the Christian understanding of God's essence and the persons of the Trinity. Secondly, as he himself is a Sufi, he intentionally presents the mediaeval mystics Meister Eckhart and Ibn al-Arabi to show that on the metaphysical level, the Christian and Islamic God is the same. Although this is an intriguing perspective, it is worth remembering that these two mystics, whilst very influential, are also controversial figures in their respective traditions.

From a theological perspective, Shah-Kazemi is aware of the difficulty of reconciliation between the Islamic doctrine of *tawhid* and the Christian doctrines of Trinity and incarnation. He examines the Qur'anic refutation of Trinity and discusses whether the persons of the Trinity are the essence of one God or attributes. From both the Islamic and Christian perception of the Trinity, in spite of all types of reasoning, he tends to regard Trinitarian doctrine as overshadowing the unity of God.[87] He further argues:

> The Trinity, being "undivided according to its common essence," is . . . nothing other than the One God of Abraham, Moses – and of Muhammad, one should add. However, neither Abraham nor Moses nor Muhammad would recognize that this One God is "distinct according to the properties of its persons"; they would not affirm any Trinity within the unity.[88]

Since theologically, it is difficult to affirm the same God, Shah-Kazemi utilises mysticism to find more common ground between the Islamic and Christian understandings of God. Here Shah-Kazemi uses Meister Eckhart's and Ibn al-Arabi's apophatic visions of God; he believes that God's oneness is 'symbolic',[89] meaning that Christian doctrine of the Trinity and Islamic doctrine of *tawhid* are subject to challenge.[90] He states:

170 *Theology of religions reassessed*

> Both the idea of oneness and that of trinity are alike to be grasped as symbolic of threshold of reality, and are not to be taken literally as definition of that threshold, or, still less, as definitions of the Essence of that reality. The first testimony of Islam, *lā ilāha illā'Llāh*, "no divinity but God," can metaphysically refer to the apophatic principle being described here: no conceivable divinity, only the inconvincible Absolute.[91]

Shah-Kazemi's overall analysis of the issue of the same God is a reflection of his theology of religions. As Sufi, he offers a universality of God. His tendency is to affirm similarity but also show awareness of differences. The most important common ground between the two faiths is that both believe in God's transcendence; however, they disagree about how the transcendent divinity relates to and is present within creation (especially the prophet Jesus). For Shah-Kazemi that difference is challenging for both Muslims and Christians, and he calls for the believers of both faiths to embrace each other and challenge the deep understanding of both faiths.

From the contributions considered here, it can be seen that any attempt to augment good relations between Muslims and Christians ends with emphasising commonality between the two faiths. Their common belief in monotheism seems to be the most effective way to find theological ground so that the believers of these two faiths might find deeper convergence and unity. Even though Vatican II and ACW have shown a tendency to insist on their own religious perspectives about others' beliefs, their efforts have been more applauded by the opposite faith's believers than criticised. As previously noted emphasising commonalities is not the only way; however, given contemporary conditions, it might be considered the more reasonable way. As demonstrated in the Malaysian case, emphasis on difference might not be good for the common good.

From the analysis of the Vatican II documents and ACW, as well as Volf's book and his critics, it can be clearly seen that it is not as easy as some Muslim and Christian pluralists think to assert that Muslims and Christians believe in the same God. The difficulty of an immediate answer to the same God idea resides in the complexity of issue. From theology of religions' perspective, it might be easier to highlight the same notion of God as both traditions have the idea of God and in certain aspects their perceptions of God look similar. However, by close attention to the specific details of both traditions' perceptions on a similar issue, we could see the complexity of such assertions raised within theology of religions. Thus, to have a better apprehension of different perceptions of both traditions' perception on the same issue urges the necessity of comparative theology.

The only thing that is obvious is that Muslims and Christians are in agreement on the notion that there is one, and only one, God who is the source of everything. In addition, to argue that despite differences, Muslims and Christians believe in the same God seems less problematic than to argue that in spite of commonality, Muslims and Christians believe in a different God.

As Christoph Schwöbel notes, '[I]t would be disastrous if Christians and Muslims would agree that they worship and believe in different gods. This would mean either that Christians and Muslims live in different realities or that there is no unitary ground for all reality.'[92]

The Christian doctrine of Trinity lies at the heart of the discussion. From the Christological point of view, any conclusion on sharing the same God should not be in contradiction with the Trinity, whereas from the Islamic perspective the oneness of God should not be challenged. Although Volf presents his argument as if the Islamic denial of the Trinity does not necessarily deny the Christian doctrine of Trinity, the Qur'anic description of God can under no circumstances accept orthodox understandings of the Trinity. On the other hand, despite different interpretations of God among Muslims, there is consensus among Muslims about the overall nature of God. Thus, the question of whether Muslims and Christians believe in the same God still remains undecided. When a positive answer is rejected, the common monotheistic belief also seems to be in danger; while if it is accepted uncritically, both faiths' specific doctrines of God seem to be challenged. Both religions' perceptions of revelation play major roles to determine the same God question. The next section will consider the concept of revelation in Christianity and Islam.

4 The concept of revelation

The concept of revelation is directly related to the same God debate. The disagreements between Islam and Christianity on the nature of God are a direct result of their disagreements on the nature of revelation. Thus, the concept of revelation in the Islamic and Christian faiths requires more careful discussion than the concept of the same God since Islam and Christianity have more disputes about revelation. In spite of some commonalities, both religions offer different explanations of the nature of revelation. The disagreement between the two religions is deep, thus further exploration is necessary.

Starting with Islam, the Qur'an uses the words *wahy* and *tanzil* to describe revelation. There are different forms of *wahy*, but only one form of *wahy* is related to prophetic revelation. The Qur'an uses this term when it refers to other prophetic revelations as well as the Qur'anic revelation. For instance, the Qur'an referring to itself says,

> And thus We have revealed [*awhainaaa*, an expression including the verb *wahy*] to you an inspiration of Our command. You did not know what is the Book or [what is] faith, but We have made it a light by which We guide whom We will of Our servants (42:52).

As for the other prophets, another verse says,

> Indeed, We have revealed [awhainaaa] to you, as We revealed [awhainaaa] to Noah and the prophets after him. And We revealed [awhainaaa]

172   *Theology of religions reassessed*

to Abraham, Ishmael, Isaac, Jacob, the Descendants, Jesus, Job, Aaron, and Solomon, and to David We gave the book (4:163).

As for *tanzil*, the literal meaning is to send down. In Islamic tradition, God sends His message down to the people. It is not God Himself who descends (as Word or Spirit), but it is his will and message which are sent down. God does not speak to people directly but sends downs his words via the angel Gabriel. Thus, it is the book of the Qur'an, as the revealed words of God, which is sent down by God to his Prophet Muhammad via the angel Gabriel over twenty-three years. The Qur'an does not use this word only to describe the Qur'anic revelation, however, but also for the Torah and the Gospel. 'Indeed, We sent down [anzalnat an expression including the verb nazala] the Torah, in which was guidance and light' (5:44) and 'let the people of the Gospel judge by what Allah has revealed therein' (5:47). From these two verses, it seems that the Qur'an presupposes that the nature of revelation in the Torah, Gospel and Qur'an is the same. All are sent down by God to his prophets.

The purpose of revelation in Islam is one and the same: to remind people of the Creator and establish a relationship between God and the people. From the Qur'anic perspective, every nation is given a prophet for the same reason.[93] The Qur'an states, 'Mankind was one single nation, and Allah sent Messengers with glad tidings and warnings; and with them He sent the Book in truth, to judge between people in matters wherein they differed' (2:213). As a result, there are multiple revelations over the course of history according to Islamic belief, but each revelation is related since they all come from God. Consequently, the purpose of the Qur'anic revelation is often seen as a confirmation and correction of other revelations. On the one hand, the Qur'an itself confirms the old revelations (the Torah and the Gospel);[94] on the other hand, Jews and Christians are criticised for distorting and corrupting their scriptures and not regarding their scriptures with proper esteem.[95] As a result of the Qur'anic accusation of corruption, Muslim theologians later thought that Jews and Christians were given a similar book to the Qur'anic revelation, but later they changed their scriptures. Some other theologians, however, developed the idea that it is not their book which is corrupted but rather the message of God was corrupted.

Looking at revelation in the Christian tradition, revelation and inspiration are interpreted as two different things. Although Christian theologians have different perceptions of incarnation, orthodox Christians agree on the fact that God made Himself present in the form of a historical figure. Incarnation is believed by Christians to be rooted in the New Testament. There are some Biblical passages referring to the incarnation of God's Word in Jesus.[96] The doctrine was subsequently formulated in the Nicaea Council in 325. In the council, the doctrine of incarnation is expressed as follows:

And in one Lord Jesus Christ, the Son of God, the only-begotten of the Father, of the substance of the Father; God of God and Light of Light;

true God of true God; begotten, not made, of the same substance as the Father, by whom all things were made, in heaven and on earth: who for the sake of us men and our salvation, descended, became incarnate, and was made man, suffered, arose again on the third day, and ascended into the heavens, from where he will come again to judge the living and the dead.

Christians believe that incarnation in Jesus (revelation) is the self-manifestation of God. They believe that in a particular time and space, the divine life transforms a particular human life by uniting it to itself.[97] The formulation of the doctrine of incarnation is related to the doctrine of Trinity. Jesus as the second person of the Trinity is believed to be fully human and divine. The purpose of the incarnation is the reconciliation of human beings to God. It is believed that 'Jesus' self-offering, his sacrifice, is the prayer that this [reconciliation] may be accomplished. Since, on the Christian view, the life of Jesus mediates the acts of God to humanity, the prayer effects what it requests.'[98] As a result of the Trinity and incarnation, Jesus has been the central figure in Christian theology. As has been demonstrated in the first chapter, the removal of these doctrines by some revisionist pluralist theologians has led to a discussion over orthodoxy and heresy in Christian theology of religions.

As for the scriptures, Christian theologians use the word 'inspiration'. The First Vatican Council describes scriptures thus: 'having been written by the inspiration of the Holy Spirit, they have God for their author.'[99] In Christian theology, the Bible is believed not to be written by the dictation of God but by the inspiration of God. Christians perceive the Bible as part of God's revelation of Himself. They tend to speak of the writers of the books, other than the prophets, not as having 'received revelation' but as being 'inspired,' that is, as having been guided in their writing by God's spirit, the Holy Spirit.[100]

From the viewpoint of Islam and Christianity, it is quite apparent that both religions have different perceptions of revelation and scripture. The common point is that both faiths assume that God has communicated with the people in revelation; the way of God's communication is, however, perceived differently. The Qur'an in Islamic theology and Christ in Christian theology are seen as God's communication with people. While the Islamic understating of revelation (*tanzil*) assumes God to have a personal engagement with people, in Christianity the meaning of revelation is that God has engaged in a historical person's life. From the literal meaning of the Qur'anic verses, one can assume that the Gospel for Christians has the same authority as the Qur'an. For Christians however, the Gospel is a record of Jesus's life, teachings, sermons and his death. Christians accept the historical nature of the Bible, but they regard it as inspirited by God. Thus, the Qur'anic account of the scriptures is complicated by the fact that Christians view their scriptures in a different way. For both Muslims and Christians there are a numerous things that can be learnt from each other's theologies. Although the nature of revelation (incarnation) in

174 *Theology of religions reassessed*

Christianity is rejected by the Qur'an, for Muslims, rather than focusing on the nature, engaging with the meaning would be more useful. Thus, if Muslims want to appreciate other peoples' scriptures, they must seriously engage with other faiths' understanding of their scriptures. 'As long as Muslims continue to impose their theory of revelation on other scriptures, the charge of the falsification of pre-Qur'ānic scriptures will remain strong.'[101]

Conclusion

Even though Christians and Muslims share some concepts in common, it seems that in certain aspects, they develop different theologies. The concept of revelation seems to lie at the heart of difference. Having different perspectives on revelation affects the question of whether Muslims and Christians can affirm wholly that both believe in the same God. The discussion on the same God should not be a matter of an either/or position. Muslims and Christians, despite having differences, can still learn from each other.

Theology of religions has its own validity, but it needs to be carried out in cooperation with comparative theology and the practice of dialogue to do justice to religious difference. Contemporary Muslims' approaches towards other religions need to be revised as they do not take into account wholly the differences of other religions. I have offered a comparative approach to certain themes in both religions which would help to contextualise a better position. Although I have tried to apply a comparative approach for the same God question and the concept of revelation, this still remains limited considering the complexity of the issue.

I will conclude this chapter by offering some imagined possibilities in a possible dialogue environment. The next chapter will offer concluding remarks for the book.

First possibility: if Christians adopt an exclusivist perspective like that of Barth, viewing all 'religion' as unbelief and Christianity as the only one which contains revelation, while Muslims continue to believe that Islamic revelation supersedes all other forms of religion, even those with valid revelations, then the situation will remain in a deadlock. It seems that there is no transition, no comparative element and no need for dialogue. This form of theology, on both the Christian and Muslim sides, cannot communicate with other forms of theology as it claims to hold the totality of truth as a whole. In Ward's terminology this is mainly 'closed' theology.

Second possibility: another possible situation involves participants who think that religions are different historical responses to the same transcendence and that there is a single God or a transcendent Reality behind all religions. This argument follows the line of thought of pluralists like Hick and Askari. Although I presented the pluralist option in the same God discussion, pluralist theologians (in particular Hick's argument) are sometimes regarded as opposing both the Islamic and Christian understandings of God; although in a dialogue environment, there are still certain things that can be developed with these kinds of pluralist presuppositions. While some Muslims would struggle to locate their religion as one form of human response to the same divine being, and some Christians would struggle to express the unique relations of divine reality with Jesus, this does not necessarily close any door to cross referencing, comparative theology and dialogue. In Ward's terminology, this is partly 'open' theology.

Third possibility: from a Trinitarian perspective, the Christian participants hold that the Holy Spirit is working in other religions; from an Islamic perspective, the Muslims propose that God has sent revelations and divided us so that we might know each other through collaboration. Thus, from both perspectives, there are true elements in other faiths. Christians and Muslims, in this situation, have distinct, tradition-specific reasons for wanting to explore other religions to find the presence of the Holy Spirit's work or prophetic revelation. It does not necessarily lead to judging other religions or to viewing common ground as having divine origin and regarding differences as human and false. There is a lot to explore to engage with deeply for the sake of learning, dialogue and practice. As a Muslim, I cannot propose a theology of religions that takes Trinitarian belief as its framework. However, I have come to think that there are some parallels between such Christian proposals and a Qur'anic vision of inclusivity. It is this kind of Islamic theology of religions, based on Islamic sources but partly inspired by Christian thinking, that I have argued for and think will be helpful for Muslims as they address the questions posed by religious pluralism and engage in dialogue with their religious others. Such an approach will allow Muslims to move towards a relatively more 'open' theology, in Ward's terms, which is capable of being affected in some way by its encounter with others.

Notes

1 See for example, Yusuf H. Seferta, "The Concept of Religious Authority according to Muhammad Abduh and Rashid Rida," *Islamic Quarterly* 30 (1986): 159–164; Fazlur Rahman, *Islam and Modernity: Transformation of an Intellectual Tradition* (Chicago: University of Chicago Press, 1984); Clinton Bennett, *Muslims and Modernity: An Introduction to the Issues and Debates* (New York: Continuum, 2005); Bassam Tibi, *Islam's Predicament with Modernity: Religious Reform and Cultural Change* (London: Routledge, 2009).
2 Hick originally put God in the centre but later offered the divine Reality or ultimate Reality as the value shared by the world religions to include non-theistic religions. Although his later theology of religions is not exempt from problems, the progress in his theology of religions shows that the critiques made against his theology have worked in certain ways. The same can be said for Knitter's theology of religions. In his early works Knitter developed a theocentric form of theology of religions. However, eventually he departed from his original theology as he thought that emphasis on a singular divine Reality might lead to disregard for the differences of other faiths. Rather than focusing on theology, he offers ethics as the common ground among religions.
3 As I have discussed in the first chapter, Barth's, Rahner's and Hick's theologies are examples of exclusivism, inclusivism and pluralism, respectively, which emerged chronologically. That does not mean that the theology which came later

176 *Theology of religions reassessed*

replaced the former one. In the contemporary period, there are still theologians promoting all three positions.

4 Jenny Daggers, "The Christian Past and Interreligious Future of Religious Studies and Theology," *Journal of the American Academy of Religion* 7/4 (December 2010): 961.
5 Ibid., 965–966.
6 Ibid., 968.
7 Ibid., 969.
8 Ibid., 973.
9 Tomoko Masuzawa, *The Invention of World Religions: Or How European Universalism Was Preserved in the Language of Pluralism* (Chicago: University of Chicago Press, 2005).
10 Hugh Nicholson, "Comparative Theology after Liberalism," *Modern Theology* 23/2 (2007): 232.
11 Paul Hedges, *Controversies in Interreligious Dialogue and the Theology of Religions* (London: SCM Press, 2010), 74–76.
12 Jacques Wardenburg, *Muslim Perceptions of Other Religions: A Historical Survey* (Oxford, New York: University of Oxford Press, 1999), 19.
13 Al-Faruqi, for instance, is an exceptional theologian. His ideas seem to be consistent with the universalist-exclusivist theology of religion, but he has played an important role for Muslim-Christian dialogue in the US.
14 Richard Schebera, "Comparative Theology: A New Method of Interreligious Dialogue," *Dialogue and Alliance* 17/1 (Spring/Summer 2003): 7–18.
15 Ibid., 9.
16 Ibid., 10.
17 Peter Feldmeier, "Is Theology of Religions an Exhausted Project?" *Horizon* 35/2 (2008): 266.
18 Ibid., 268.
19 Ibid.
20 The Qur'an, 9:29.
21 Rifat Atay, "Religious Pluralism and Islam: A Critical Examination of John Hick's Pluralist Hypothesis" (PhD diss., University of St. Andrew, 1999), 3.
22 The Qur'an uses the word *tahrīf* and *tabdīl* (meaning change or corruption) while referring to the books of beliefs and practice of the People of the Book. This issue is complicated. There is no straightforward Qur'anic position towards the scriptures of other religions. As has been noted, the Qur'an offers complicated statements, both positive and negative, regarding the scriptures of Jews and Christians. For a good overview on the issue of *tahrīf* and *tabdīl*, see Munim A. Sirry, "The Falsification of Jewish and Christian Scriptures," in *Scriptural Polemics: The Qur'an and Other Religions* (New York, Oxford University Press, 2014), 100–132.
23 Lamptey, *Never Wholly Other*, 48.
24 Gavin D'Costa, *The Meeting of Religions and The Trinity* (Edinburg: T&T Clark Ltd., 2000), 22–24, 116.
25 D'Costa, "Holy Spirit and the World Religions," *Louvain Studies* 34 (2009–2010): 279–311.
26 D'Costa does not only argue all truths which are seen non-Christian religions should be considered as the Holy Spirit's action; he also says some truths can be achieved through natural law without Holy Spirit's intervention (Ibid.).
27 Ibid.
28 D'Costa, *Meeting of Religions*, 138.
29 Jenny Daggers, *Postcolonial Theology of Religions: Particularity and Pluralism in World Christianity* (London: Routledge, 2013), 161–165.
30 Ibid., 165–167.
31 Ibid., 167–171.

Theology of religions reassessed 177

32 Daggers, "Thinking Religions," 984.
33 Daggers, *Post Colonial Theology*, 206.
34 Ibid., 207. She is referring to Amos Yong, *Discerning the Spirit(s): A Pentecostal-Charismatic Contribution to a Theology of Religions* (Sheffield: Sheffield Academia Press, 2000).
35 Ibid., 208.
36 See the Quran, 5:3.
37 See Jeannine Hill Fletcher, *Monopoly on Salvation: A Feminist Approach to Religious Pluralism* (London: Continuum, 2005). See specifically chapter four, *We Are All Hybrids*, 82–101. She argues that we are all hybrids and that not only religious tradition but also other factors such as culture, gender and social class complicate our sense of religious identity.
38 See, for example, the Qur'anic verses in which God articulates belief and right deeds: 2:25, 2:2, 2:277, 3:57, 5:69 and 18:88.
39 Yasir Qadhi, "The Path of Allah or the Paths of Allah? Revisiting Classical and Medieval Sunni Approaches to Salvation of Others," in *Between Heaven and Hell: Islam, Salvation and the Fate of Others*, ed. Mohammad Khalil (New York: University of Oxford Press, 2013), 119.
40 Keith Ward, *Religion and Revelation: A Theology of Revelation in the World Religions* (Oxford: Clarendon Press, 1994), 339–340.
41 Ibid., 340.
42 Ibid.
43 John Hick, *God Has Many Names* (London: Macmillan Press, 1980), 45–46.
44 See Hasan Askari, "Within and Beyond the Experience of Religious Diversity," in *Spiritual Quest: An Inter-Religious Dimension*, eds. John Hick, and Hasan Askari (Pudsey: Seven Mirror, 1991), 39–58.
45 Mehmet Sait Reçber, "Hick, The Real and al-Haqq," *Islam and Christian Muslim Relations* 1/1 (January 2006): 3–10.
46 Al-Haqq is one of the ninety-nine names of Allah, which means the Truth or the Real.
47 John Hick, "Response to Dr. Reçber," *Islam and Christian-Muslim Relations* 16/1 (2010): 11–14.
48 Denys Turner, "Christians, Muslims and the Name of God: Who Owns It, and How Would We Know?" in *Do We Worship the Same God? Jews Christians and Muslims in Dialogue*, ed. Miroslav Volf (Grand Rapids: Eerdmans Publishing, 2012), 26.
49 Although, in eleventh century, Pope Gregory VII (1073–1085) wrote to a Muslim emir that 'You and we . . . believe in and confess one God, admittedly in a different way, and daily we praise and venerate him, the creator of worlds and ruler of this world,'(quoted from Rollin Armour, *Islam, Christianity and the West: A Troubled History* [Maryknoll, NY: Orbis Books, 2002], 103) that did not lead to any positive relations between Muslims and Christians.
50 Declaration on the Relation of the Church to Non-Christian Religions (*Nostra Aetate*), available at: http://www.vatican.va/archive/hist_councils/ii_vatican_coun cil/documents/vat-ii_decl_19651028_nostra-aetate_en.html (accessed in 26 August 2015).
51 Dogmatic Constitution on the Church (*Lumen Gentium*), available at: http://www.vatican.va/archive/hist_councils/ii_vatican_council/documents/vat-ii_const_19641121_lumen-gentium_en.html (accessed in 26 August 2015).
52 See for example, David Marshal, "Roman Catholic Approaches to the Qur'an since Vatican II," *Islam and Muslim-Christian Relations* 25/1 (2013): 89–100. He examines Catholic scholars approaches of Islam such as Giulio Bassetti-Sani, George Dardess, Jacques Dupuis, Hans Küng, Jacques Jomier and some others who mainly comment on the authenticity of Qur'anic revelation.

178 *Theology of religions reassessed*

53 Addressing of His Holiness John Paul II to Young Muslims: Morocco (Monday 19 August 1985), available at: http://w2.vatican.va/content/john-paul-ii/en/speeches/1985/august/documents/hf_jp-ii_spe_19850819_giovani-stadio-casablanca.html (accessed in 20 April 2015).
54 John Paul, *Crossing the Threshold of Hope* (London: Jonathan Cape, 1994).
55 Ibid., 93.
56 All information, including the letter, signatures, responses and several other things regarding the ACW, can be found here: http://www.acommonword.com/ (accessed in 30 April 2015).
57 See third part of the letter. Available at: http://www.acommonword.com/.
58 'Say: O People of the Scripture. Come to an agreement between us and you: that we shall worship none but Allah, and that we shall ascribe no partners unto Him, and that none of us shall take others for lords beside Allah. And if they turn away, then say: Bear witness that we are they who have surrendered (unto Him)' (Qur'an, 3:64).
59 All responses can be found here: http://www.acommonword.com/category/site/christian-responses/ (accessed April 30, 2015).
60 Christian Troll, *Towards Common Ground between Christians and Muslims?*, available at: http://www.sankt-georgen.de/leseraum/troll46.pdf (accessed in 30 April 2015).
61 Ibid.
62 Rowan Williams, *A Common Word for the Common Good*, available at: http://rowanwilliams.archbishopofcanterbury.org/articles.php/1107/a-common-word-for-the-common-good (accessed in 30 April 2015).
63 Ibid.
64 John Hoover, "A Common Word: 'More Positive and Open, Yet Mainstream and Orthodox'," *Theological Review (Near East School of Theology)* 30/1 (April 2009): 65.
65 ACW letter, Ibid. Tim Winter in an interview with Joseph W. Edwin, states that 'they (referring to ACW) cannot take a viewon the Trinity since they are aware that there is no Christian consensus on Trinitarian doctrine. Many Christians, in the reformed traditions at any rate, now do not accept it at all. The *Daily Telegraph* (31 July 2002) recorded that a quarter of Anglican priests now state that they do not believe in the Trinity. Amongst lay Christians in the UK, in my experience, the proportion is still higher. The ACW's policy is to give Christians the benefit of the doubt (*husn al-zann*) and engage with them on the basis that many hold theories about the Trinity that can indeed be defined, as Muslims understand it, as monotheistic. This is necessary for the sake of reconciliation. Cappadocian views, rather than the rival Augustinian theory, may be somewhat more amenable to definition as monotheistic. But the CW certainly cannot offer a view on all Christianunderstandings of this doctrine.' Joseph W. Edwin, "A Common Word between Us and You: A New Departure in Muslim Attitudes towards Christianity" (Master diss., University of Birmingham, 2010), available at http://www.acommonword.com/category/new-fruits/publications/ (accessed in 30 April 2015).
66 Daniel Madigan, '*A Common Word between Us and You': Some Initial Reflections*' (18 January 2008), available at: http://www.thinkingfaith.org/articles/20080118_9.htm (accessed in 30 April 2015).
67 While Vatican II documents have not directly used the Qur'anic verses, when referring to Muslims, they implicitly used the Qur'anic verses. See S. J. Christian Troll, "Changing Catholic Views of Islam," in *Islam and Christianity: Mutual Perceptions since the Mid-20th Century*, ed. Jacques Waardenburg (Leuven: Peeters, 1998), 23–27.
68 Miroslav Volf, *Allah: A Christian Response* (New York: HarperOne, 2011).

Theology of religions reassessed 179

69 Ibid., 9.
70 Ibid., 49–50.
71 Ibid., 50.
72 Ibid., 75.
73 Ibid., 91.
74 Ibid., 97–102.
75 Ibid., 104–108.
76 Ibid.
77 Ibid., 102.
78 Ibid., 110.
79 Ibid., 133–135.
80 Ibid., 135.
81 Ibid., 144.
82 Ibid., 43.
83 Sidney H. Griffith, *Is Their God Ours: A Review of Allah: A Christian Response by Miroslav Volf*, available at: http://www.firstthings.com/article/2011/10/is-their-god-ours (accessed in 30 April 2015).
84 Gavin D'Costa, "Do Christians and Muslims Believe in the Same God? Reflections on Miroslav Volf's Allah: A Christian Response," *Islam and Christian-Muslim Relations* 24/2 (2013): 151–160.
85 Volf, *Allah: A Christian Response*, 80–81, 130, 188.
86 Reza Shah-Kazemi, "Do Muslims and Christians Believe in the Same God?" in *Do We Worship the Same God? Jews Christians and Muslims in Dialogue*, ed. Miroslav Volf (Grand Rapids: Eerdmans Publishing, 2012), 78.
87 Ibid., 103.
88 Ibid., 140.
89 Ibid., 120.
90 Ibid., 121.
91 Ibid.
92 Christoph Schwöbel, "The Same God? The Perspective of Faiths, the Identity of God, Tolerance and Dialogue," in *Do We Worship the Same God? Jews Christians and Muslims in Dialogue*, ed. Miroslav Volf (Grand Rapids: Eerdmans Publishing, 2012), 1–17.
93 The Qur'an, 35:24, and 10:47.
94 The Qur'an, 10:95: 'If thou wert in doubt as to what We have revealed unto thee, then ask those who have been reading the Book [the Torah and the Gospel] from before thee: the Truth hath indeed come to thee from thy Lord: so be in nowise of those in doubt' and 29:46: 'Do not debate with the people of the Book unless it is in the best manner, except with those of them who commit injustice. And say, "We believe in what is sent down to us and sent down to you, and our God and your God is One, and to Him we submit (ourselves)." '
95 The Qur'an, 4:46 and 5:15.
96 The most formulate passage is Philippians 2:5–11. The first passages of the Gospel of John also indicate how Word become flesh (incarnate in Jesus).
97 Ward, *Revelation and Religion*, 194.
98 Ibid., 185.
99 Vatican Council I, Dei Filius 2, in J. Neurer and J. Dupois (eds.), *The Christian Faith in the Doctrinal Documents of the Catholic Church* (London: Collins, 1983), 75, cited in Ward, *Revelation and Religion*, 209.
100 Montgomery W. Watt, *Islam and Christianity Today: A Contribution to Dialogue* (London: Routledge, 1983), 58.
101 Mun'im Sirry, *Scriptural Polemics: The Qur'an and Other Religions* (New York: Oxford University Press, 2014), 131.

Theology of religions reassessed

Bibliography

Armour, Rollin. *Islam, Christianity and the West: A Troubled History*. Maryknoll, NY: Orbis Books, 2002.

Askari, Hasan. "Within and Beyond Experience of Religious Diversity." In *The Experience of Religious Diversity*, edited by John Hick and Hasan Askari, 191–218. Gower, Aldershot: Gower Publishing, 1985.

Atay, Rifat. "Religious Pluralism and Islam: A Critical Examination of John Hick's Pluralistic Hypothesis." PhD diss., University of St Andrews, 1999.

Bennett, Clinton. *Muslims and Modernity: An Introduction to the Issues and Debates*. New York: Continuum, 2005.

Daggers, Jenny. "The Christian Past and Interreligious Future of Religious Studies and Theology." *Journal of the American Academy of Religions* 7/4 (2010): 961–990.

———. *Postcolonial Theology of Religions: Particularity and Pluralism in World Christianity*. Abingdon, Oxon: Routledge, 2013.

D'Costa, Gavin. "Do Christians and Muslims Believe in the Same God? Reflections on Miroslav Volf's Allah: A Christian Response." *Islam and Christian-Muslim Relations* 24/2 (2013): 151–160.

———. "Holy Spirit and the World Religions." *Louvain Studies* 34 (2009–2010): 279–311.

———. *The Meeting of Religions and the Trinity*. Edinburg: T&T Clark, 2000.

Edwin, Joseph W. "A Common Word between Us and You: A New Departure in Muslim Attitudes towards Christianity." Master diss., University of Birmingham, 2010. www.acommonword.com/category/new-fruits/publications/ (accessed April 30, 2015).

Feldmeier, Peter. "Is Theology of Religions and Exhausted Project?" *Horizon* 35/2 (2008): 253–270.

Fletcher, Jeannine Hill. *Monopoly on Salvation? A Feminist Approach to Religious Pluralism*. New York: Continuum, 2005.

Griffith, Sidney H. *Is Their God Ours: A Review of Allah: A Christian Response by Miroslav Volf*, 1 October 2011. www.firstthings.com/article/2011/10/is-their-god-ours (accessed April 30, 2015).

Hedges, Paul. *Controversies in Interreligious Dialogue and the Theology of Religions*. London: SCM Press, 2010.

Hick, John. *God Has Many Names*. London: Macmillan, 1980.

———. "Response to Dr. Reçber." *Islam and Christian-Muslim Relations* 16/1 (2010): 11–14.

Hoover, John. "A Common Word: 'More Positive and Open, Yet Mainstream and Orthodox'." *Theological Review (Near East School of Theology)* 30/1 (April 2009): 50–77.

Lamptey, Jerusha. *Never Wholly Other: A Muslima Theology of Religions*. New York: Oxford University Press, 2014.

Madigan, Daniel. *A Common Word between Us and You': Some Initial Reflections*. 18 January 2008. www.thinkingfaith.org/articles/20080118_9.htm (accessed April 30, 2015).

Marshall, David. "Roman Catholic Approaches to the Qur'an since Vatican II." *Islam and Muslim-Christian Relations* 25/1 (2013): 89–100.

Masuzawa, Tomoko. *The Invention of World Religions: Or How European Universalism Was Preserved in the Language of Pluralism*. Chicago: University of Chicago Press, 2005.

Nicholson, Hugh. "Comparative Theology after Liberalism." *Modern Theology* 23/2 (2007): 229–251.

Qadhi, Yasir. "The Path of Allah or the Paths of Allah? Revisiting Classical and Medieval Sunni Approaches to Salvation of Others." In *Between Heaven and Hell: Islam, Salvation and the Fate of Others*, edited by Mohammad Khalil, 110–122. New York: University of Oxford Press, 2013.

Rahman, Fazlur. *Islam and Modernity: Transformation of an Intellectual Tradition*. Chicago: University of Chicago Press, 1982.

Reçber, Mehmet Sait. "Hick, The Real and al-Haqq." *Islam and Christian Muslim Relations* 1/1 (January 2006): 3–10.

Schebera, Richard. "Comparative Theology: A New Method of Interreligious Dialogue." *Dialogue and Alliance* 17/1 (Spring/Summer 2003): 7–18.

Schwöbel, Christoph. "The Same God? The Perspective of Faiths, the Identity of God, Tolerance and Dialogue." In *Do We Worship the Same God? Jews Christians and Muslims in Dialogue*, edited by Miroslav Volf, 1–17. Grand Rapids: Eerdmans Publishing, 2012.

Seferta, Yusuf H. "The Concept of Religious Authority according to Muhammad Abduh and Rashid Rida." *Islamic Quarterly* 30 (1986): 159–164.

Shah-Kazemi, Reza. "Do Muslims and Christians Believe in the Same God?" In *Do We Worship the Same God? Jews Christians and Muslims in Dialogue*, edited by Miroslav Volf, 76–147. Grand Rapids: Eerdmans Publishing, 2012.

Sirry, Munim. *Scriptural Polemics: The Qur'an and Other Religions*. New York: Oxford University Press, 2014.

Tibi, Bassam. *Islam's Predicament with Modernity: Religious Reform and Cultural Change*. London: Routledge, 2009.

Troll, Christian. *Christian, towards Common Ground between Christians and Muslims?* 22 October 2007. www.sankt-georgen.de/leseraum/troll46.pdf (accessed April 30, 2015).

Turner, Denys. "Christians, Muslims and the Name of God: Who Owns It, and How Would We Know?" In *Do We Worship the Same God? Jews Christians and Muslims in Dialogue*, edited by Miroslav Volf, 18–36. Grand Rapids: Eerdmans Publishing, 2012.

Volf, Miroslav. *Allah: A Christian Response*. New York: HarperOne, 2011.

Waardenburg, Jacques. *Muslim and Others: Relations in Context*. Berlin: Walter Gruyter, 2003.

———, ed. *Muslim Perceptions of Other Religions*. New York, Oxford: Oxford University Press, 1999.

Ward, Keith. *Religion and Revelation: A Theology of Revelation in the World Religions*. Oxford: Oxford University Press, 1994.

Watt, Montgomery W. *Islam and Christianity Today: A Contribution to Dialogue*. London: Routledge, 1983.

Williams, Rowan. *A Common Word for the Common Good*, 15 July 2008. http://rowanwilliams.archbishopofcanterbury.org/articles.php/1107/a-common-word-for-the-common-good (accessed April 30, 2015).

Conclusion

In this study I have examined diverse Christian and Muslim responses to religious diversity. Liberal understandings of religious diversity have brought many challenges to both Christian and Islamic theology of religions. Those who have integrated enlightenment philosophy and empirical study of other religions into their theological approaches have started to offer more inclusivist approaches towards the other. This trend in Christian theology of religions started with Karl Rahner and has continued with more pluralistic positions offered by John Hick and some others. Their pluralistic approaches have been considered more open to religious others than other approaches as they reject claims for the superiority of a specific religion by equalising them. However, on the one hand post-liberal theologians have proposed a cultural-linguistic theory of religious difference which considers religions as incommensurable. By arguing for the incommensurability of religions, post-liberal theologians have aimed to recognise both the distinctiveness of Christianity, which retains its particular claims to superiority, and to accept the real difference of other religions. On the other hand, comparative theologians have carried the discussion of religious diversity to another level, which basically proposes that theorising other religions should take place after inter-religious engagement, not before. Comparative theologians have also sought a better understanding of their own religions in the light of learning from other religions. Thus, pluralism's rejection of the superiority of a single religion, post-liberalism's acceptance of the real difference of other religions and comparative theology's attempts at a better understanding of other religions and simultaneously of their own religions seem to be the main insights of these different approaches.

Rowan Williams's theology of religions, though it has some unresolved issues, seems to acknowledge, for the most part, the insights of different approaches which are usually offered as alternatives to one another. His theology of religions, on the one hand, retains the orthodox beliefs of Christian faith, while on the other hand, it shows a surprising level of radical openness towards the believers of other religions. His openness towards others has been considered to be the consequence of his Trinitarian theology of religions, which respects the real differences of other religions and, simultaneously, does not claim to hold the totality of truth.

When we came to Islamic theology of religions, I noted that Muslim theologians' responses to religious diversity have also been somewhat affected by modernity and liberal ideas. On the one hand, the sociopolitical exclusivist position has challenged modernity by rejecting Western values, while subsequently affirming Islamic superiority; it has also rejected any values of different religions, primarily Christian and Jewish values. On the other hand, pluralist Muslims have also challenged modernity by accepting liberal values as something which can be accommodated within Islamic faith. From this perspective, like their Christian liberal counterparts, they have offered a more pluralistic approach which makes a distinction between historical and universal Islam. Thus universal Islam was seen as a religion of God that includes different religious traditions, including historical Islam. While these two different approaches have shown up modernism's effect on Islam, theologically exclusivist theologians have modified the traditional form of exclusivism that locates Islam as superseding other religions. Although some approaches have significant insights, the exclusivist position devalues non-Islamic religions by its supersessionist theory, whereas the pluralist position ignores the real difference of other religions by putting too much emphasis on the sameness of religions.

In contrast to these two main Islamic responses to religious diversity, Jerusha Lamptey has contextualised her theology of religions by firstly looking at the differences of other religions. Unlike pluralist positions, by turning the direction of focus from sameness to difference, her theology of religions makes a new and significant contribution to Islamic theology of religions. She has combined several methodological approaches and offered her own Muslima theology of religions, which aims at equal treatment of similarity and difference among religions. While her theology of religions successfully locates Islam among world religions, it also uses Islamic presuppositions for understanding other religions, which to some extent are inadequate as a response to non-theistic and polytheistic religions.

To correspond sufficiently with the real difference of non-Islamic religions, I have proposed an Islamic theology of religions which works together with comparative theology. However, since the main focus of this study is to analyse Islamic and Christian theology of religions, I have offered only a short comparative overview of two important notions: the concept of God and revelation. Although these two concepts also need more careful comparison, requiring in-depth focus on the two religions' scriptures and investigation of specific themes, my primary aim was to illustrate that the Islamic and Christian understanding of certain notions is not as similar as pluralist theologians might think. However, they are also not as different as post-liberal and exclusivist theologians think. Thus, the concern I raised could be more carefully analysed in further researches. A potential Islamic response to non-theistic religions also needs to be developed within Islamic theology of religions, and I have suggested that as Islamic presuppositions based on the Qu'ran and Sunnah are not sufficient for taking into account the real difference of these religions, a type of theology of religions which works in conjunction with comparative theology will be a useful way of advancing a more satisfactory solution.

Index

Abduh, Muhammad 93, 103
Abraham (scriptural) 89, 106, 108, 163, 169, 172
Abrahamic religions 87, 89, 90, 94, 95, 100, 102, 104, 105, 112, 120n105, 168; *see also* Christianity; Islam; Judaism
Acceptance Model 34, 36, 40–1, 57, 58, 130; *see also* post-liberal theology
Afghani, Jamaluddin 93, 103
agnosticism 27, 59
al-Banna, Hasan 93, 118n59
al-Faruqi, Ismail Raji 131, 176n13
Al-Ghazali 98, 99, 119n91
al-Haqq 162
Allah: A Christian Response (Volf) 166
al-Maturidi, Abu Mansur (Imam) 84–5, 116n13
al-Qaradawi 120n98
al-Razi 167
Anglican Church. *See* Williams, Rowan
"anonymous Christian", theory of 14–16, 17, 18–19, 20, 69
apostates 156
Arkoun, Muhammad 85, 107
Askari, Hasan 103, 104–6, 110, 111, 162, 174
Aslan, Adnan 86, 103
Atay, Rifat 84–5, 86, 156
Ateş, Süleyman 85
atheism 16, 139
Aydin, Mahmut 85–6, 103, 104, 121n113, 128
Ayoub, Mahmoud 103, 112

Barlas, Asma 133–5, 137
Barth, Karl 9, 10–12, 33, 99, 161, 174, 175n3
Benedict XVI (pope) 164

Bhakti Hinduism 11; *see also* Hindus and Hinduism
Bible: Christian study of 70; and the concept of revelation in scripture 173; different role from that of the Qur'an 165; as final source of religious truth 12–13; on the incarnation 172; as source of common Christian identity 29; verses supporting commonality with Islam 164, 166–7; verses supporting exclusivist view 9, 117n44; *see also* New Testament
binary oppositions 133
blind men and the elephant parable 60, 76n29
Boutin, Maurice 19
Brecht, Mara 41
Brunner, Emil 13–14
Buddha 24, 26, 112
Buddhism and Buddhists 19, 112, 113, 122n166, 140, 168
Building Bridges Seminars 56, 75n7

Calvin, John 97
Calvinism 97
capitalism 94
Catholic Church: inclusivist approach 14, 17; official view of other religions 45n43; on salvation for non-Christians 9, 17–18; *see also* First Vatican Council; Second Vatican Council
Catholic Model 35
Catholic scholars 177n52; *see also* Clooney, Francis; D'Costa, Gavin; Knitter, Paul; Küng, Hans;
Chalcedonian Council 23
Charter of Medina 108

Index

Children of Israel 138
Christ *see* Jesus Christ
Christ alone (*solus Christus*) doctrine 9
Christian churches: Evangelical 9, 22, 24, 29, 35; Fundamentalist 9; Pentecostal 158; Protestant Reformed 10, 11, 96–7; *see also* Catholic Church
Christianity: chauvinist history of 65; commonalities with non-Christian religions 1, 20; and the concept of religion 152; conflict with other Abrahamic religions 105; differing theologies within 27; and the God of Islam 161–71; institutionalism of 22; Islamic vision of 3, 42; liberal 1, 21, 112, 153; Mystery of 65; negative views of 95–6, 142, 156; neo-orthodox 12; as only true religion 4, 32; orthodox 2, 3, 12, 22, 23, 26, 33, 54–5, 57–9, 73, 85, 112, 114, 127, 142, 157, 162, 167, 171, 172, 173, 182; post-liberal 157; Qur'an verses regarding 89–92, 142; on revelation 171–4; shared commandments with Islam 167; shared concept of God with Judaism 167; superiority of 11, 13, 42, 157; Trinitarian 164, 165, 169–70, 171, 173, 175, 182; understanding of God compared to Islam 161–71; as universal religion 152; *see also* Abrahamic religions
Christians: criticism of 97–8; in Islamic states 156; Muslim view of 113
Christians and Religious Pluralism (Race) 1, 8, 9
Christian theologians: on belief in the same God 161; Catholic 9, 14; comparative 154; exclusivist 17; on the ioncarnation 172; inclusivist 14, 84; Pentecostalist 158; pluralist 1, 3–4, 21, 59, 103–4, 114, 150; on religious diversity 42; response to ACW by 165–166; on revelation 12; on salvation 17, 119n94, 160; Trinitarian 157; *see also* Barth, Karl; Brunner Emil; Clooney, Francis; D'Costa, Gavin; DiNoia, Joseph A.; Griffiths, Paul; Heim, Mark; Hick, John; Knitter, Paul; Kraemer, Hendrik; Küng, Hans; Lindbeck, George; Race, Alan; Rahner, Karl
Christian theology of religions 1, 3, 8, 37, 39, 82, 142, 151, 154

Christian Uniqueness Reconsidered: The Myth of a Pluralistic Theology of Religions 59
Christology 14, 15, 22–5
Clarke, James F. 49n157, 152
Clooney, Francis 8, 38; comparative theology of 38–40
cognitive-linguistic approach 47n124
colonialism 26, 65, 153
A Common Word document (ACW) 2, 162, 164–6, 170, 178n65
comparative religion 39
comparative theology 5, 6, 8, 32–3, 37–8, 43, 49n157, 58, 141, 154, 174, 182, 183; as alternative to theology of religions 42; assessment of 40–2; Clooney's approach to 38–40; vs. comparative religion 39; defined 38–9; goals of 38; Islamic 4; problems of 41
Conservative Evangelical Model 35
Controversies in Interreligious Dialogue and the Theology of Religions (Hedges) 9
Council of Christians and Jews 56, 75n9
Crossing the Threshold of Hope (John Paul II) 164
crusades 26, 65
cultural-linguistic systems 29, 30–1, 41, 61, 157, 182; criticism of 33–4

Daggers, Jenny 48n138, 152, 157–8
D'Costa, Gavin 14, 19, 27, 28, 34, 35, 36, 41, 56–7, 58, 62, 64, 84, 86, 100, 157, 176n26; critique of Volf 168; theory of seven "centrisms" 35
'Declaration of the World Parliament of Religions' 2
democracy 94
dhimmi status 82
Different Equations (J. Smith) 133
din al-fitra (natural religion) 131, 140–1
DiNoia, Joseph A. 32–3
divine transcendence 131; *see also* Transcendent Reality
Dupuis, Jacques 39

Eckhart, Meister 169
Ecology and Economy (Williams) 72
Engineer, Ali 103, 104, 128
Enlightenment philosophy 11, 20, 33, 153

epistemology 4, 23, 37, 83–7, 100, 130
Ernst, Cornelius 63
Esack, Farid 3, 103, 104, 106–9, 113, 131, 159
eschatology 31, 32, 67, 156
ethical-practical bridge 21, 24, 104, 106–7, 113, 121n112
Eucharist 72
Eurocentrism 152, 158
Evangelical Christian churches 9, 22, 24, 29, 35
exclusivism: in Barth's theology of religions 10–12, 35; basis for 9–10, 25–6; Brunner's view of 13–14; and the Catholic Church 17; Christian 9–14, 21, 22, 26, 29, 32, 42, 44n28, 62, 65, 99, 105, 117n44, 157, 174; in D'Costa's typology 35, 36, 48n146; Islamic condemnation of 107–8; in the Islamic context 5, 83–4, 87, 95–8, 99, 100, 115, 130, 151, 155–7; Islamic definition of 84; in Islamic theory of religions 5, 92–103; Jewish 105; Kraemer's view of 13–14; move away from 9; objections to 12–14, 22; other forms of 12–14, 28, 32, 36, 56; parallels with other forms 3; pluralism as form of 27, 28; in Race's typology 1, 4, 8, 37, 38, 43n2, 47n131, 48n138; restrictive-access 48n136, 56–7, 84; social 151; sociopolitical 93–7, 100–3, 114, 130, 151, 153, 183; subdivisions of 35; and the supersessionist theory 91; theological 97–8, 101–3, 130; universal-access 35, 56–8, 62, 67, 73, 74, 84, 86, 100, 116n24, 176n13; view of salvation 140; in Williams' theology of religions 57–58, 62–64, 67–9
exegesis: Qur'anic 90, 92, 93, 94, 96, 102, 103, 110, 151; sociopolitical 93
Experience of Religious Diversity, The (Aksari) 104
extra ecclesiam nulla salus doctrine 9, 17

Fahman, Fazlur 103
fatwa 101
Feldmeier, Peter 155
feminism 65, 127, 157; Islamic 132
fides ex auditu doctrine 9, 31, 32
Finality of Christ (Williams) 63
Finality of Christ in a Pluralist World (speech by Williams) 64

First Vatican Council 173
fitra (primal and fundamental consciousness of God) 153; *see also din al-fitra* (natural religion)
fi Zilal al-Qur'an (Qutb) 93
Fletcher, Jeannie Hill 136
Ford, David 59
Fredericks, James 38, 41
Fulfilment Model 35
Fundamentalist Christian churches 9

Generous Love: The Truth of the Gospel and the Call to Dialogue: An Anglican Theology of Interfaith Relations 70, 71
German idealism 20
Global Ethic 60
global ethics project 28
globalisation, and the non-Christian neighbor 31
God: devotion to 138; expressed as the Real 23; finding 40; humans called to relationship with 15–16; and the issue of salvation 160; Jesus Christ as revelation of 64–5, 157; learning about 71; means of sending message to the people 172; Muslim and Christian understanding of compared 161–71; as Mystery 21–2, 68–9; oneness (unity) of 165, 169–70, 171; in other cultures 78n85; revelation of 10, 12; shared concept of in world religions 22–3, 162; of theistic traditions 23; trusting 139; as Ultimate Reality 175n2; universal awareness of 15–16; universality of 22, 103, 105, 110, 111, 113, 114, 115, 170; see also *taqwā*
good deeds (ethics) 108, 111, 113, 139, 159
'good neighborhood' policy 34, 71, 73
grace: and the non-Christian 14–16, 20; and salvation 10–11, 15–16, 68
Gregory VII (pope) 177n49
Griffith, Sidney 168
Griffiths, Paul 32
Gunton, Colin 12

hadiths: and the supersessionist theory 91, 109, 134; verses supporting exclusivist view 98; verses supporting inclusionist view 164
hanif (nondenominational monotheism) 138, 139

188 *Index*

Hassan, Riffat 133–4, 135
Hebrew prophets 24, 171–2
Hedges, Paul 9, 36, 37, 38, 57, 58, 62
Heim, S. Mark 28, 33
Hick, John: on common religious objects 21, 23, 162; definition of pluralism 85; on the incarnation 23–4, 46n78, 112; objections to 26–8, 58, 60, 162; objections to Rahner's theology 18–19; and philosophical-historical pluralism 22–4; philosophy of 65–6; as pluralist example 9, 21, 22–4, 95, 104; on salvation for all 65; as theocentric pluralist 35, 104, 112, 128–9, 175n2; on world religions 36, 110, 121n113, 129, 162, 174
Hindu-Christian Forum 56
Hindus and Hinduism 12, 38, 40, 113, 168; Bahakti form of 11; and the Catholic Church 17–18; and the concept of God 162
Holy Spirit 57, 70, 157–8, 173, 175, 176n26
Hoover, John 166
Huntington, Samuel 2
Hütter, Reinhard 33, 47n124

Ibn al-Arabi 99, 109, 162, 169
Ibn Taymiyya 99
iman (faith) 107, 109, 113, 131, 138–40, 139
imperialism 26, 94, 152, 153
incarnation 3, 23–4, 58, 68, 97, 105, 112, 114, 162, 169, 172–3
inclusivism: Catholic 35; Christian 4, 14, 22, 30, 37, 151, 182; in Clooney's theology 39–42; criticism of 4, 22, 33; in D'Costa's typology 35, 157; development of 14; diverse responses to 35; examples of 44n28, 46n66, 155; Islamic 4, 5, 83–9, 99–100, 108, 109, 111, 114–15, 156, 182; Khalil's interpretation of 99; Lamptey's view of 130, 136; liberal 86; objections to 18–21, 22; other forms of 17–18; parallels with other forms 3; in Race's typology 1, 4, 8, 35, 37, 38, 43n2, 48n138, 83, 84, 87, 130; in Rahner's theology 9, 14–17, 39; restrictive 14, 18, 84, 86, 100; on salvation 21, 42; structural 14, 84; subdivisions of 35; in Williams' theology 56, 60, 63, 64, 69–70, 73

incommensurability 25, 28, 33, 41, 61–2, 129, 168, 182
intercession, doctrine of 98
interfaith dialogue 19, 26, 28, 30–1, 37, 39, 55, 57, 66, 69, 71, 72, 73, 74, 160, 175; Williams' commitment to 55–6; *see also* A Common Word (ACW)
intratextuality 38, 40, 61, 137
Introducing Theologies of Religion (Knitter) 35, 40
Invention of the World Religions, The (Masuzawa) 152
invincible ignorance 100
Islam: Christian approaches to 3; commonalities with Christianity 2, 167; and contemporary political situations 82; on ecology 73; historical 106–8, 110, 111, 121n113, 159, 183; inclusivist 83–5, 86, 87, 99, 114; as the only valid religion 1, 4, 89, 90, 95, 99, 183; orthodox 98, 102, 107, 142, 156, 159–60, 162, 166; relationship with other religions 82, 83, 126; on revelation 171–4; and Second Vatican Council 163; as superior religion 83, 85, 129, 138; as system under God's direction 94–5; understanding of God compared to Christian 161–71; as universal religion 106, 115, 138, 183; as a world religion 183; *see also* Muhammad (Prophet); Muslims; Muslim theologians; supersessionist theory
islam (submission) 91, 106, 107, 113, 121n113, 131, 138, 139, 140, 159
Islam and the Fate of Others (Khalil) 84
Islamic denominations 164
Islamic law (shari'a) 88, 91, 95, 103, 120n105, 143n5
Islamic studies 151
Ismalian Islam 164
Izutsu, Toshihiko 134, 137

Jaafari Islam 164
jahiliyyah societies 94
Jesus Christ: divinity of 23–5; faith in 57; finality of 63–4, 66, 77n56; as the fulfillment of all religion 14; as God's Word incarnate 172–3; identity of 168; incarnation of 3, 23–4, 58, 68, 97, 105, 112, 114, 162, 169,

172–3; Islamic denial of divinity of 105; Islamic understanding of 165; Judaism transformed by 105; as necessary for salvation 48n136, 63, 66, 73, 74, 83; as normative 18, 42; objections to finality of 64–5; and the reshaping of human history 68; as revelation of God 64–5, 157; sacrifice for all humanity 57; as Son of God 24, 46n78; uniqueness of 62–7; universality of 67

Jesus studies 23

Jewish state 93

Jews: and the Catholic Church 17–18; criticism of 97; in Islamic states 156; Muslim view of 113, 138; *see also* Judaism

jihad 91, 95

John Paul II (pope) 163–4

Judaism: and the concept of God 162; on ecology 72; exclusivism of 105; and the 'jubilee' principle 72; negative views of 95–6, 156; in the Old Testament 45n38; Qur'an verses regarding 89–92; shared concept of God with Christians 167; *see also* Abrahamic religions; Jews

kāfir (disbelievers) 156; see also *kufr* (disbelief)

Kant, Immanuel 12, 28, 47n102, 152

Khalil, Muhammad 84, 86, 99, 119n91, 151

Khan, Sayyid Ahmad 103

Kilby, Karen 20

King, Ursula 136

kingdom centered approach 25

Knitter, Paul: Acceptance Model 34, 36, 40–1, 57, 58, 62, 130, 155; compared to Kant 47n102; criticism of Rahner 19; on the divinity of Christ 24–5; and ethical-practical pluralism 24–6; on interfaith relations 12, 34, 71, 47n102, 120n99; *No Other Name* 25, 44n28; objections to 26–8; pluralist theology of 3, 9, 24–6, 104, 151, 175n2; Replacement Model 35, 83; on salvation 25–6, 45n42; on types of pluralism 21, 34; typology of 35–7, 57–8, 59, 62, 118n54; on Williams 54

Koçyiğit, Talat 85

Kraemer, Hendrik 12, 13–14

Krishna 26

kufr (disbelief) 107, 113, 138, 139; *see also kāfir* (disbelievers)

Küng, Hans 2, 18, 28, 60

Kwok Pui Lan, 136

Lamptey, Jerusha: analysis of Islamic theology of religions 127–31; biographical background 126; methodology of 132–7; Muslima theology of 127, 143n5, 159–60; on Muslim theologians 102; "open" approach of 161; on the religious Other 103; theology of religions 5–6, 115, 126–7, 132–43, 150, 151, 155, 183; typology compared to Race 130–1

Legenhausen, Muhammad 129, 151

liberalism 33, 54; *see also* post-liberalism; theology, liberal

liberation theology 9, 25, 26, 104, 107, 113, 131

Lindbeck, George 9, 29, 30, 47n124, 61, 62, 67, 157; criticism of 33–4

Logos 22, 24, 27, 63

Lumen Gentium (Second Vatican) 1, 17, 163

Luther, Martin 97, 166–7

Lutheranism 97

MacGarvey, Kathleen 136

Madigan, Daniel 166

Magians 138

Malaysian case 168–9, 170

Markham, Ian 37

Masuzawa, Tomoko 152

Maturidi, Imam 84–5, 116n13

Maurice, Frederick D. 49n157

Milbank, John 33

missionary work 8, 13, 17

modernism, exclusivist 28

modernity 27, 151–2, 183

monotheism 153; as common belief 170; Trinitarian 165

Moses (scriptural) 106, 169

Moulasion, Jane Barter 55

Muhammad (Prophet): on farming 73; followers of 106, 121n113, 142; hadiths of 98; and the Islamic system 118n63; in Mecca 117n52; message of 96, 107, 157; on the Qur'an 87, 172; as representative of God 26; as the seal of the prophets 61, 105, 119n72, 140, 163; Sunnah of 106

Muslim Brotherhood 101, 118n59

Muslim-Christian Forum 56, 75n8

190 *Index*

Muslim Perceptions of Other Religions (Waardenburg) 82

Muslims: and the Catholic Church 17–18; relationship with non-Muslims 101–2, 103, 107–8, 113–14, 120n98, 159; response to religious pluralism 5; *see also* Islam; Muslim theologians

Muslim theologians: contemporary 128; exclusivist 89, 100, 115; in Khalil's book 99; liberal 83, 126, 152; pluralist 5, 85, 87, 104, 112, 114–15, 131, 150, 151, 161–2; relationship with Christians 1, 160, 172; supersessionist theory 156; theology of religions 3–4, 90, 128, 155; *see also* Askari, Hasan; Atay, Rifat; Esack, Farid; Khalil, Muhammad; Lamptey, Jerusha; Qadhi, Yasir; Qutb, Sayyid; Shah-Kazemi, Reza; Winter, Tim

Mutuality Model 34, 35; *see also* pluralism

Mystery, God as 21–2, 68–9

Myth of Christian Uniqueness, The (Williams) 59, 60

naskh (supersessionism) 91; *see also* supersessionist theory

Nasr, Seyyed Hossein 103, 104, 128–9

natural theology 13

Nazarenes 138

necessity of inter-religious apologetics (NOIA) principle 32

Never Wholly Other: A Muslima Theology of Religious Pluralism (Lamptey) 126

New Testament 172; Christocentric message of 24; eschatology of 32; on the need for Jesus Christ 66; as source of revelation about God 12; universality of 65; view of Jesus Christ 23, 26; *see also* Bible

New Testament studies 23

Nicene Council 23, 172

Nicholas of Cusa 166–7

Nicholson, Hugh 152

nifaq (hypocrisy) 138, 139

nihilism 59

Nishitani, Keji 19

Noah (scriptural) 106

non-Christian religions: as equally valid 33; grace-filled elements of 15; as lawful religions 16; salvific efficacy of 14, 17, 18, 57, 67, 109, 113, 129; spiritual power of 14; supernatural elements of 15; *see also* Buddhism and Buddhists; Hindus and Hinduism; Islam; Judaism

non-Muslims: in Muslim societies 117n52; protection of 82, 95; salvation for 86, 98, 99, 111, 113, 129, 130–1, 140–1, 156; taxation of 82; *see also* Christians

non-theistic religions 23, 85, 112, 140–1, 175n2, 183

No Other Name (Knitter) 25, 44n28

Nostra Aetate (Second Vatican) 1, 17, 45n43, 163, 166

Old Testament religion 45n38

On Christian Theology (Williams) 58

oppression 25, 107, 114, 131

orthopraxy 98, 159–60

Other/other: acceptance of 37, 68, 73, 127, 142; attention to 69, 74; divinity of 109; exclusion of 121n113; inclusion of 182; marginalized 107; Muslim attitude toward 98; pluralist view of 145n60; proximate 103, 133, 142; religious 3, 5, 32, 39, 60, 62, 73, 103, 107, 108, 110, 111, 115, 131, 132, 133, 135–6, 138, 156, 157, 159, 175, 182; remote 133; theological attitudes toward 102; unrighteous 107; women as 136

Palestine 93

Panikkar, Raimon 21, 27, 46n66, 60, 68, 157

particularism 4, 5, 9, 36, 40, 43n2, 57, 58, 63, 67, 73, 74, 135, 151; post-liberal 130

People of the Book 85, 107, 108, 131, 142; exclusivist verses from the Qur'an 89–92, 113

People of the Scripture 138

phenomenology 36, 162

philosophical-historical bridge 21, 104

philosophy 27, 65–6; Enlightenment 11, 20, 33, 153

pluralism 1, 2–3, 4, 5, 8, 9, 13, 20, 21–8, 35, 42–3, 46n66, 48n138, 48n146, 57, 58, 59–60, 64–5, 135, 142, 151, 152, 175, 175n3; attractive aspects of 26; Christian 153, 161, 162, 170, 182; Christian and Islamic responses to 4; ethical form of 104; ethical-practical 24–6, 104, 106–9, 113; as form of exclusivism 27, 28; Hick's view of 22–4, 85; in the Islamic context 1, 5, 43, 83–4, 85, 86, 87, 94, 103–14, 115, 121n113,

153, 161, 162, 170, 183; Islamic definition of 84; Knitter's view of 24–6; Lamptey's concept of 127; mystical 129; nonreductive 129; objections to 26–8; philosophical-historical 22–4, 104; as philosophical hypothesis 36; problems of 145n60; Real-centered 28; subdivisions of 35; theocentric 28, 104–6, 111–12, 113, 127–8, 138; universalist 109–10; view of salvation 140–1; as Western imposition 145n59; Winkler's definition of 85

polytheists 156

post-liberalism 25, 182; *see also* liberalism; theology, post-liberal

poverty 25, 72

praeparatio evangelica 157, 158

Protestant theology 10, 11

purgatory, doctrine of 33, 67

Qadhi, Yasir 97–8, 151

quasi-religions 36

Qur'an 24, 72, 84, 183; approach to non-Islamic religions 87–92; authority of 44n18; as central to Islam 114; contextual reading of 91–2, 113; criticism of Christianity 142; as God's means of engagement with people 173; interpretation of 107, 132; on People of the Book 89–92, 142; perfection of God's message in 158; semantic analysis of 137; verses pertaining to non-Islamic traditions 156; verses referring to revelation 171–2, 179n94; verses regarding other Abrahamic faiths 102; verses regarding other scriptures 176n22; verses relevant to Christians and Jews 108; verses supporting commonality with Christians 164, 165, 166; verses supporting exclusivist view 89–92, 97, 118n69, 119n72, 128; verses supporting pluralist view 88–9; women's interpretations and reinterpretations of 132–3, 134

Qur'anic revelation 155, 171–2, 177n52

Qutb, Sayyid 101, 114, 118n63, 161; on sociopolitical exclusivism 93–7; on theological exclusivism 99

Race, Alan 1, 4, 5, 8, 9, 14, 19, 37, 43, 83

Race's threefold typology 154; application to Christianity 4, 8–9, 115; application to Islam 4, 83, 84–7, 115, 128; compared to Lamptey's 130–1; criticism of 43; evaluation of 28, 35–7; and feminist theology 136; moving beyond 109; overview of 154; utility of 48n138; in Williams' theology of religion 37, 56, 64, 67; *see also* exclusivism; inclusivism; pluralism

Rahman, Fazlur 91–2, 107, 113, 120n95

Rahner, Karl 9, 39, 99–100, 122n166, 175n3, 182; criticism of 20

reason, and ethical truth 47n102

Reçber, Mehmet Sait 162

Reformation Movement 96–7

relativism 33, 34, 54, 58–60, 66, 72, 134

religion(s): cultural-linguistic systems 29; difference of 58, 60, 61, 62, 72, 74, 104, 127, 141; experiential-expressivist approach 30; incommensurability of 25, 28, 33, 41, 61–2, 129, 168, 182; Lindbeck's models for understanding 29–30; as manifestation of Reality 28; non-theistic 23, 85, 112, 140–1, 175n2, 183; Old Testament 45n38; propositional-cognitive model of 29–30; as unbelief 10, 11; untranslatability of 32, 62; *see also* Abrahamic religions; Buddhism and Buddhists; Christianity; Hindus and Hinduism Islam; Judaism; non-Christian religions

religious diversity 4, 5, 42, 94, 110, 154, 182, 183; Anglican approach to 70; and Islam 83

religious-mystical bridge 21–2, 104

religious pluralism 1, 8, 35, 133, 134, 150, 175

religious violence 65

religious wars 26

Replacement Model 35, 83

revelation: in Christianity 10–12, 14, 61, 62, 141, 172–3; general 13; in Islam 61, 62, 141, 171–2; Islamic and Christian concepts compared 171–4; through Jesus Christ 10, 13, 15; progressive 105; and religion 11

Rida, Rashid 99

Rose, Kenneth 41

Ruether, Rosemary R. 65

Rumi 104, 162

Sabeanism 102, 112, 117n52

Sabians 112, 117n52, 138

192   *Index*

Sachedina, Abdulaziz 91, 128
Saeed, Abdullah 93
salafi school 99, 101, 114
salvation: for all people 15–16, 44n28,
  65; Christological perspective on
  22; Church as requirement for 9,
  17–18, 114; exclusivist view of
  14, 84; God as final arbiter of 74;
  and grace 10–11, 15–16, 68; as
  individually achieved 137, 140; in
  Islamic theology 114; Lamptey's
  concept of 140–1; for non-Christians
  18, 20, 42, 56–7, 62–3, 67, 83, 140,
  157; for non-Muslims 86, 98, 99,
  111, 113, 129, 130–1, 140–1, 156;
  outside of the Church 17; plan of 15,
  67, 111; problem of 5, 8; question of
  110, 159–60; through faith in Christ
  9, 10, 21, 31, 57; through grace 10;
  through Jesus Christ 14, 48n136,
  63, 66, 73, 74; through post-mortem
  confrontation with Christ 31–2,
  67; totality of truths 73; and the
  uniqueness of Jesus Christ 62–7
Schebera, Richard 154
Schleiermacher, Friedrich 152
Schmidt-Leukel, Perry 36, 37
Schwöbel, Christoph 171
"Scriptural Reasoning" 78n76
scriptures: Christian 38; different
  perceptions of 173; Hindu 38;
  Islamic 54, 85–90, 105–8, 112;
  Jewish 54; of other faiths 70; *see also*
  Bible; New Testament; Qur'an
Second Vatican Council 1, 14, 17,
  45n42, 70, 100, 162, 163, 166, 170,
  178n67
semantic analysis 137, 146nn63–64
Sermon on the Mount 72
Shah-Kazemi, Reza 103, 104, 109–10,
  111, 128–9, 169, 170
shari'a (law) *see* Islamic law (shari'a)
Shia Islam 164
shirk (ascribing partners to God) 105,
  128, 138, 139
Sikhism, and the concept of God 162
Smith, Jonathan 28, 104, 133
social justice 26
solus Christus doctrine 9
soteriocentrism 25, 26
soteriology 36, 57, 62, 67, 83, 84, 130
*Spiritual Quest: An Inter-Religious
  Dimension* (Askari) 104
Sudworth, Richard J. 71
Sufi tradition 104, 109, 169, 170

Sunnah 42, 103, 106, 132, 151, 183
Sunni Islam 164
supernatural existential 15
supersessionist theory 5, 83, 91, 97,
  102, 108, 114, 130, 156, 174, 183

Tabatabai, Muhammad Husayn 73
tabdīl (change or corruption) 176n22
tahrif (corruption) 141, 176n22
taqwā 107, 131, 135, 137–41;
  categories of 139–40; understanding
  of 140
tawhid 169
Theocentric Model 35
theocentrism 25, 28, 60, 103, 111–12,
  113, 127–8, 138, 175n2
theologians: Asian 158; comparative
  1, 37–8, 40–2, 154, 182; European
  158; exclusivist 9–10, 12, 17, 20,
  21, 57, 63, 87, 89, 100, 115, 128,
  140, 183; feminist 136–7; inclusivist
  14, 18, 19, 21, 39, 99, 137; liberal
  1, 29, 45n60, 83, 86, 103, 112,
  126, 152–3; mediaeval 99, 102;
  non–Christian 84; particularist 57,
  63, 167; pluralist 5, 13, 21, 26–8,
  34, 40, 45n60, 58, 59, 60, 62, 64,
  76n29, 83, 85, 87, 88, 104, 114,
  115, 135, 138, 140–1, 152–3,
  161–2, 173, 174, 183; position of
  toward other religious 1–2, 57, 82;
  post-liberal 5, 13, 28, 29, 33, 37,
  48, 67, 129, 182; theocentric 113;
  see also Catholic scholars; Christian
  theologians; Muslim theologians
theology and theologies: academic 39;
  celebratory 58–9; communicative
  58–9; comparative 32–3; critical
  58–9; intratextual 61; liberal pluralist
  83; Muslima 127, 132–3, 136–7,
  143n5, 183; natural 13; "open" vs.
  "closed" 160–1, 174–5; post-liberal
  28, 29, 32–5, 36, 40–1, 57, 182,
  183; Protestant 10, 11; Trinitarian
  74, 157–8; Williams' definition of 59
Theology and Religious Pluralism
  (D'Costa) 35
theology in dialogue 33; *see also*
  interfaith dialogue
theology of religions: Barth's view of
  12; contemporary Islamic 127–32;
  cultural-linguistic 41; diversity of
  approaches to 150–1; Islamic 4,
  44n18, 142–3, 150–1, 154–61, 183;
  Kraemer's view of 13; Lamptey's

concept of 127, 137–42, 143, 155; objections to post-liberal approach 33–5; origin of 82–3; outcomes and problems 150–5; post-liberal 8, 9, 12, 29–35, 41–3, 120n99; Rahner's view of 14–17; Sufi-based 109; Trinitarian 5, 56, 58, 67–74; utility of 154; validity of 174; of Williams (locating on the map) 56–8; of Williams (on Christ's uniqueness and the problem of salvation) 62–7; of Williams (Trinitarian) 67–74; of Williams (understanding) 58–62; Williams' concept of 5, 127, 143, 155; *see also* Christian theology of religions; exclusivism; inclusivism; Islamic theology of religions; pluralism; universalism; Williams, Rowan
theory of excuse 99–100, 119n91
Thomas Aquinas 100, 119n94
Transcendent Reality 36, 106, 110, 140, 162, 174
Trinitarian theology 74, 157–8, 164, 165, 169–70, 171, 173, 175, 182; and the Islamic concept of God 166–7
Trinity, doctrine of 22, 27, 57, 58, 67, 70, 97, 114, 169–70, 171, 173, 175, 182
Trinity and Pluralism (Williams) 67–8
Troll, Christian 165
truth: ethical 47n102; propositional 47n124
Turner, Denys 162

unitarianism, neo-pagan 27
universalism 99, 104, 109–10, 111, 129, 152

Vatican Councils *see* First Vatican Council; Second Vatican Council
Volf, Miroslav 163, 166–8, 170, 171

Waardenburg, Jacques 82, 153
Wadud, Amina 133–5
Ward, Keith 6, 160–1, 174, 175
Williams, Rowan 5, 6, 37, 43, 141, 157, 160; biographical background 54; as exclusivist 54–7, 64, 67; foreword of *Generous Love* 70; as inclusivist 56, 69, 70; locating theology of religion on theological map 56–8; "open" approach of 161; as particularist 55, 67, 73, 74; as pluralist 54; theology of religions 58–74, 127, 143, 155, 182
Winkler, Lewis 85, 86
Winter, Tim 98, 99, 129, 151, 178n65
Wittgenstein, Ludwig 29
women: interpretation of the Qur'an by 144n41; as interpreters of the Qur'an 133–6; in Islamic tradition 133; non-Muslim feminist theologians 136–7; *see also* Lamptey, Jerusha
world peace, promotion of 164–5, 168
world religions discourse 152, 153, 183; and the shared concept of God 162

Yale University 166
Yodoism 11
Yodo Shin-shu Buddhism 11
Yong, Amos 158

Zen Buddhism 19, 122n166
Zoroastrians 156